A Sheaf of Leaves:
Literary Memoirs

OTHER BOOKS BY LEWIS TURCO

The Book of Dialogue, 2004
The Green Maces of Autumn: Voices in an Old Maine House, 2002
The Book of Forms, A Handbook of Poetics, Third Edition, 2000
The Book of Literary Terms, 1999
A Book of Fears, 1998
Shaking the Family Tree, 1998
Bordello: A Portfolio of Poemprints, with George O'Connell, 1996
Emily Dickinson, Woman of Letters, 1993
The Public Poet, 1991
The Shifting Web: New and Selected Poems, 1989
The Fog: A Chamber Opera in One Act, with Walter Hekster, 1987
Visions and Revisions of American Poetry, 1986
The Compleat Melancholick, 1985
American Still Lifes, 1981
Poetry: An Introduction Through Writing, 1973
Pocoangelini: A Fantography & Other Poems, 1971
The Inhabitant, 1970
Awaken, Bells Falling: Poems 1959-1967, 1968
First Poems, 1960

A Sheaf of Leaves

Literary Memoirs

Lewis Turco

Star Cloud Press
Scottsdale, Arizona

A Sheaf of Leaves:
Literary Memoirs

Copyright © 2004
by Lewis Turco

All rights reserved. No part of this book may be used or reproduced in any manner whatsoever without written permission from the publisher, except in the case of brief quotations embodied in articles and reviews.

Published by

Star Cloud Press

an imprint of

**CLOUDBANK
Creations, Inc.**

6137 East Mescal Street
Scottsdale, Arizona 85254-5418

*Cover and Book designed by Retha Schlabach Elmhorst
Front cover photo by Lewis Turco
Author photo by Gentile Camera, Oswego*

ISBN:0-9651835-6-4 cloth $36.95
ISBN: 0-9651835-4-8 softcover $24.95

Library of Congress Control Number: 2003115036
Printed by Lightning Source
La Vergne, TN

Acknowledgments

"The Hillsdale Epistles" in its original version first appeared in *The Carleton Miscellany* and is here used by permission of the author.

A version of "Introduction: A Brief Life" was published in *Contemporary Authors Autobiography Series*, Joyce Nakamura, editor, Vol. 22, Detroit: Gale Research, 1995, and is here used by permission of the author.

"The Cherub" appeared in *The Edge City Review* and is here used by permission of the author.

"Our Friend Dan Chaucer" was published in *The English Record* and is here used by permission of the author.

A version of "Ideologies: The Chronicle of a Conflict" appeared in *Escarpments*; the original review of "The Suspect in Criticism" was published in *Mad River Review*, i:2, Spring-Summer 1965, and reprinted in *"Struggling for Wings": The Art of James Dickey*, ed. Robert Kirschten, Columbia: University of South Carolina Press, 1997 and is here used by permission of the author.

"A Remembrance of Howard Nemerov" appeared originally in *The Formalist* and is here used by permission of the author.

"Upstairs" first appeared in *How We Work*, edited by Marla Morris, Mary Aswell Doll and William F. Pinar, New York: Peter Lang, 1999 and is here used by permission of the author.

"Musing about Students" was published originally in *Poesis* in 1986 and is here used by permission of the author.

The sections of "Lydia and Douglas" on Cuba, Haiti, Japan, Singapore, and Hong Kong were first published in *The 1954 World Cruise of the U. S. S. Hornet (CVA 12)*, edited by Gareth Lewis, all rights reserved 1954.

Two portions of "Engle's Workshop" appeared as "The Iowa Workshop: An Assenting View" in *Prairie Schooner* and as "The University of Iowa's Writers' Workshop Golden Jubilee" in *The Dictionary of Literary Biography Yearbook 1986*, edited by J. M. Brook for Gale Research, 1987. An abbreviated version appeared in *A Community of Writers* edited by Robert Dana for the University of Iowa Press, © 1999. The version used here has never before been published.

An early version of "My Old Pal Walt" appeared as "Whitman and I" in *The Public Poet: Five Lectures on the Art and Craft of Poetry*, Ashland: Ashland Poetry Press, © 1991 by Ashland Poetry Press; "The City's Mask" was published in *Quartet* in 1964; both are used here by permission of the author.

"Great Poets I Almost Met" appeared in *Spring, The Journal of the E. E. Cummings Society*; one portion of it also appeared as "Corresponding with Conrad Aiken" in *Conrad Aiken, A Priest of Consciousness*, edited by Ted R. Spivey and Arthur Waterman for AMS Press, © 1989; by permission of the author.

"A Friend in Need, A Friend Indeed" appeared in *Voices in Italian Americana*; portions of it were included in *Bread Loaf Writers' Conference: The First Thirty Years (1926-1955),* by Theodore Morrison, Middlebury College Press, © 1976, and in *Whose Woods These Are, A History of the Bread Loaf Writers' Conference, 1926-1992,* by David Haward Bain and Mary Smith Duffy, Ecco Press, © 1993; by permission of the author.

Contents

Introduction: A Brief Life   1

Upstairs   39

Our Friend Dan Chaucer   47

My Old Pal Walt   57

Lydia and Douglas   69

Friends at Last   89

Engle's Workshop   95

Ideologies: The Chronicle of a Conflict   121

Meters and Missiles   141

The Cherub   161

Musing about Students   171

A Remembrance of Howard Nemerov   195

The Hillsdale Epistles   201

Great Poets I Almost Met   219

A Friend in Need, A Friend Indeed   237

Poetry, the Tag-End of the Entertainment Industry   243

INTRODUCTION: A BRIEF LIFE

My father, Luigi Turco, was a Sicilian immigrant who came to America and was welcomed by the missionaries of the Episcopal Church; however, he was not converted from Roman Catholicism but from indifference to religion. In fact, his family in Sicily had for generations been Waldenses, not Catholics.

The founder of the ancient Protestant sect known as Waldenses, a movement that opposed the ecclesiastical establishment, was Peter Waldo of Lyons (c. 1140-1217), a wealthy French merchant and religious reformer who began to preach during the early twelfth century using as his text vernacular translations of the Gospels. His followers were known as the "poor men of Lyons," itinerant preachers who took a vow of poverty and taught a simple, Bible-based type of religion.

Waldo attended the third Lateran Council in 1179 where his vow of poverty was confirmed by Pope Alexander III who, however, forbade him to preach. Nevertheless, he continued to do so, and subsequently, in 1184, he was excommunicated and banished from Lyons together with his followers. The Waldenses spread through Europe, including Italy, especially the Cottian Alps which now mark the border between Italy and France and are known still as the Waldensian Valleys. The Waldenses have over a hundred organized churches throughout Italy, one of these being located in Riesi, Sicily, seat of my father's family. In the 1950s my father returned to Riesi and preached in the Waldensian church there.

The Episcopalians who welcomed my father, however, did not really want Italians as fellow worshipers. As a result, he became the minister of the First Italian Baptist Church of Meriden, Connecticut. Early on, in my *First Poems* (1960), I wrote "An Immigrant Ballad" which, despite my mother's scandalized disapproval, papa felt was rather accurate:

AN IMMIGRANT BALLAD

My father came from Sicily
    (O sing a roundelay with me)
With cheeses in his pocket and
A crust of black bread in his hand.
He jumped ashore without a coat,
    Without a friend or enemy,
Till Jesus nailed him by the throat.

My father came to Boston town
    (O tongue a catch and toss one down).
By day he plied a cobbler's awl,
By night he loitered on the mall.
He swigged his wine, he struck his note,
    He wound the town up good and brown,
Till Jesus caught him by the throat.

He'd heard of Hell, he knew of sin
    (O pluck that wicked mandolin),
But they were for the gentle folk,
The cattle broken to the yoke.
He didn't need a Cross to tote:
    His eyes were flame, his ears were tin,
Till Jesus nabbed him by the throat.

He met a Yankee girl one day
        (O cry a merry roundelay)
Who wouldn't do as she was bid,
But only what the good folk did.
She showed him how the church bells peal
        Upon the narrow straitaway,
And Jesus nipped him by the heel.

My father heard a sermon said
        (O bite the bottle till it's dead).
He quit his job and went to school
And memorized the Golden Rule.
He drained his crock and sold his keg,
        He swept the cobwebs from his head,
And Jesus hugged him by the leg.

The girl was pleased: she'd saved a soul
        (O light a stogie with a coal).
No longer need she be so wary:
Daddy went to seminary
To find how warm a Yankee grows
        When she achieves her fondest goal.
And Jesus bit him on the nose.

At last he had a frock to wear
        (O hum a hymn and lip a prayer).
He hoisted Bible, sailed to search
For sheep to shear and for a church.
He asked the girl to share his life,
        His choir-stall and shirt of hair,
For Jesus bade him take a wife.

My father holds a pulpit still
        (O I have had enough to swill).
His eye is tame, his hair is gray,
He can't recall a roundelay.

> But he can preach, and he can quote
>   A verse or scripture, as you will,
> Since Jesus took him by the throat.

Pappagallo — as I liked to call my father, somewhat to his annoyance, for it means "parrot" — met May Laura Putnam — Mom May as she liked to call herself, because of the pun, I suppose — at a Methodist camp in Wakefield, Massachusetts, where she was working as a missionary. At the time she was an old maid in her thirties who had pulled herself out of rural poverty in Superior, Wisconsin, by sheer wit and strength of will. Despite the desperate penury of her second generation Danish mother, born Laura Christine Larsen; her shiftless father, William Herbert Putnam, descendant of an old New England family, her six brothers and two sisters, Mom May had made something of herself, becoming the only one of the Putnam siblings to graduate from college — Boston University School of Religious Education. I wrote about her in my first book as well:

REQUIEM FOR A NAME

> Believe it or believe it not,
>   My mother was a Putnam once.
>   On her ancestral tree she swears
> The Lowells and the Deweys too
>   Hang pendulous as lovely pears.
>   My grampaw was a sort of dunce
> Who rather let things go to pot —
>
> Himself, his offspring, farm and wife.
>   My grampaw was a sort of dunce.
>   His homestead I remember well:
> The floors were warped, the doors askew,
>   And now and then the rafters fell.
>   My mother was a Putnam once —
> She led a less than social life,

So she went East from grampaw's West.
        My mother was a Putnam once
    Till she was married, woe O! woe.
No longer was she maiden free —
        She cursed her pa from pate to toe.
        My grampaw was a sort of dunce
To cheat the eaglet in its nest

By willing her a woman's form.
        My grampaw was a sort of dunce,
            But what a hefty name he wore!
He gave my middle name to me;
        It fits me like a saddlesore.
        My mother was a Putnam once,
I'd be one too, come sun or storm.

The Deweys and the Lowell hosts
        Are pendant from a hollow tree.
Now with this rime let them be felled,
        Let me be nothing more to me
Than windfalls blasted by the frosts.

        My mother was a Putnam once;
        My grampaw was a sort of dunce.

Mom May was wrong about the Lowells, but right about the Deweys.

So my parents married and I was born into their middle age. We lived a while in Buffalo near my father's sister, Vita Sardella, and her family. I was christened Lewis (my mother was having no other "Luigi" in the family) Putnam (hyphenated last names were not yet current in the U.S.) Turco, and then we moved to Meriden, where I was brought up unaware of how poor we were. Thinking back on my early life, I consider it remarkable that my parents, given their own histories, brought up their children as members of the middle class who had no doubt at all we were as privileged as anyone else. Though we had no money, the house was full of books of all sorts.

My parents read to me from the cradle, and I was soon reading for myself.

From an early age, also, I was aware that my mother's family had a long and fascinating, if not always distinguished, history. In my adulthood I traced my Grandfather Putnam's genealogy with some accuracy back to fourteenth century Puttenham, Penne, and Aston Abbots in Buckinghamshire, England. Mother was a direct descendant of Constable Carolina John Putnam of Salem Village, now Danvers, Massachusetts, who in 1692 was throwing the accused and hapless New England witches into jail, but *her* mother was a full-blooded Dane. Because the Putnams of Aston Abbots were also originally Danes living in the Danelaw, my brother and I are really as much Danish as Sicilian.

But long before I discovered all this, when I was five years of age, my brother, Gene, was born in Meriden. His middle name is "Laurent" — probably the female version of "Laura," and it was many years before I realized the derivation of "Gene": it is the American version of "Gino," which is short for "Luigi" — my father had named both his sons after himself! In my second collection of poems, a chapbook titled *The Sketches of Lewis Turco and Livevil: A Mask* (1962), I wrote about our childhood:

GENE

    "Ragtail Gene, don't tag along here;
        scram on home or I'll bop your nose."
Brother, come the first of April,
        that was the word the second of May
        and all you heard when our lead pipe cannon
        swallowed a cherry bomb and belched a stone
        that boomed across the Fourth of July,
        nearly crocking you where you hid
        to spy on all the older kids.

    If the world grew huger in your eyes,
        that was because they went wide
        to hear the clubhouse secrets told

in the dark garage where gasoline
smelled about good enough to swill.

For, the first you knew of going,
    you knew because we swore our raft
    was not a raft, but a ship to float
    a boy's body out of sight
    and a man's voice too deep for sounding.

That's the way that I am going;
    ragtail Gene, don't tag along here.

When I was in the eighth grade my father sent me off to Suffield Academy in Suffield, Connecticut. He told me that he was doing it to give me the best education he could, but he evidently told my brother that he sent me away to save Gene's life. I don't recollect that I was all that homicidal toward my sibling. The worst thing I remember doing was tying him to the porch of the parsonage on Windsor Avenue when I was supposed to be baby-sitting him. I wanted to play with my neighborhood buddies instead, and I knew he was safe because I could hear him screaming.

My father's money and credit ran out after I had spent two years at Suffield, and I returned to Meriden to attend high school. By that time I'd been writing for several years. I had begun to publish in Suffield's student publication, *The Bell*, and when I returned home I won several writing prizes locally including honorable mentions and a Key Award in the National Scholastic Writing Awards. In the local papers, *The Morning Record* and *The Journal*, I published poetry, articles, and even fiction, for I had become the *Record*'s morgue clerk, high school correspondent, and cub reporter. I also wrote for the Meriden High School publications and during my junior and senior years was, first, undergraduate editor and then co-editor of *The Annual*, the yearbook. Ray Staszewski and I collaborated on the Senior Class Poem:

GRADUATION

The morning years of life, for us, are through.
We leave a training-ground of mind...this school.
Our thoughts, diversified ahead, behind,
Find us more than a bit perplexed with life.
In retrospect, our memories are sweet...,
Like morning sunbeams spread on dampened earth,
Or sparkle of a dew-dropped, dawning day.
Our free, young past we'll cherish close to us;
A bulky mass of mixed-up incidents
To be relived in later dreams of youth.
But ah, how swiftly change the tunes of life!
Our present soon becomes the passive past;
The future, perfect...yet, in all our hopes
There runs a thread of fear, for through the haze
Of college, working, fighting, on the road
That lies before us all, a question mark
Rears up its hoary head and asks, "But what
Of Age, of Death's cold, bony hand, whose slave
Is Time, with sickle cutting ever-widening swaths
Through youth, which cannot mend itself again?"
But still we look with firm, convincing thought
Into the foggy future that is ours...
Which holds some love, yet hate; some joy, but pain.
We therefore look to Fate and humbly say,
"Our lives are yours, harsh world. Please use them well!"

    Neither Ray nor I could afford to attend college immediately, so we decided to join the Coast Guard for the Korean G. I Bill. Through sheer laziness we wound up joining the Navy instead — not as safe, perhaps, but safer than the infantry. The point was soon moot, however, for before our second year was spent the war was over. Although my future wife and I had been members of the same crowd in high school, we didn't begin to date until she was a co-ed at UConn and I had gone to sea aboard an aircraft carrier, the *U. S.*

S. Hornet, as I recorded in a poem from my chapbook *Curses and Laments* (1978), published under the anagram pen-name "Wesli Court":

HORNPIPE EPITHALAMIUM

The sea blows high and the wind blows cold,
      The *Hornet* sails out to sting.
We bellbottom boys are bully and bold,
Young at the moment but growing old,
And it's no damn good that I bought Jean a ring,
      I bought pretty Jean a ring.

The Gunner's Apprentice is cute as a pin,
      The Yeoman can really swing.
Those almond-eyed girls all know how to sin
To make your eyes swivel and your head spin —
But I had to go buy Jeannie a ring,
      A yellowish diamond ring.

Davy Jones flirts with the mermaids below.
      Down there where Neptune is king
The seacows come swimming along in a row
With nothing more on than a green weed bow
While the drowned sailors gather around in a ring
      And dance till the fathoms ring,

For each wooed a maiden of iron and steel,
      Then took her out for a fling.
She had a pert hull and a lovely keel,
But one day she just wouldn't answer her wheel —
I wonder if Jeannie's still wearing her ring,
      That beautiful bargain ring.

> The wind blows cold, the sea blows high;
>   I stand here trying to sing,
> But the salt spray rises to spit in my eye
> Till I'm ready to kill and fit to die
> While Jeannie sits home and stares at her ring,
>   For I gave sweet Jean my ring.

It was while I was in the Navy, at the age of nineteen, that I published my first verses in 1953 in a national literary journal, *The American Poetry Magazine*. Shortly thereafter my work began appearing widely in the "littles." By the time I was discharged, married to Jean Cate Houdlette, and myself a student at UConn, I was heavily involved in the literary scene. My friends included my fellow undergraduate James Scully and a graduate student, Alexander Taylor, both poets — Sandy Taylor had been the editor of *Patterns*, one of the magazines that had published my early poems

Two of my instructors were Norman Friedman and John Malcolm Brinnin, the man who had brought Dylan Thomas to America. I emulated him by getting myself put in charge of the Student Union's Fine Arts Festival committee which brought visiting writers to campus to read their work: E. E. Cummings, Richard Eberhart, Donald Hall, Philip Booth, James Wright, James T. Farrell, and many others. As editor of *Fine Arts Magazine* I published original work by some of our visitors, and as president of The Connecticut Writer, the undergraduate literary organization, sponsored events by student writers, including a "Beatnik" reading at which everyone wore white bucks! Jean worked for the university (on the information desk at the administration building — people enjoyed calling her "Miss Information," and when she told them she was married they said, "All right, then, Mrs. Information!" and laughed and laughed); we lived, therefore, in the Northwood Apartments faculty housing. Still, the winters could be bitter:

A Sheaf of Leaves: Literary Memoirs

LETTER FROM CAMPUS

It somehow seems the campus owns no end,
No boundaries save those of season's change.
The students make no bones at fall, but wend
Their leaf-run courses out of shouting's range

And in again, four sheets to compass lawns
Extending, dun on green, toward the rout
Of hill on which this world is built. The tawns
And hint of fawn in autumns hereabout

Extend no hint of leniencies of snow
This winter. There will be the ague to pay:
The weather holds three mortgages on woe
Till March steps in to steal the march on May.

June's like a pregnancy not long conceived:
More wonderful in dreaming than in fact,
Perhaps. Yet, none of pain may be perceived
Except in execution of the act

Of proving life. I must believe the warmth
Is worth the winter, worth this boundless hill.
The third month has transpired. So will the ninth.
Leaves fall no longer and the wind is still —

The blizzard's will is stronger than my own.
This letter wrinkles on and must be done,
For chill has breached the window, scorned the stone
Around my room. December has begun.

    Graduating in mid-year of 1958-59, I applied to attend the Iowa Writers' Workshop in the fall and was accepted. I spent the spring semester at UConn as a graduate assistant and part-time instructor of English teaching an introduction to the short story / composition course to sophomores, then several weeks during the summer as the youngest resident of Yaddo, the artists' colony at Saratoga

Springs, experimenting with writing unrhymed quantitative syllabic poems. Yaddo is located next to the Saratoga Raceway; this poem is from my third collection, *Awaken, Bells Falling: Poems 1959-1967* (1968), and it depicts an actual event:

RACEWAY

I.
>>>>>>My raceway of sheets last night became
a cool trotter, unwinding with grace. Today,
>>>>autumn peeps imponderably out of
>>>>>>the soggy drought July had posted
>>>>>>>>on the foothills. It is August

>>>>here in Saratoga; the races
open tomorrow. Yesterday a filly
>>>>>>worked out her own odds, snapping two of her
>>>>>>>>ankles while we watched. She was done in
>>>>>>>>>>by a green syringe. She lounged on

>>>>the turf, staring from one farthest eye,
both her forehooves angled like ballerina
>>>>>>slippers. With her, summer has stagggered: it,
>>>>>>>>too, soon will drop and the jockey sun
>>>>>>>>>>grow gray above the world's brown hide.

II.
>>>>>>When a thoroughbred loses its
pins, there's no more running. Snort if you
>>>>>>will, but reason, too, exhausts itself when
>>>>>>>>cause falters. Men have run down when barred from the
>>>>>>>>>>race. Summer is a fragile courser

>>>>here in the North; our racers are
all imports from the southland. Summer
>>>>>>will not slow for falling leaves, nor haul our
>>>>>>>>sleighs: it will linger, pawing its reluctance
>>>>>>>>>>to leave, but its strength is of only

> short will, meant for one swift effort.
> Watch the summer run its oval, it's
> a winner now — nothing can stop it! The
> stands urge their encouragement upon open
> air; shouts fall and rise like the fall wind
>
> that moves out of the foothills now, sure,
> pervasive, wild.
>   Blooded summer shies.

At Iowa some of my fellow students were George Keithley, Robert Mezey, Vern Rutsala, Morton Marcus, and Kim Merker; Curtis Harnack was there with his wife, my fiction professor Hortense Calisher, and Verlin Cassill labored away in the quonset hut where the poetry workshop was held. My professors were Paul Engle, director of the Workshop, and Donald Justice who has remained a lifelong friend — in fact, I am writing these words on the 5th of May, 1995, having returned to Oswego this morning from Oneonta, New York, where last evening I witnessed Don receive a well-deserved Doctor of Humane Letters Degree from Hartwick College. I reminded him that at Iowa I had asked him whether he thought a comprehensive handbook of verse forms traditional to English and American poetry might be useful, as no one, incredibly, had ever compiled one before, not even George Puttenham. Don had said he thought so, and with that encouragement I'd begun working on the book that would be published eight years later as *The Book of Forms: A Handbook of Poetics* (1968) and later still as *The New Book of Forms* (1986) and *The Book of Forms, Third Edition* (2000).

Influence is reciprocal sometimes, however, even between student and teacher. When he saw my new Workshop poems back in 1959 Don said, "But, Lew, you're cheating. Your poems don't rhyme." Dylan Thomas and Marianne Moore had been writing rhymed syllabics, but no one other than haikuists had been writing just plain syllabics. A few years later I couldn't help noticing (because I was asked to review it) that Don's second book, *Night Light*, consisted of unrhymed syllabic poems.

I didn't stay at Iowa as long as I might have wished, though, for I needed to find a position and begin earning some money:

Old News

"Six weeks gone," the doctor said,
that odd good luck look walking his lips along

the trail blazed by the tip of
his tongue. "Six weeks gone, son. She'll be fine. Lousy

in bed, though," shaking his head.
"You'll be used to the idea come daylight,"

and off he went, his eyes propped
wide with a good call's work — blasé, not quite bored

by the old wonder with which
I was left: the old bride whose acquiescence,

I now find, can swallow down
this house with its carpet silences; stillness

of pillows; the couch couching.
Outdoors, the dark lies in the hollows of trees.

Night descends like a muffled
lamp. These eyes seize on ancient things: the roadway

sleeping between its curbs, the
lurking swell of a still flat belly, and the

lidded moon risen, unwinking, on the world.

I left without taking my degree, but my publication record was strong enough to land me a job at what was then Fenn College in Cleveland, later to be Cleveland State University. My *First Poems* was published, and in Meriden our daughter, Melora Ann, was born during the summer of 1960:

A CAROL FOR MELORA'S FIRST XMAS

When I came out of the bunting's hive
I stung the world with my bumble eyes
    With a hey! ho! rockabye boy,
And it was a kick to be alive —
I dug this chuckle and mammary jive
    Come dumpling, precious, dear little goy.

When I hopped out of the cradle's croon
I counted the cash in my purse of skin
    With a hey! ho! rockabye boy,
And I spent my time like a new doubloon
On liquid propellants to the moon
    Come thumper, jiminey, jumping for joy.

When I blew off to my windy school
I kissed Miss Tuttle and told her lies
    With a hey! ho! rockabye boy,
For I played the scholar like a fool,
And she broke mine, and I broke her rule
    Come cunning, clever, fresh little goy.

But when father preached, he tried to tell
Me the last damn word in the works of sin
    With a hey! ho! rockabye boy!
I caught on quick, and the breezy bell
Went swinging above us halfway to hell,
    Come organ, keyboard, an end to joy.

When I buzzed out of that web of pain
Death was a spider, we were flies
    With a hey! ho! rockabye boy,
And Christ dripped blood on the windowpane
      From a sky of tears and a world of rain
      Come sad, solemn, sorrowful goy.

Now my Melora has bumble eyes
That prickle and prod my purse of skin.
Shall I say there's fear in the belfry's din,
And the flesh of the world is a bag of lies?
Shall I teach her to love, but teach her to sin,
To look for Hell in her grandfather's skies? —

    With a hey! ho! goodbye, old boy!
    Come sweat, sweet, as you stretch for joy.

During the summer of 1961 I went as a Poetry Fellow to the Bread Loaf Writers' Conference in Middlebury, Vermont, where I made the acquaintance of John Ciardi, director of the conference, who remained a friend and mentor until his death. Others there stayed friends as well: Richard Frost, whom I introduced to Robert Frost one evening in Treman Hall and whom I saw at Hartwick College yesterday; Richard Emil Braun, with whom I had been publishing in the little magazines for years (people at Bread Loaf thought I ought to be much older than I was, as Dick Frost reminded me; I told him that I'd caught up with and passed myself); A. R. Ammons, and Miller Williams who, many years later, as Director of the University of Arkansas Press, would publish two of my books: *Visions and Revisions of American Poetry*, which in 1986 won the Poetry Society of America's Melville Cane Award for criticism, and in 1989 *The Shifting Web: New and Selected Poems*. I've just finished revising an essay for a forthcoming Arkansas book edited by David Baker, *Meter in English*, and some years back I contributed an article to another, *John Ciardi, Measure of the Man*, edited by Vince Clemente.

When I got back to Cleveland in the fall of 1961 I founded the Cleveland Poetry Center aided and abetted by Loring Williams, Hart

Crane's uncle by marriage and publisher of American Weave Press. Before either of us knew I would be coming to Cleveland, Loring had been one of the members of the board of editors of The Book Club for Poetry, which had made my *First Poems* one of its selections. He presided over the Center's Poetry Forums which soon became a major focus for literary activity in the city. I put the UConn experience to good use by bringing William Golding for a reading that founding year, followed by John Crowe Ransom who read the first poem he had written in forty years at a session of the Ohio Poetry Society convention, and a Jazz Poetry Benefit reading. Subsequent visitors included Richard Wilbur, Robert Huff, W. D. Snodgrass, Donald Justice, Hollis Summers, Mac Hammond, Howard Nemerov, Richard Frost, Don Petersen — also an Iowan and Oneontan, Alberta Turner — who eventually succeeded me as director, and many others.

In 1962 Loring published *The Sketches* from his own press and I returned to Iowa briefly to finish my master's degree. In 1964 I left Fenn to go to Hillsdale College in Michigan where, in the fall, the nation completed a year of mourning for its fallen president:

ODE ON ST. CECILIA'S DAY 1964
For J. F. K., One Year Later

I. Of the Past
Some music, then, for this day. Let it be
Suitable to the mood of fallen snow,
The veil of a virgin saint. Quietly
Let it come now, out of the silence; now
While the birds inexplicably forsake
The elm, the oak, the seed in the lilac....
Instead, drumrolls muffled in an old year,
An echo of trumpets in the streets. Clear
But muted, there is a ragged tattoo
Of hooves, image of a sable horse, wild-
Eyed, resisting the rein, skittish among
The twin rows of witness citizens who,
Their voices frozen, give up to the cold
Air of the marble city an old song.

II. Of the Present
But it's another year, Cecilia's day
Again, another part of the land. So,
Let the phantoms of those dead days lie
Under these new burdens of snow. Allow
That chorus of stricken men to dim like
Shadows into blackening film, the dark
Merging with the riderless horse. Feature
By feature, let the scene fade into near
Distance, into perspective, then shadow.
This is music for St. Cecilia. Yield
To her the lyric due her. Let us sing
For her patronage — her martyrdom grew
Out of a summer heart: she is our shield
Against the winter. She is always young.

III. Of the Moment
Here beyond the window the campus lies.
The students pass in mufflers and coats, eyes
Almost hidden against the wind. The sound
Of radio music settles around
The furniture, into the carpeting.
Choral voices: a requiem. Distant
And urgent, the November church bells ring.
Outdoors a dog rags something. An instant
Pause in his play — he has caught a squirrel
Which tosses and tosses in the gray air.
The mongrel, in the midst of his quarrel
With life, is assaulted by three girls. There,
At the base of a tree, the limp ruff falls
From insensate jaws, starts to inch up walls
Of oak bark toward some invisible
Sanctuary. The dog begins to howl.
The girls watch the squirrel into the limbs.
Cecilia's radio is done with hymns.

I stayed at Hillsdale just long enough to produce the Conference of Midwestern Poets during the summer of 1965. The morning after the conference was over, a portion of the town was destroyed by a tornado while I snored. In June "While the Spider Slept," a ballet choreographed by Brian Macdonald to music by Maurice Karkoff, titled from and based upon my poem "November 22, 1963," was debuted by the Royal Swedish Ballet in Stockholm. Subsequently the Royal Winnipeg Ballet performed it in Canada and throughout the United States. My family moved to Oswego, New York, where I began to teach in the State University College.

During the summer of 1968 I returned to Bread Loaf as a member of the teaching staff, and in the fall my family moved temporarily to Potsdam, a sister college in the S.U.N.Y. system, where I was visiting professor for a year. No sooner had we settled in than my father died in Meriden. Mom May said he had been sitting watching the news on television when suddenly he pitched forward and was gone, a circumstance that gave rise to a recurring dream which was not exorcised until I wrote this sestina:

THE OBSESSION

Last night I dreamed my father died again,
A decade and a year after he dreamed
Of death himself, pitched forward into night.
His world of waking flickered out and died —
An image on a screen. He is the father
Now of fitful dreams that last and last.

I dreamed again my father died at last.
He stood before me in his flesh again.
I greeted him. I said, "How are you, father?"
But he looked frailer than last time I'd dreamed
We were together, older than when he'd died —
I saw upon his face the look of night.

I dreamed my father died again last night.
He stood before a mirror. He looked his last

Into the glass and kissed it. He saw he'd died.
I put my arms about him once again
To help support him as he fell. I dreamed
I held the final heartburst of my father.

I died again last night: I dreamed my father
Kissed himself in glass, kissed me goodnight
In doing so. But what was it I dreamed
In fact? An injury that seems to last
Without abatement, opening again
And yet again in dream? Who was it died

Again last night? I dreamed my father died,
But it was not he — it was not my father,
Only an image flickering again
Upon the screen of dream out of the night.
How long can this cold image of him last?
Whose is it, his or mine? Who dreams he dreamed?

My father died. Again last night I dreamed
I felt his struggling heart still as he died
Beneath my failing hands. And when at last
He weighed me down, then I laid down my father,
Covered him with silence and with night.
I could not bear it should he come again —

I died again last night, my father dreamed.

In 1968 also *Awaken, Bells Falling* and *The Book of Forms* were published. When I returned to Oswego I took up the directorship of the Program in Writing Arts which I had put together before I left for Potsdam. It became eventually one of the largest undergraduate writing programs in the nation, and I directed it until this year, 1995, when I stepped down on January 1st. The College subsequently appointed me Poet-in-Residence, perhaps to comfort me, though I needed no consolation — I'm not J. Edgar Hoover, and more than a quarter-century of doing something is long enough.

My colleague and fellow (but much younger) Iowan, Leigh Allison Wilson, became the new director.

At Oswego in those early days I met and began working with the printmaker Thom. Seawell. We did several poemprints together and then, in 1970, we collaborated on a book of prose poems and prints, *The Inhabitant*, about a man who, in midlife, discovers he no longer understands who he is and begins to wander about his house in search of himself:

THE HALLWAY

The Inhabitant stands in his hallway. A long way from the door, still
    the gentleman has a distance to go before he can leave, or
    enter, or simply resume.

Here there is small illumination. The only window is of squares of
    stained glass, in the door behind him which is closed.
Things wait in the narrow aisle. Objects beguile him — each has its
    significance, in and beyond itself; each is an obstacle in a way
    to be touched and passed:

Touched and repassed, and with each touching to become more
    than the original substance. The Inhabitant stands in his
    hallway, curiosities looming ahead and behind.

It is as though, almost, this furniture had become organs, extensions
    of his body. If he listens, the gentleman may find his pulse
    booming in the hallseat, under the lid, gently, among artifacts
    and mathoms.

Let him proceed; let his footfall say *clum*, silence, *clum*. Let the
    stained light lie amber on a black umbrella in its stand, fall
    scarlet on the carpet, make a blue haze of a gray hatbrim rising
    in shadow to the level of his eye to rest on an iron antler in the
    hall.

> The Inhabitant is home. Let him go down the hallway, choosing
> to pass the stair and banister this time, pass these things of
> his, levelly, moving from light to light, shadow to shadow.

In the same year my monograph bibliography, *The Literature of New York* appeared — books at opposite ends of the spectrum, no doubt — and S.U.N.Y. published a study guide for a correspondence course, *Creative Writing in Poetry*.

In 1971 *Pocoangelini: A Fantography and Other Poems* appeared; it was followed in 1973 by an expansion of the study guide as a college text, *Poetry: An Introduction through Writing*; a second study guide, *Freshman Composition and Literature*, and a chapbook, *The Weed Garden*, but the most important thing was the birth of my son, Christopher Cameron:

MINOTAUR

> In my dream there is light
> in the underground passage
> turning between stone block walls.
> The floor is a shallow stream.

> How have I come to be
> here in this place with my son,
> not yet a yearling? Danger
> waits nearby — one can feel it.

> He must be preserved. At
> the end of the passage there
> is safety — another thing
> I know, but cannot tell how.

> The water moves slowly,
> but it can bear him in this
> frail shell in which I place him.
> And he has been set afloat.

As he drifts through stone, through
light, he rises, leans upon
the rim to fathom water.
It is true: Pain is depthless.

My feet move to follow,
to seat my child again, but
the fluid drags at my flesh.
I call; he does not look back.

As he diminishes
in the curve of his passage,
I sense the beast I have feared
in the distance between us.

This poem is from a chapbook, *A Maze of Monsters*, with illustrations by Louise Dickinson, published in 1986, but the series from which the chapbook was culled is an unpublished (in its entirety) alphabestiary, *A Book of Beasts*, which had fostered an earlier chapbook in 1978, *A Cage of Creatures*.

"Wesli Court" published his first chapbook in 1977, *Curses and Laments*, from Mathom Publishing Company of Oswego whose founder, Charlie Davis, had at one time been a jazz musician and composer of the all-time jazz classic, "Copenhagen." On a second sojourn at Yaddo that year I lived and worked in The Tower room where Edna St. Vincent Millay and Theodore Roethke had also worked, and I reacquainted myself with the millpond about which I had written on the first occasion:

MILLPOND
Yaddo, Saratoga Springs, New York

This is the place where peace grows
like a green frond set among waters aerial
   with dragonflies. Where, at noon,
the trees section the broad falling
leaf of light, and space color upon the millpond,

    yet do not move because motion
        might be lost upon silence.

    This is the place where a stone,
given its occasional career, could disturb
        little with an arc and fall,
    for the pond would swallow all voice
and shrug circling ripples into its banks until
        moss had absorbed this small wet gift,
            showing a fancy darker.

    This is the place where one may
abet his heart's romance, deceiving his eyes by
        unconsciously confusing
    slow change with no change. But even
here, dream makes way for declensions of wind and sun.
        The alders will grow, moss will dry.
            Wings will pulsate, then plummet.

    This is the place where peace rests
like ferns beyond lilies. The trick is to wear it
        as a mantle, but to know
    cloaks for cloaks, shelters for shelters.
Beneath this revery of surfaces, fish wait
        for the dragonfly's mistake. The
            trick is to lose, but to own.

    Curses and Laments, another chapbook, followed in 1978, as did a children's storybook, *Murgatroyd and Mabel* illustrated by "Robert Michaels" (Robert Sullins), and a third chapbook, *The Airs of Wales*, modern versions of Medieval Welsh poems in the bardic forms, all by "Wesli Court." In Maine, on the farm where my family and I spent nearly every summer, my father-in-law, John Cate Houdlette, who had been my seventh-grade shop teacher in Meriden, died just before Christmas. The summer before, the family had spent one lovely day at the beach before learning the diagnosis:

Cancer

We did not know, then, what the wen
   was on his heel. The gulls wheeled
in the summer sun, the combers
     broke and broke; the sand siled.
   On the beach the grandchild ran
   and stopped, dug wells, ran again

while the old man slept in a round
   shadow cast against the light.
The old wife dreamed beside his dream,
     wound in a shawl, as shade
   fretted the edge of waking.
   But all the while, as the tide

pulsed, moving by moments toward
   the drying seaweed of high
water, through the web of his veins
     the crab sidled, stalking.
   The day was perfect, then. Now
   a sea-change has taken it;

rather, it has become two days,
   that fair one and another
in which sandworms rise from the child's wells,
     segmented, mandibled.
   The beach umbrella sends its shade
   casting over the rising surf

to meet the east wind. The seabed
   is calm and murderous with
life. The boats toss like dreams, their nets
     seining the undertow.
   Now the ocean is almost
   upon us — our eyes are stars

   with spines; our minds are eight-armed; they
grope and coil in the darkness of the sun.

The following summer while Curtis Disbrow, a Houdlette son-in-law like me; Jean's cousin Joe Packard, and I were converting the ell and shed of the ancient Dresden farmhouse into heatable living quarters for Bertha Houdlette, my newly widowed mother-in-law, and Jean's oldest sister Nathalie Ahern, I began a seasonal enterprise, The Mathom Bookshop, in Dad Houdlette's tractor garage. (Joe's brother's middle name, like mine, is "Putnam Packard," for the Packards and a branch of my mother's family had intermarried generations before.) My bookstore is still operating, and this summer I will move it into a newly renovated section of the barn, as the garage has become too small and the sills have disintegrated. Because many people ask, I will record here that "Mathom" is a Tolkien word meaning "useless treasure."

My chapbook *Seasons of the Blood*, poems on the Tarot, appeared in 1980, and I began collaborating with a second Oswego printmaker, George O'Connell, with whom I have been working ever since. My old Yaddo poem, "Millpond," was coupled with his intaglio "Dark Light" in *The New York Landscape: Poems by Twenty State University of New York Poets, with Visual Responses by Twenty S.U.N.Y. Artists*, an exhibition that opened at The Plaza Gallery in Albany in 1981 and subsequently toured the State, with reprises in 1982-83 at the Pratt Manhattan Center Gallery in New York City and at S.U.N.Y. Plaza in the fall of 1994. This collaboration led to a permanent exhibit, the Jeffrey Sisson Memorial, in the lobby of the Aurelia Fox Memorial Hospital in Oneonta, which I had the pleasure to see for the first time when I went down to the investment of Justice this week. Also in 1981 *American Still Lifes*, a book of poems with drawings and design by O'Connell, was published by Charlie Davis.

In 1982 I was Bingham Poet-in-Residence at the University of Louisville, and in 1983 an awardist in the NEA/PEN Syndicated Fiction Project. *The Compleat Melancholick*, supported through a grant from the National Endowment for the Arts, was published in 1985 and exhibited at international book fairs in Europe. The next year I returned to Cleveland for the first time since 1964 to participate in the Poetry Center's silver anniversary. The same year, 1986, saw the publication of *A Maze of Monsters*, *The New Book of Forms* (which was introduced to the world by its publisher in a reception at the M.L.A. convention in New York City with a dinner afterward at The Algonquin — ah! if only poets could live like that a bit more often), and *Visions and Revisions of American Poetry*. However, in Connecticut my mother died — she was the same age as the century, and in Oswego I was a pall bearer several times:

THE SHADOWMAN

This is the year when everybody died —
This is the year when friends and neighbors died,
Took that short trip or ended the long slide.

Jim shot himself on Cemetery Road,
Left an ironic note beside the road.
No one heard his desperate heart explode.

Our frightened former next-door neighbor went —
Rita, the fearful widow from next-door went
To join her husband John in the firmament.

Paul's heart quit because his cough would not.
His life went up in smoke, for he could not
Stop smoking soon enough — so he would trot

Along our streets slower than folks could walk,
Jog the streets slower than we could walk
And slower than the shadowman can stalk.

Cooper's blood sluggishly turned to whey
In his pale veins — slowly turned to whey
Beneath the translucent skin now turned to clay.

Kermit and Dorothy lost this chilly spring
To the sickle and the crab — lost the spring
To the dim weather and the scorpion's sting.

And Mag, our neighbor on the other side,
Next door toward the lake on our north side,
Father of my son's best friend, has died

Because he loved his beer more than his life,
Loved his suds more than his very life,
Let alone his daughter, his son, his wife.

The shadowman comes tapping down the street,
His feet come stuttering along the street.
Nobodaddy's patrolling, walking his beat.

Hear him, townsmen, between the curbs of night,
Among our yards, towing the craft of night
Whether the hour is dusky or dark or light.

Listen to him breathing in the walls
Of all our houses, breathing in the walls,
In our kitchens and in the empty halls.

Stop when you listen and whisper to the dust,
"These are the names of neighbors scrawled in dust,
Whistled to shadow, scattered in a gust."

One of our high school crowd, Alice Van Leuvan, had married the Dutch composer Walter Hekster. When the Twents Conservatorium in Enschede, Holland, wanted to commission a chamber opera on an English script, Walter asked me for one. The result was *The Fog*, published in 1987 in Amsterdam. In 1989 both *Dialogue: A Socratic Dialogue on the Art of Writing Dialogue in Fiction* and *The Shifting Web: New and Selected Poems* appeared.

For many years, all of my married life, I had been writing family poems about the Houdlettes and the Getchells of Dresden, Maine, most of whom I loved as though they were blood relatives rather than in-laws, but I had never been able to develop a format into which I might fit them in an organic manner. At last I evolved a sequence titled *The Green Maces of Autumn, Voices in an Old Maine*

House, in which people who had lived on the farm for over two centuries, since 1754, spoke with one another across the generations. From this I culled two chapbooks of poems, the first of which was *A Family Album* in 1990; [the complete series would be published in 2002]. This was the prologue:

ALBUMS

        The ancient albums lie
   behind the parlor door spinning fine
tintype fables between plush covers: straight stares
    line out over handlebars and whalebone

        stays. They were familiars,
   once; now the summer eyes of the old
farm run through evenings of conjecture, try names
    against heydays, trace the features of these

        generations peering
   over collars and boas. A jowl
sags here, beneath this rafter. An eye is gray,
    like the sky over the hill. A fire

        flickers at the grate, flares
   and settles. Someone lights a pipe. Now
the pictures come to life and walk the halls: this
    bone is the old lady's, that tooth the man's.

        Whose child is this that sits
   in the dusty shadows — whose dust, whose
shade? Who made the bed of webs above the ell?
    Who sleeps, who wakes, whose footfall on the floor

        disturbs the carpet beetle in its lair?

The following year, 1991, I was Writer-in-Residence at Ashland University in Ohio which published a series of talks I gave there during my tenure, *The Public Poet: Five Lectures on the Art and Craft of Poetry*. A British edition of *Dialogue* was published in London as well, and a poem from the manuscript *Green Maces*, "Priscilla Bourne," was chosen to appear in *The Family*, a national juried visual art and poetry exhibition mounted by the Peconic Gallery of Riverhead, Long Island, New York. For four years in a row different judges took poems from the manuscript for the annual Peconic exhibitions. In 1992 a second chapbook culling from *The Green Maces*, titled *Murmurs in the Walls*, was published, and "Francis Pullen," was chosen to appear in the Peconic exhibition titled *Heroes*. In 1993 "William Mason" was selected for the *Imagination* exhibition, and in 1994 "Jason Pullen" hung in the fourth and final Peconic show, *Passion*, which subsequently traveled to the Rathbone Gallery of Page Junior College in Albany where I read from the chapbooks at the gallery's reception.

In the spring of 1992 the Alumni Association of my *Alma Mater*, the University of Connecticut, presented me with a Distinguished Alumnus Award, and later in the year *Il Dialogo*, the Italian edition of *Dialogue*, was published in Milan in a translation by Sylvia Biasi. Although I'd not been overseas since the *U.S.S. Hornet* had made its world cruise during 1953-1955, I'd always meant to go to England, but at the last moment something always seemed to go wrong: the roof blew off the house, the driveway sank out of sight in spring mud, the ancient sewer system collapsed. In 1992, however, Jean and I actually managed to go. We spent a week in London, and then during the second week drove around the rest of Britain, up to Wales and Scotland, in a whirlwind trip with two friends from Oswego, Tom and Mary Loe.

The following year I was granted a sabbatical, and I went back for a month, Jean joining me for the second fortnight. I spent the first two weeks in London, and then we went to visit friends in the Lake District and in Devon, where at the University of Plymouth at Exmouth I participated in the opening day class of a course in Modernism conducted by the English poets John Daniel and Tony Lopez.

In London I renewed my acquaintance with Gavin Ewart, who had read at Oswego in 1986, and got in touch with Ian Hamilton, for whom I had been writing entries on American poets for his *Oxford Companion to Twentieth Century Poetry*. He was associated with the literary periodical *Agenda*, and I made a point of attending its silver anniversary celebration at the Turret Bookshop where I heard various people read and chatted with some of them, including William Cookson and Sam Milne. It was there also that I made the acquaintance of a young American poet who had been living in England for eight years and had published two collections of poetry with Oxford University Press, Michael Donaghy. A few days later Michael took me to another reading at the Terrible Beauty Coffee House where I met some young expatriate Americans and Canadians and talked at some length with one of the readers, Charles Boyle. Then it was my turn to introduce Donaghy to David Ricks of the King's College, London, with whom I had been corresponding. At last Jean joined me, and when we got back to Oswego it was winter. I went back to work in my attic study with its huge window that looks out over our neighborhood.

Since 1982 I had been living inside Emily Dickinson's head, reading her work and writing about her in my garret on West 8th Street in Oswego. At last, in 1993, *Emily Dickinson, Woman of Letters*, was published; it included "A Sampler of Hours: Poems and Centos from Lines in Emily Dickinson's Letters":

BROWN STUDY

   His son's dinosaurs surround me.
Overhead in his attic study
     antique maps slant away
     between me and the stars.

   The kneewall set into the eaves
is sated with books. Down the garret,
     charts and prints cascade from
     the eastern wall — its slit
   window — to the western

>   door with a panel of glass stained
>   green and faint lavender,
>   the *fleur-de-lis* aqua
>   in a field of frost. The gable
>   end displays portraits of him, the boy
>   whose ancient animals
>   walk this landscape of books,
>
>   that pause of space which we call 'Father!'

Also published that year was a chapbook, *Legends of the Mist*. Though I liked the poems in it well enough, it was so badly produced that I got rid of every copy I could find. In October I was installed in the Hall of Fame of my home town in Connecticut, an event that was belittled by a fellow Workshop poet. I wrote him a letter that read in part,

> I saw your remarks in the Iowa Workshop *Newsletter* and feel constrained to write. Meriden, Connecticut, a city of about 50,000 souls, is the place where I grew up. When one's home town chooses to confer upon one of its sons or daughters its highest honor it is, indeed, an *honor*, because those people know you; they watched you walk the streets and play in their back yards; they noticed you in your best and worst moments over a period of years. The standard by which they judge you is stringent and personal.
>
> The man who nominated me was my high school choral director, Tony Parisi, now nearly blind. The person who seconded the nomination was the ancient editor of the *Morning Record*, for whom I had worked as a cub reporter, morgue clerk, and high school correspondent forty years earlier. The people who attended were citizens for whom as a child I had delivered newspapers, my classmates and schoolmates and playmates, the parishioners of my father's church including my Sunday school teacher, the organist with whom I had sung in the choir, the man with whom as a student I had collaborated to write the Meriden

High School Class of 1952's graduation song [Walter Carey].

The day I was installed in the Meriden Hall of Fame alongside the diva Rosa Ponselle and my classmate Tomie DePaola, winner of the Caldecott Award, was without a doubt the most gratifying day of my life. When another classmate [Jim Masterson] asked me whether I had truly enjoyed the day, I told him my only regret was that it could never come again.

My acceptance speech was a poem that I had written years earlier in Meriden about the family, the town, Hubbard Park, and Castle Craig, a stone tower on East Peak that looked down upon the place where Jean and I had grown up:

A FAMILY CELEBRATION

>That fourth of July a sly laugh
>>dogged our fancy. Uncle John,
>the old wag, taled off again. The children
>clamored in bushy shadow, and green
>>grass grew all around all around
>
>under the vintage windows, rosé
>>with the last of the sun. Like
>time shrunken and drawn taut across the evening,
>the lawn tapped out its cricket sounds and
>>Melora rapped her doldrums on
>
>the tabletop. Muzzy Aunt Nat
>>turned over turning forty-
>one, gave the women the once-over, thumbed
>down the thought. Who'll describe it? The park
>>that day was ducks like sparks about
>
>the pair of snowflame swans burning
>>out of blue sconces. The kids

had crackers and quacks — as many as they
    could swallow or toss; the trees had leaves
        thick as Moorish rugs. Their silhouettes

        blotted sunlight, drank it off thick
            banks and gravel walks. And flowers!
Bows of them, beds massed beneath Old Glory
    poling it over the bandshell, green
        benches applauding its rustic

        orchestration: flagstone, sandstone,
            half-timber. All told, it was
a period piece, a dash of Edward —
    a pause. But not ours, and surely not
        the children's. Perhaps we elders

        could remember when it was like
            this all day long, nearly, day
in, well-nigh, and out. And what were we to
    say when the night came mooning? When light
        lay draped lightly about the hill,

        and on the hill the old stone tower,
            in it the four flights of iron
stair that we climbed counting that afternoon
    to see the world unroll there beneath
        the parapet? Not even the world,

        merely our town: a tall tale told tongue-
            in-cheek — to a child holding
buttercups and clover — by a sly old
            mountebank, it well may be.

    During the winter of 1995 Tony Parisi died. Both Jean and I had sung in many of his choruses and a production of Gilbert and Sullivan's *H.M.S. Pinafore* while we were high school students and shortly afterward. We still sing in productions of the Oswego

Opera Theater; just this spring we were in the chorus of William Schuman's *The Mighty Casey*, a tortuous piece of music. Afterward we went to Meriden during spring break and made a point of visiting Tony's widow Tata, the Warren Gardners, the Jim Mastersons, Dorothy Van Leuvan, the mother-in-law of Walter Hekster, and others of our friends.

Recently I have been working on several projects, notably a manuscript volume of memoirs titled *A Sheaf of Leaves*, of which this essay will become an integral part, and *The Book of Literary Terms*, a test draft of which, on a Faculty Development Grant from S.U.N.Y. Oswego, has been given a field test this spring in various classes and schools. George O'Connell is working on a portfolio of prints incorporating my ancient "Bordello" series, and if all goes well we will exhibit them at the Rathbone Gallery in Albany during the spring of 1996.

Reading through this brief account of my professional life, I can see one might get the impression that all has been clear sailing for me during the last forty-five years or so. Such is far from the case. For instance, no one publisher till now has published more than two of my books, which means that I have had to sell each manuscript separately, without benefit of an agent. Early on there were long dry periods — eight years passed between the publication of my *First Poems* and my next full collection, *Awaken, Bells Falling*. I don't want to leave the reader with the notion that the writer's life is anything but frustration and rejection...but then, what life isn't? It's much more like this:

CANZONE

> *"Whatever you set your mind to, your personal total obsession, this is what kills you. Poetry kills you if you're a poet, and so on. People choose their death whether they know it or not."* — Don DeLillo in Libra, p. 46.

Canto Uno. Obsessive Ottavi
It's said we choose the thing that will destroy us:
The plumber picks the scalding pipe that bursts.

We seize upon the obsession to employ us
All our days — the butcher among his wursts
Will gasp his last on the sausage he embraces,
The cobbler strangle in his own shoelaces.
The tease will die in a way that will annoy us,
The sweetie-pie in a manner sure to cloy us.

The fiddler will pass away in some vile inn
Between gigs on the road. The hypnotist
Will suffer stroke and spend a little while in
Staring into nothingness; the dentist
Will feel the drill slicing through his sinus,
The banker's columns add at last to minus.
The model shall come to end her days in style, in
Styli the engraver; the clerk shall file in.

Who makes these rules? One wishes it were so,
But only poets smother in their words
That spill like cottage cheese out of their vents
In swollen streams throughout their lives. Although
The words are for the world, the world says, "Hence!
Take back this whey, take back these pallid curds."
And so we eat our words all our lives long,
Stifling finally in a mound of song.

Canto Due. Terminal Capitolo
Why is it when we've worked our will and won,
Some goomba comes along and trips us up?
Just when we're on our toes he knocks us down.
The ewe's in place, and now here comes the tup —
The ram is blind! He misses by a mile!
Basta! It does no good to mope and gripe —

We ought to groan and berate with a snile;
We ought simply to turn the other cheek,
But when we do we're met with another snarl

And batted from today into next...month.
That's to the good! for there we'll find the sun
Filling the halcyon sky with light and warmth.

Basta! again — smoke rises between our toes!
Just when the eyes have it, so does the nose.

Canto Tre. Aria Gone Awry
Everything is gall and bile at last,
A dagger in the liver or the spleen,
A splash of acid from the acrid past,
A dash of bitters in life's chipped tureen.
No matter what we do it comes out wrong,
Our voices crack in the middle of the...aria.

The world is a martini mixed, not stirred,
Its twist of lemon sere as August's rind.
Search as one may to find the proper word,
A synonym will have to do: "behind"
Becomes *arrears* and smells a little strong,
And that's the short of it, the short and...interminable.

So, what to do? Drink up the curdled broth;
Quaff the quotidian cocktail at the sink;
Choke down the peel that tastes like pickled moth;
You'll never swallow finer food or drink —
For future food becomes what you have passed,
And everything is gall and bile...in the final analysis.

Commiato. Elegiac Barzeletta
No one can tell which way the wind is blowing
Unless it's snowing; then the eyes can wrinkle
And an inkling — just a hint — of the future
Lash its way beneath your eyelid. Your cornea
Will be abraded. You will be all but blinded.
You'll long for California, or perhaps you'll
Wish that you'd been born dead. You take my meaning?

The weather of the world's demeaning, *non e*
Vero? The temperature is zero even
On a summer evening: Here comes the sunset;
The azure of the heavens slowly deepens
To violet. The sun on the horizon
Cloaks itself in velvet mists. It is lovely...,

Until the hailstones fall upon our foreheads
As we look up. The wind comes whistling meanly
Among the fuschias, knocking down the bluebirds'
Happy house. Outstanding among the headstones
We find our fortune: "He who lies here sleeping
Cares not for hail or gallstones, earth or ether,
Nor for songs of the plaining poet's making,
But for dreams that rise from a gravel pillow."

Upstairs

On the theory that after more than four decades of marriage my wife Jean might possibly know more about how I work at my writing than I do, at least consciously, I asked her to help me with this essay. "When you're working," she said, "you're upstairs," meaning upstairs in my garret study in Oswego, New York, on blue Ontario's shores.

I waited for further information, but none was forthcoming. "That's it?"

She thought for a moment. She smiled. "When you come downstairs you're in a good mood." And that *is* it in a nutshell: writing makes me happy. I'm one of those people who enjoy writing, but to begin with, of course, I enjoyed reading.

In order to enjoy reading, however, one must be introduced to the practice. This is critically important, and one's early environment, I believe, is the key. Some people come to reading by accident, others are lucky to have parents who read, and often one's cultural heritage is either a help or a hindrance. In an essay titled "In Search of Italian / American Writers" Fred Gardaphé wrote the following:

There were no bookshelves in my home. Reading anything beyond newspapers and the mail required escaping from my family. I soon developed a chronic reading problem that identified me as the "merican" or rebel. My reading betrayed my willingness to enter mainstream American culture, and while my family tolerated this, they did little to make that move an easy one.

Prof. Gardaphé came to reading circuitously:

> Once, while I was being chased by the police for disturbing local merchants so my partners could shoplift, I ran into the public library. I found myself in the juvenile section and grabbed a book to hide my face. Safe from the streets, I spent the rest of the afternoon reading, believing that nobody would ever find me there. And I was right, so whenever I was being chased, I would head straight for the library, which became my asylum. (Gardaphé, 1997).

Nothing could have been further from my own experience; however, thinking back on my early life, I consider it remarkable that my own parents, given their individual histories — impoverished childhoods in Sicily and Wisconsin, my mother a product of rural American penury, my father someone who wanted to be "someone," the only evident way to that goal being to join the local Mafia, a course he contemplated for a time — brought up their children as members of the middle class who had no doubt at all we were as privileged as anyone else. Thus, *attitude* is important, how one regards oneself, no matter what one's background may be.

Somehow, without what we now call a "role model," unless it was one or more of her teachers, my mother had managed to pull herself out of her parents' Superior, Wisconsin, shack, and work her way, first, through secretarial school and then through Boston University's School of Religious Education. Likewise, my father had extricated himself from Riesi, Sicily, and all sorts of menial jobs, to become pastor of the First Italian Baptist Church of Meriden, Connecticut.

Though we had no money, our house was full of books of all sorts. My mother read to me from the cradle, and I soon learned to read for myself. Nor was writing an abstruse act, because every week for as long as I can remember I watched my father hunched over his typewriter hunting out and pecking at his two weekly sermons, one in English and one in Italian.

From an early age, also, I was aware that my mother's family had a long and fascinating, if not always distinguished, history. George Puttenham, back in the sixteenth century, had been the author of *The Arte of English Poesie*, a fact that was fraught with omens for me, omens of which I was not completely aware when in 1959 I began writing my own *The Book of Forms A Handbook of Poetics*, published first by Dutton in 1968.

I knew, too, that Israel Putnam had been a general in Washington's colonial army and that Amelia Earhart had been married to George Palmer Putnam, the publisher. There have been many writers, librarians and teachers among the Putnams (my daughter, Melora, is a librarian), but there had been lots of farmers and artisans as well (my brother is a toolmaker). From my reading I knew of the involvement of the Putnam clan in the Salem Witch Hunt of colonial America — in high school I wrote an addendum chapter to Hawthorne's *The House of the Seven Gables* and a Senior Skit for the Fantaseers, our "science fiction reading club," about the trials of the Salem witches.

In retrospect I can see that I was subjected to anti-Italian prejudice, even on the part of at least one of my teachers, but either I did not recognize it or I ignored or disdained it, for I always felt myself to be seminally involved with English and American literature because of my family connections with the majority culture. Felix Stefanile, reviewing *Pocoangelini, A Fantography & Other Poems* (1971) said, "Turco seems to have the whole of the English lyric tradition at his fingertips..." (Stefanile, 1975). That's because I have studied it closely all my life, taught it for more than three decades, and write out of it perfectly "naturally."

This business of prejudice is not uncomplicated. The title of my entry, during my senior high school year, in the school's Hicks Prize Essay Contest — one of the six finalists — was "A Row of Hedges," and it made an elaborate metaphor: the hedges outside the English Honors classroom represented the succession of our school years; the window cut off the view of the downhill end of the hedges, which represented the future, etc., etc. Quite corny, but decently written for a high school senior, evidently. I was told by other teachers that two of the three faculty judges thought my essay was the best one submitted that year, but that one judge, Mark Bollman, refused to support it for the prize. In 1993 our old music teacher, Antonio Parisi, confirmed what I had long suspected: "Bollman hated Italians," he said. "You never stood a chance."

At Fenn College (now the Cleveland State University) at the beginning of my second year of teaching in 1961, I was asked to address the incoming freshmen at the fall convocation. Reaching back into my not-so-distant past, I refurbished "A Row of Hedges" and turned it into an exemplary talk about the importance of writing in college. Afterward one of the freshmen approached me to say, "I hope you don't expect us to write as well as that!" I didn't, but I wished I could have done so.

One supposes that teachers ought at least to try to be even-handed with all their students and to recognize and reward merit no matter where it arises, but there is prejudice toward Italians even among members of the Italian-American community itself. Some of my father's Italian parishioners were unhappy because they had a "Sicilian" pastor, a standard distinction and bias, for Sicily is considered by Italians to the north to be ethnically part of Africa. And one can perhaps also imagine what the Italian Roman Catholics thought — they called my brother and me "the priest's kids".

Most of our parishioners lived in the neighborhood of the church, like the Poles who lived on Polish Hill near St. Stanislaus church. The Irish had their section of the city, as did the Germans, but none of the "ethnic" families that I knew wanted their children to be "Italian-Americans" or whatever-"Americans." They wanted them to be "Americans." The sooner into the melting pot, the better. My view of my "Italianness" has always been much closer to that of John Ciardi than it is to that of Gardaphé.

Vince Clemente, in an essay titled "The Writer as Hyphenated-American," wrote, "The critic Harold Bloom once came down heavily on the poet Stanley Kunitz for 'evading his Jewish heritage' in his poetry. Kunitz thought about that for a long time, and in his response articulated perfectly the plight of those American writers who carry with them, along with the burden to recreate the truth as they see it, the freight of ethnicity, this 'dual citizenship.' In a spring 1982 *Paris Review* interview Kunitz remarked:

> It's obvious that Jewish cultural aspiration and ethical doctrine entered into my bloodstream, but in practice I am an American free-thinker, a damn stubborn one, and my poetry is not hyphenated.... True, I have no religion, but I have strong religious feelings. Moses and Jesus and Lao-tse have all instructed me...and three of the poets who most strongly influenced me — Donne, Herbert, and Hopkins — happen to have been Christian churchmen."

Clemente continued, "The American poet and translator of Dante, John Ciardi, himself the son of Italian immigrant parents, wrote in an early letter to me, 'I have poured out endless poems about my Italian "roots." Yet Jefferson, Tom Paine, and even — God save the mark, Emerson — are as much at the roots of my mind and feeling as the It[alian] of my Am[erican]. I am an American man of letters!' Like Kunitz, Ciardi insisted his 'poetry is not hyphenated.' In fact, he once told me, 'In truth, my boyhood (in Boston's Little Italy and Medford, Massachusetts) was not so much an Italian-American one as *my* boyhood.' And just two weeks later, in another letter, he recalled, 'I had a longish poem about Italy in the *Atlantic* some years back, and when Robert Lowell wrote to praise its Italo-Amer[ican] voice, I took offense. Did the S.O.B. suppose I had used an Amer[ican] Eng[lish] inferior to his, or that I inherited and made mine less Amer[ican] Eng[lish] than his?'

"About that time," Clemente wrote, "I proposed to him the prospect of an anthology of 'Italian-American Poets.' He never really warmed up to the thing and wrote to the poet-critic Lewis Turco, 'I've never thought in terms of Italian-American poetry; I don't know any Italian-American poets, as such. Lew Turco is an American poet who happened to have [an Italian father]. Theodore Roethke is a ditto with German parents.' Now, all these years later," Clemente discovered, "I know just what Ciardi meant: Why isn't Archibald MacLeish a Scottish-American poet? Whitman, on his mother's side, a Dutch-American one? I like to feel the American experience is broad enough, indeed all-encompassing as Whitman's vision of it, to include all of us as simply 'Americans' without the hyphen" (Clemente, 1996).

In a videotaped interview that he made for the "Writers' Forum" series at the S.U.N.Y. College at Brockport (a tape I played about once a year for two decades in my contemporary American poetry class), Robert Hayden was asked about "Black poetry." His response was that such a term, which had the approval of many militant Black poets, was useful primarily to white academics who wish to ignore poetry written by blacks. The inference to be drawn therefrom, Hayden said, is that somehow poetry written by black Americans is not good enough, or not universal enough to be included in the Anglo-Saxon literary canon.

In a letter dated February 24, 1976, Radcliffe Squires, in his capacity as editor of *The Michigan Quarterly Review*, published by the University of Michigan where Hayden was teaching at the time, wrote to one of his regular reviewers who happened to be a white academic — myself, to be specific, "to ask you if you could review Robert Hayden's *Angle of Ascent*.... He feels bad that every place seems to feel it must have him reviewed by another black. I agree that is both silly and intolerable. Anyway, I hope you will be willing to undertake this...." I was, and I did.

Hayden always wanted to be judged merely as a poet among poets, not one to whom special rules of criticism had to be applied in order to make his work acceptable in more than a sociological sense. His stance, reiterated in the Brockport interview, was well known for a long time both to militant blacks and to "liberal" whites. Thus, if the latter relegated Hayden to the literary ghetto along with the other Black poets, the former have seen him, if not as an "Uncle Tom," at least as a reluctant resident. Perhaps this situation best explains why Hayden was virtually ignored during his lifetime. Yet Hayden, like Ciardi, wrote as much out of his ethnicity as anyone else. He was a paradigmatic poet of the English language who was also true to his roots and history, though not circumscribed by what is merely racial, ethnic, or personal.

Just as Stanley Kunitz, John Ciardi, and Robert Hayden did, I sometimes write out of my ethnic "heritage." Writing in their book *La Storia: Five Centuries of the Italian American Experience* (Mangione, 1992), Jerre Mangione and Ben Morreale said, "Not all of the immigrants' offspring who became poets were as much at ease in America as Ciardi. But the most gifted of them were able to transcend the specifics of the Italian American experience through the more subjective and symbolic language of their craft. For poets deeply imbued with the experience of trying to straddle two cultures, such as Lewis Turco and Frank Polite, poetry became the vehicle by which they could transmit the loneliness of their alienation with impunity, without denying or betraying their Italian connection."

But I don't remember being alienated as an *Italian* American, though I certainly do as a *Protestant* Italian American. Mangione and Morreale continued, "Lewis Turco, one of the most prolific of the Italian American poets, gradually distanced himself from his past as he journeyed toward the mainstream. By the time he was in his thirties, in 1973, when he published *Pocoangelini: A Fantography*, Italianate poems constituted only a third of the contents. They were a group of so-called 'Sketches,' which A. R. Ammons characterized as 'an autobiography of biographies,..'" (Mangione, 1992). Although it is true that I distanced myself from my youth, of course (everybody does), I never distanced myself from my ethnicity. I simply write poems and stories — and, of recent decades, essays — as they occur to me, and if later on I feel that older material can be mined, transformed, or linked together to form longer works or sequences, as I first did in "Observations" and *The Sketches*, so be it. Now that I think of it, that was how Walt Whitman worked, too.

Lewis Turco

Our Friend Dan Chaucer

My daughter, Melora, was the chief librarian of the Bailey Library in Winthrop, Maine. She is now the director of the Outreach Program of the Maine State Library in Augusta, she chairs the Committee on Intellectual Freedom of the Maine Librarians' Association, and she is active on the national level of the Modern Library Association. Unlike some of her colleagues, especially many small-town librarians, Melora does not believe in the censorship of books. She takes a considerable amount of flak for this liberal position, though she has many backers as well. She thinks that the truth is important.

John of Salisbury wrote in the twelfth century that "The lies of poets are lies in the service of truth." I used to read those lies, those tall tales and fables, day in and day out. I would walk down the streets of my home town reading books, and somehow I was never hit by a car or in any other way seriously injured because my nose was buried in a sheaf of dry leaves. I first made the acquaintance of "Dan" Chaucer, as Jonson or Donne or someone once called him, when my parents invested in *The Book of Knowledge*. As I recall, they bought the encyclopedia more for my younger brother's than for my use; although I was perhaps a bit old for a schoolboy's reference work, I was the one who pored through it. Gene never was much interested in reading. It was in the pages devoted to modern versions of *Beowulf* and *The Canterbury Tales* that I began to understand something of the unchanging drives and characteristics of human nature. Later, in college, under the tutelage of Charley Owen at UConn, I read the *Tales* in the original Middle English and learned something of the subtleties of the language, but I regret to say that I never mastered the old English of *Beowulf*.

To no book in the English language is John of Salisbury's statement more applicable than *The Canterbury Tales*. These tales are mere fiction. The characters depicted in these pages never existed. Although there were during the Middle Ages pilgrimages from London and other cities to the holy center Canterbury, and the route Chaucer's travelers took existed, this particular group of people never got together for the trip, never knew each other, never spoke the words the poet put into their mouths. Nevertheless, in a very real sense this is a book of history. How can this be?

The answer to the question is that some books of fiction depict the life of an era and we have no other books to tell us what that era was like. Are *The Iliad* and *The Odyssey* of Homer merely ancient novels, or do they tell us of events that actually took place? Was there a city of Troy? Did the Greeks and the Trojans actually go to war over a beautiful woman named Helen? Was there, in fact, a poet named "Homer" who wrote these poems? For years, during the nineteenth century, all these questions were debated, but then Heinrich Schliemann found the site of what many scholars and scientists believe to be the fabled city, and partial answers to the questions began to be formed. A great deal of this "history," however, is still conjecture, yet we act as though what "Homer" wrote were "gospel."

What of the Bible? Was there a historical Garden of Eden? Were there two people named Adam and Eve? Did Genesis take place? Was there an actual Exodus? Whether or not mankind is able to answer these questions with any degree of certainty or faith, we know logically that there had to be a first human being somewhere in the dim past; there had to be the First Mother and the First Father of the race, and they existed in an environment that was conducive to their survival.

Who were the Cro-Magnon men and women? What happened to their contemporaries, the brutish-looking, yet intelligent race called Neanderthal man? On Sunday, the fourth of July, 1993, in *The New York Times Book Review* there was an essay that discussed three new books on the subject: Did Cro-Magnon destroy Neanderthal, or did he die out naturally, cataclysmically, because of some inherent flaw in his constitution?

Back in the mid-'forties when I was a fifth or sixth-grader living on North Third Street in Meriden, Connecticut, I was crazy about prehistory. One day I walked down to Ciotti's sundries store a couple of blocks away, on West Main Street, and I purchased a pamphlet about cavemen. As usual, I walked back home with my nose buried in the book, and soon I was standing in front of my house showing it to Bob Strauss, my best friend from across the street, who looked over my shoulder as I turned the pages. Shortly we came across the picture of a Neanderthal, a reconstruction of what he must have looked like, with his strong-featured face displaying its heavily-ridged brow (a bit like the brow-ridge I have myself).

As we stood before my two-storied house reading we happened to glance at my upstairs neighbor, old Mr. Longo, who was leaning over the railing. To say we were startled is to understate, for the picture in my book could have been a photograph of our neighbor. Bob and I stood comparing the man with his likeness for several minutes. There was no doubt about it, the man and the reconstruction were practically identical.

From that moment I felt certain I knew what had happened to Neanderthal man: he had been absorbed into the general Cro-Magnon population. I have remained interested in the subject of mankind's origins all my life. We know that the race of Mankind spread across the globe from some point of origin. Therefore, we can invent stories, like the book of Genesis, to explain our beginnings, and in those stories, though they be "lies," there will be a core of fact, and they will be lies in the service of truth. This is a lie I invented to explain our origins to myself, from my chapbook of poems having to do with the legendary prehistory and history of the race, *Legends of the Mists* (1993):

Lewis Turco

DAWN SONG

"...world of the first rose, and the first lark's song." —
Margaret Mead

I am the first to know dawn for the dawn —
it breaks across my mind as across the eyes
of the beast I was, of the beasts from whom I come,
and the swift sun slows, and I know it for the sun
in the world of the first rose, and the first lark's song.

I am the first to see the sharp sun dawn,
breaking across my terror and my surprise;
to know that I am the beast who knows his name:
Beast of the Sun, beast of the spinning sun
of the world of the first rose, and the first lark's song.

I am the first to see stone for a stone,
to heft it in my hand, to feel its weight
and know what it may do to the brittle bone
of the beasts of the sun, in the morning of the sun,
in the world of the first rose, and the first lark's song.

I see, and my sight is hard, hard as the stone
held in my hand, and this stone will be my fate.
The beast is my brother — beast is his only name.
He is the child of dust. I am stone's son,
born of the first rose and the first lark's song.

How many people have lived and breathed in this world since the first man or woman recognized him- or herself as a human being? How many have eaten and made love and raised children and suffered famine and plague and drought? How many have died and no one remembers who they were or where (or if) they were buried? But how many are acquainted with Tom Sawyer and Huckleberry Finn? With Hercule Poirot? With Scrooge and Uncle Tom and Hamlet? With the Wife of Bath? Do these characters exist or don't they? Are they less real than the nameless hosts who have existed and disappeared without a trace? Have they had an effect on the lives of other people? Do readers know them as well as they know their next-door neighbors? Better, perhaps? Are these fictive personalities as substantial as the woman who works down the hall?

The Canterbury Tales is the best document we have from the period in which it was written to tell us what that era was like. Some books of fiction are also history, and this is one of them. How do we know that the fifteenth century in England was like the times portrayed in Chaucer's book? Because the author convinces us that it was. If these are merely characters in a story, Chaucer makes us believe in their reality. If we know in our minds that these people never lived, nevertheless we are certain that people just like these existed. As a matter of fact, we know people like these who are still alive, that we have run into in the course of our daily lives.

We know that these things have happened, that they still happen. We are convinced that there are still people around who, like the clerk Nicholas in "The Miller's Tale," are capable of seducing a neighbor's wife and playing dirty, frat-style tricks on others. We know that there are evil mothers-in-law, like those that preyed upon Constance in "The Man of Law's Tale." In some cities and towns school officials and parents have been upset with the depiction of the corrupt Church of Chaucer's time, as portrayed in the hilarious "Friar's Tale" and the retaliatory "The Summoner's Tale." But what is the point of being upset with what we know was the case in those long-dead days? Why do we suppose there was a Protestant reformation and a Catholic Counter-Reformation later on in the sixteenth century? As a matter of fact, in Chaucer's own time the Englishman John Wyclif led a dissident religious movement.

Again, perhaps Chaucer makes these people too real for us to disbelieve. It is one thing to read a list of dry facts in a history of the period, quite another to experience them vicariously in the pages of the *Tales*, for there they take on life and substance. As we read we breathe the air these pilgrims breathed and we walk the road they trod on their way to Canterbury to perform a religious ritual.

Is that another thing that bothers some readers? That these people are engaged in a purportedly holy trek but on the way they tell stories ranging from the tragic to the coarse, from the pious to the scatological? Isn't that what one might have to label hypocritical? But does it come as a surprise to us that there are hypocrites in the world? Do we want our children to grow up believing that they can take everyone at face value? Do we think they would have no other exposure to hypocrisy? Deception, honesty, infidelity, constancy, injustice, kindness — these are the topics of the stories Chaucer's characters tell, most of them adapted from stories that other writers, such as Giovanni Boccaccio and Chaucer's contemporary John Gower, had already told, but more important than these considerations are the characters of the travelers themselves which give us the flesh and blood of the fifteenth century. For instance, I knew The Wife of Bath personally, or someone just like her — she lived in my back yard when Mr. Longo lived upstairs.

We'll call her "Mrs. Boone." Like Chaucer, I am going to tell the truth, but I am going to tell some partial lies to get at the truth for the good reason that I don't wish to hurt the feelings of those who are still living, should they happen to run across this memoir.

My family lived at 43 North Third Street in Meriden, and Mrs. Boone lived with her family at 43-1/2 North Third; in effect, in our back yard. Like the old woman in the shoe, she had so many children I was never able to count them all, and they ranged in age from three to around thirty. Most of them lived at home, but some were out in the world on their own and only visited. Mrs. Boone was lusty, loud, and always carrying on at the top of her lungs. She was dark-haired, dark-eyed and middle-aged, and she lived in a medium-sized house with her children, Mr. Boone, and "Uncle Zack." Mr. Boone was on the short side; he was thin, and he had a swarthy complexion and black hair. His face was long and his eyes were dark and sorrowful. I never saw him smile. For some reason I thought of him as being French, and I don't recall his ever speaking, although he must have done so.

Uncle Zack, on the other hand, was tallish, blond, thick in the middle, round-faced, and often laughing. His skin was so fair that it always looked flushed, and perhaps it was — he was most likely a drinker. Some of the Boone kids looked like Mr. Boone, but others looked a lot like Uncle Zack. The youngest child, in particular, was the spit and image of his "uncle" — I remember at the time thinking the resemblance was odd, even though I knew little or nothing about genetics or heredity. But when I read "The Wife of Bath's Prologue and Tale" in college (I don't believe it was included in the version published in *The Book of Knowledge*), I recognized Mrs. Boone immediately.

The Wife of Bath tells us (please blame and forgive me for this rough prose translation of Chaucer's spritely verse), "Experience, though there were no other authority in this world, is good enough for me to speak of the woe to be found in marriage; for, lords, since I was twelve years old, (thanks be to the eternal Lord!) I have had five husbands at the church door, if I might have been married so often, and each one was a worthy man in his own degree. But I was told...that since Christ never went but once to a wedding, in the Cane of Galilee, his example taught me that I should be wedded only once." And the Wife of Bath had outlived all five of her "husbands."

The story she spins is your standard tale out of folklore, about a knight who is given the task of answering correctly, within a year, the question, "What do women most love?" The answer, "sovereignty," is given to him by a witch, but in return he must agree to marry the hag. A man of his word, he carries out his promise reluctantly, upon which the old woman is transformed into a lovely young woman — moral: always keep your promises and you will be rewarded. But it isn't the story that parents object to, it is the prologue in which the Wife of Bath rises off the page a substantial, a nearly palpable personality, as easy of virtue as she is of religion.

The Wife of Bath rationalizes her behavior and resorts to the Bible to vindicate her actions. How many real people do the same? How many nations have interpreted the scriptures so as to vindicate some act of war or inhumanity while people on the other side do the same thing? One need only look at Northern Ireland, or Bosnia, or Africa or Palestine today to see it being done.

What having five husbands, or one husband and four live-in lovers, boils down to is this, she says: "Men may foresee and justify up and down, but I know well and say without lying, God bade us wax and multiply — that gentle text I can well understand. I know as well that He said my husband should forsake his father and mother and cleave to me, but he mentioned no particular number, nor 'bigamy' or 'octogamy.' Why, then, should men speak of it as villainy?" Perhaps that philosophy of life is what some readers object to. Have they never heard it before? Do they know nothing of people who have practiced what is called "common law marriage?" The term "live-in boyfriend" is one that has become commonplace during my lifetime.

Chaucer's "fault" is that he made his characters true-to-life. We cannot disbelieve in their existence. They walk around among us, and their types are always with us. There are Mrs. Boones and Uncle Zacks living in houses throughout the nation. We can close our eyes to Chaucer, and perhaps we can put blinkers on the eyes of our children, but we cannot obliterate the life that goes on around us.

If our children have eyes, they will see that life; if they are unlucky, they will make the same mistakes that characters make in the pages of books. But if our children read about such lives, they will have experienced vicariously a reality that they do not, themselves, have to live through in order to learn something about how to deal with the world.

What is it, after all, that we wish schools to do for our children if not to train and educate them to get along in the world? In his poem "Cliff Klingenhagen" the American poet Edwin Arlington Robinson tells of a fellow who had a neighbor in to dine, and after the meal "Cliff took two glasses and filled one with wine / And one with wormwood. Then, without a sign / For me to choose at all, he took the draught / Of bitterness himself," and gave the neighbor the glass of good wine. Why?

For the same reason that the poet in A. E. Housman's "Terence, This Is Stupid Stuff" tells the story of King Mithridates. The "stupid stuff" is literature, poetry. A friend of the poet wants him to put down his pen and come out for a drink. "...good Lord, the verse you make, / It gives a chap the belly-ache." The poet replies that he would face the trouble-filled world "...as a wise man would, / And train for ill and not for good. / 'Tis true, the stuff I bring for sale / Is not so brisk a brew as ale," but it will do his friend more good than liquor, for to read of the world's ills is the same as doing what Mithridates did: he took small doses of all the poisons of "the many-venomed earth," until he had built up immunities to them all. Then, when his enemies "...put arsenic in his meat," they "stared aghast to watch him eat; / They poured strychnine in his cup / And shook to see him drink it up." But the king was immune to their malice; " — I tell the tale that I heard told. / Mithridates, he died old."

We inoculate our children against diseases by vaccinating them with organic material made from the viruses that spread the disease. Literature is harmless material that can prepare us to cope with the lives we must lead. It can be history; it can introduce us to friends who will walk beside us until the day we die; it can give us insights into why our neighbors do what they do...into why we do what we do. Writers of fiction and poetry were the first, and they are still often the most effective psychologists, sociologists, theologians and historians, even though they are also liars, for they invent stories, like *The Canterbury Tales,* that hold up mirrors to the many-faceted world in which we move and have our being.

Lewis Turco

My Old Pal Walt

As I mentioned earlier, I first read Walt Whitman's poem "Mannahatta" in "Doc" Michel's 11th-grade English class. Miss Michel was a wonderful French teacher with a Diplôme Supérieur from the Universite de Rennes and a Ph.D. from Laval University in Quebec, but like many of the teachers at Meriden High School in 1950, she had to teach both in and out of her discipline, and I was glad she did.

My other outstanding English teacher in high school was Mary Flynn, whom I was fortunate to have in my sophomore year. She counseled me to concentrate on writing fiction rather than poetry because, she thought, I would have a better shot at making money from it. I had been writing both, and, in fact, had begun publishing both in the local paper and in school publications. For a while after Miss Flynn's counsel my literary fate hung in the balance. Perhaps it was reading Whitman's upbeat, Pollyanna-ish effusion and a subsequent trip to the Bowery that brought me down on the poetic side of the fence. Or maybe not — perhaps it was something as pragmatic as going into the Navy where my situation was more conducive to writing shorter pieces rather than prose narratives.

I'd not yet been exposed to a great deal of Whitman, and it was shortly after Doc Michel's class had read "Mannahatta" that I took my first trip to Manhattan and saw for myself what Whitman's glorious city had become in the twentieth century. The vague sense of offense I'd felt when I read his poem crystallized, after the trip, into a lifelong aversion to the work of "The Good Gray Poet." Yet, in a curious sense, my negative response to Whitman was as formative for me as a positive response has been for many another writer. He was the motivating force behind the writing of my first ambitious poem, which was also my longest poem to that date, the most serious, and the most consciously formal, in contrast with what I perceived at the time to be the aformal splatter of Whitman's good gray prose poetry.

I don't recall the occasion of the field trip to New York City, ninety miles away from Meriden, Connecticut, down the Merritt Parkway, but it was an excursion by bus. Not much remains in my memory of the outing. I do remember we saw "Chinatown" and the Bowery. I recollect the skyscraper canyons and the dirt. But there is one image that is still vivid — it was of a derelict on the Bowery.

He was, or he seemed to be, an old man. I saw him up close. He wore a tattered T-shirt and a pair of the palest blue denim "dungarees," frayed around his ankles, no shoes, his toenails long and filthy. An old piece of rope was knotted around his waist for a belt. The creases of skin on his face were filled with dirt, and in his ears the dirt was caked like topsoil. His hair was white; it fell down over his eyes, which were as pale blue as his jeans — washed out, empty, the eyes of a chronic alcoholic. He was panhandling. It was a dismaying and disillusioning experience, to say the least, to be brought face-to-face with this wrecked human being amid the squalid alleys of New York. I returned home considerably troubled by what I had seen of the reality behind Whitman's "prophetic" vision of America.

Not long after the trip I began to write some poems about my experiences in and impressions of Manhattan. I must have shown them to Doc Michel, but it was not until the next year, in Mark Bollman's twelfth-grade English honors class, that I conceived of the epic scheme of my adolescence, "Observations of a Resurrected Corpse," as I originally titled my English Honors project. When we all had finished our projects, we spent several days discussing them and deciding which examples were to appear in the class magazine, *The Leaky Pen*.

Bollman was a graduate of Muhlenberg College in Allentown, Pennsylvania, but he had taken his M. A. from Yale University, just a couple of towns south of Meriden in New Haven. He struck me as an upright, if not an up-tight Yankee type, but I was unprepared for his reaction to my poem, a response more violent than mine had been to Whitman's.

I was as apolitical as anyone might imagine a 1950s teenager could be. I recall one day when Arthur von Au, another member of Bollman's class and co-editor with me of the yearbook, remarked that we would probably soon be at war with the Russians. I was incredulous. How could we go to war with our beloved ally of World War II? Now, in 1991, the Soviet Union is spontaneously self-destructing, we love the Russian people again, and it turns out that I was right, after all, but who could have imagined it? I venture back along the pathway of recollection and wonder exactly when it was that we stopped worrying about the atomic bomb, and I realize that it has been something like twenty years since anyone actually thought that one would be dropped anywhere.

Somewhere along the line the world, at least most people in the world if not their governments, stopped believing in the likelihood of atomic mass destruction. I never thought the Russians would "bury us," as Khrushchev said later on, but on the other hand I never thought that Communism was any kind of viable system, either. In fact, in my senior year I didn't even have a handle on what the word meant. I was therefore unprepared when Bollman, in the middle of the class' discussion of "Observations," without forewarning, smashed his fist down upon his desk and roared — and this is a near quote — "It is from such works as this that the seeds of Communism spring and grow to bear evil fruit!"

No, the word "unprepared" is insufficient to describe not only my astonishment but that of the class as well. I remember everyone sitting bolt upright, our mouths open and eyes wide, first staring at

Bollman and then turning to look at each other. I leaned forward and whispered to my friend Ray in the seat ahead of me, "What's 'Communism'?" Even when I found out later, I was baffled by Bollman's outburst. Could he possibly imagine that a senior in Meriden High School was a raving Bolshevik? Though it was true at the time that I assumed it was the government's responsibility to take care of the sick, the poor, and the aged. I would not be rudely disabused of my misconception of the role of government until I entered the Navy after my graduation from high school and discovered that only those actually in government service were thus protected from the worst ravages of fate and nature.

Bollman's view of my work notwithstanding, I thought well enough of "Observations of a Resurrected Corpse" to enter it in that year's Scholastic Writing Awards competition, sponsored by Scholastic Magazines, Inc. My attack upon Whitman received a citation, one of several I won that year in the State competition in both fiction and poetry, and it was the only poem from Meriden that won a Key Award in the national contest.

A dozen years later I still thought well enough of my first earnest attempt to court the Muse to take it out and revise it once more, this time for full publication in a little magazine, *Quartet*. That version is sufficiently like the original to give a fair impression of the work Bollman felt was a threat to democratic society. In revising the poem I changed its title to "The City's Masque," and I emphasized its inherently dramatic form:

THE CITY'S MASQUE

Persons of the masque:
A **Corpse**
Chorus of Townsfolk

Place of the masque: a graveyard near a city at the present time. During the first portion of the masque the city is nearly obscured by a fog. As the action progresses the city becomes more clearly defined, until at last it is illuminated by a garish yellow light. As the masque opens, the Corpse is discovered standing outside the graveyard.

Corpse. The earth is good.
I am grateful, satisfied with life.
Nature's treasure is my heritage,
and equilibrium of mind is mine —
worldly things I neither own nor want;
tranquility and work suffice for me.
My life is pleasure's bed.

(*He moves inside the graveyard, kneels before a stone*).

But I come to Death.
Abysms engulf my tired flesh.
Sleep enfolds me; the darkness here is dense.
Dreams writhe fitfully upon the verge
of consciousness, but cannot penetrate
this stratum of existence. Now and then
I sense a surge towards life...,

(*He rises*).

I awaken!
Up, dank bones! and walk among mankind.
Wind and sun once more caress my flesh.
Let me pause a time and look about;
nearby, what? — here stands a morose crowd
of men and women who deploy like sorrow
about this granite forest.

At this point the reader might pause and look at the form a high school poet chose to use for these soliloquies by his protagonist — that form has not been changed from the original. The first line of each stanza is iambic dimeter, accentual-syllabic verse, and each last line is iambic trimeter; thus, the first and last lines of each stanza, taken together, equal one line of iambic pentameter verse which was, in effect, broken at the caesura (a medial pause) into two lines. The five lines intervening are iambic pentameter as well. Whenever the Corpse talks to himself, he uses this stanza. His dialogues with the Chorus, however, are in rhymed heroic couplets: this is a change from the original, which used iambic tetrameter rhyming couplets. Perhaps when I revised the poem for publication I wanted a little extra space in the line to orate, or tetrameters felt too short for the gravity of the speeches. The Corpse is still speaking:

> As I stand among these muted graves
> beggar, churchman, chandler, — saints and knaves
> wearing their solitary cloaks of gloom —
> stand in the shadow of my cast-off tomb.
> Their mouths begin to writhe. I hear them sigh:
>
> **Chorus.** What was it like to sleep in the soil, to lie
> breathless beneath the rock, your mortal breath
> stopped by a mute of sand? Tell us of Death —
> what song does he strum upon his solemn lute?
> Does Peace come piping quietly with his flute,
> filling the earth with the harmony of things?
> Or do men's frenzied bones dance in the night
> to the drums of Fear? Is there second sight,
> or only the blind worm tunneling through recall?
> Is Death a passage through this mortal wall?
> Tell us. We wish to know, for we have seen
> all that we care to of this wild careen
> of planets and futile works through vacant space.
>
> **Corpse.** You amaze me, mortals. Of what place
> and time are you, of what hopeless race?
> Are the men all gone, replaced by mannequins
> hollow inside? Or is this Hell were sins
> shall be scourged by mockery instead of flame?
> Don't ask me to number things I cannot name.
> Rather, if you be made of virile marrow
> go live in the world. Rejoice before you sorrow.
>
> **Chorus.** We've known the world, and were it not for fear
> of the unknown, we'd trade you our career

for your contentment, if Death be content.
This planet's virile youth, and ours, is spent
with waste and wars; Nature's vicious rape
has been accomplished by the hairless ape.

Since you cannot impart your history
of sleep, we'll tell you ours — a wakeful story
that has to do with people piled on people
in dens of stone taller than any steeple.
We'll talk of a place called Megalopolis...

(The **Chorus** points in the direction of the city, which is now clearly defined):

...it lies there yonder. Listen, we'll speak of this,
the contagious city.

    Here, in the original, I broke into what my teachers had been trying to define as "free verse," a concept I struggled to understand then and for many years thereafter. I wanted to answer Whitman directly, in his own idiom. These tirades were the original portions of "Observations of a Resurrected Corpse," written the year before in Doc Michel's class, and everything else had been written to frame them. But when I came to revise the poem, I had learned enough of poetics and the traditions of English poetry to realize that, rather than writing "free verse," I had come very close, altogether unwittingly, to writing in Anglo-Saxon prosody; that is to say, in the alliterative accentual verse of the anonymous Old English poet who had written Beowulf, rather than in prose parallels in the manner of Whitman. Therefore, in revising I went all the way and deliberately cast the fulminations of the **Chorus** in Anglo-Saxon prosody:

See it clearly:
a ghetto of grime, of grit and mire,
a roiling, roaring, raging torrent
of life passing, pressing, pushing along
the narrow alleys, canyons of brick;

the clash and clamor of crowds and engines,
the pyramids of people peering and leaning
from towering tenements, tainting the air
with curses and calls, the cries of Cain;
the acrid aroma, the air leaden;
the rich growing richer, the poor still poor,
rich or poor, greedy alike
with the avarice of vermin, vicious, despairing.

[It was this passage in particular that infuriated Mark Bollman.]

This is the city, citadel of Man —
decadent, desperate, dollar-driven,
its veneer of glass a transparent mockery,
a mural of mirror masking a core
of misery and madness: humanity's castle,
the fabulous fortress of a futile race,
the pinnacle of pride, the prime of civility.
See it clearly. This is the city.

Corpse. I have to see.
Let me emerge from the chill crypt's mouth.
I shall judge this world of which the folk
standing near my grave have thus discoursed.
Out upon the wings of the bruiting wind
and swiftly through the countryside I'll go
to find the fabled city.

(*as he speaks he moves quickly into the city*).

Where trees once stood there stands a wall;
where once grass grew, grim buildings rise;
where forest lanes wandered, there writhes a highway;
where once was solitude, a city screams.
Lights, noise impinge on revolted senses;
soot and dust and smog and grease

replace cool, silent leaves and loam.
Neons flaring, glaring; carhorns blaring
cacophonies of crimson sound!
Where once flowed lucid, plashing brooks
there now splash streams of sewage and silt;
where there once were scents of the subtle spices
of summer and winter, spring and fall,
slums exude the stench of Death.
The world is an apple, once plump and ripe,
now smitten with the bitter blight
of burgeoning burgs — a blitz of cities!

Through the streets
of Megalopolis I walk and wonder.
On every side the city's squalor gasps.
I must gasp myself, for none of this
is part of my green remembrance of the past.
Sense revolts within me as I look
at the squalid town.

The city screams! see its furor;
hear its raging, madcap uproar!
Watch the crushing, cursing, nerve-crazed crowds
prowling around the spires and towers
that stand like sticks stuck in an anthill
under the unctuous, oily clouds.
The city stands, surly and painted,
a festering female whose foul wares
are hawked and bought with ostentation.
The sin-slaked lips and sallow flesh
of this lusting leper are lent to lechers
who flock like flies to her flimsy skirts —
the silken skirts that screen her body.
The city stands and screams her trade.

(*as the Corpse retraces his steps toward the graveyard, the city begins to fade*).

I'll return
to the graveyard where I should have stayed.
At least, Death is tranquility compared
with this. Time, in your mercy, let me lie...

[I am astonished to discover, or I should say to realize, for the first time as I type this memoir, that this last line, which was part of the original draft, is a paraphrase of lines from Dylan Thomas' "Fern Hill." But perhaps it should not be surprising, for the Red-eyed 'fifties were the years when Thomas was wandering about the United States declaiming his wonderful verse, though I was never to encounter him in the living flesh. I do remember picking up, in 1953 at the Yale Co-Op in New Haven, the new edition of his *Collected Poems*.]

...once more beneath the sod! Take back these bones
that they may fuse once more with stone. Give me
my niche with the forgotten.

Upon my marker lies my threadbare shroud,

(*he picks it up and puts it on*);

and nearby there still stands the mortal crowd
which once I envied, now may only pity
since I have made my survey of the city.
What is that sound they make as I approach? —

Chorus. You've seen why we'd be thankful to encroach
upon your simple slot of hallowed earth.
The lives of men in mass have slender worth.

Corpse. Oh! Lord of all creation, is this your Man?
Image of the Ideal, whose life began
swaddled in primal Nature's verdant sheets
but ends within the city's sordid streets?
Farewell, mortals, Death shall be my choice.

> I shall respond henceforth to no carnal voice,
> but lie in clay until all cities sink
> into the muck of ages, until the stink
> of their hacking funnels exhale the scent of night
> and neon fades beneath Aurora's light.
>
> (*once more he kneels before his stone*).
>
> To sleep again —
> back to blankness, back to the nether-land.
> Sanity's a figment and a fraud;
> only madness reigns eternally.
> Reliquary, hold my bones until
> the morning after history, when Earth
> is frost among the stars.

Of course, I ought never to have published this poem. Its faults are too evident: The minister's son in his adolescent Victorian disillusionment stood embarrassingly naked there in cold print for those few who read the little magazines of the 1960s to see. And perhaps I should not now, again, exhume that old resurrection, but many people have asked me over the years why I dislike Whitman so much, and this will help explain it. I answered his optimism with the pessimism of disillusion; his secular religious vision with religiously secular naturalism; his aformalist Romantic effusions with artfully literary forms and diction; his affirmations with the self-conscious cynicism of youth.

Furthermore, I was offended by Whitman's use of prose as a vehicle for poetry. I agreed with Robert Frost's criticism of Carl Sandburg's work, that writing poetry in prose was "like playing tennis with the net down." I am somewhat more liberal in my views now, but I was delighted recently to run across an essay by Grace Schulman, poetry editor of *The Nation*, that quotes "An unsigned review of Walt Whitman's Drum-Taps that appeared in *The Nation* on Thursday, November 16, 1865. The reviewer (Henry James at 22) said that the poem 'exhibits the effort of an essentially prosaic mind to lift itself, by a muscular strain, into poetry.'" James seems to have been as outraged as I for the same reason. He wrote that "Drum-Taps begins for all the world like verse and turns out to be arrant prose." But that was not the worst of old offenses: "To sing aright our battles and our glories it is not enough to have served in a hospital (however praiseworthy the task in itself), to be aggressively careless, inelegant, and ignorant, and to be constantly preoccupied with yourself." Amen.

Whitman may have convinced the masses, or at least the masses of academics who read his work, that he speaks for America, but he never spoke for me, and I have never been able to understand why so many people enjoy reading his obtuse prophecies through the rose-colored glasses he provides — but maybe I have just answered my own question. Life is hard, and it gets harder every day.

Lydia and Douglas

I think of myself as a New Englander, but in fact I've spent most of my life in my native state, New York. I was born in Buffalo, and for thirty-one years the upstate city of Oswego was my place of residence and work. Nevertheless, I'd been brought up in Meriden, Connecticut, and since 1956 when I was discharged from the Navy and had begun to attend the University of Connecticut at Storrs, Jean (also a UConn alum) and I have spent our summers and, since 1996, our retirement, in Dresden, Maine.

When we moved to Oswego in 1965 I thought it was passing strange to be located on the shore of a huge body of water, Lake Ontario, that ought by rights to have smelled of salt and clam flats, and it was years before I got used to the north-flowing Oswego River, part of the New York State Barge Canal, once a branch of the Erie Canal. If one counts my earliest four years in Buffalo on Lake Erie, and four in Cleveland, also on Erie, I spent almost forty years on the Great Lakes.

The fourteen years in Meriden, however, and the four spent in the Navy just after my graduation from Meriden High in 1952 —

two of them aboard the *Hornet* — were the seminal years, for they saw me begin my career as a writer. Aside from my influential high school English teachers, "Doc" Michele and Mary Flynn, and my editorial bosses, Herman Angel and Warren F. Gardner at the Meriden Record-Journal Publishing Company where I worked during high school, two other people were important to me as mentors during this time: Lydia Atkinson, editor of the "Pennons of Pegasus" column in *The Morning Record*, and Lieutenant J/G Douglas Kiker of the *Hornet*, later to become famous as a television reporter for NBC News.

I suspect it was because my surname ended in a vowel that I was not selected to go to Tufts University after having passed the NROTC Prep School at Bainbridge, Maryland. Being transferred to sea duty aboard the *USS Hornet* was a sort of mixed blessing for me. On the one hand, throughout the Navy going to sea seemed to be the thing universally to be avoided, odd when you think about it — why would anyone join the Navy to avoid going to sea? On the other hand, while it was waiting to be commissioned the new *Hornet* was berthed in Brooklyn Naval shipyard, only ninety miles from my home town.

At first the crew were berthed ashore, but eventually we moved aboard and the ship was commissioned at a ceremony that included the participation of the World War II legend, Admiral Bull Halsey. I was a yeoman seaman assigned to the Gunnery Division under a third-class yeoman named Fairall who soon proved to be the Navy's version of Sgt. Bilko, the Army television con-man made famous later on by Phil Silvers. The Gunnery Officer was LCDR R. E. Edwards, a fine man whom I soon liked a good deal, a "mustang" officer who had worked his way up through the ranks over a long career. Douglas Kiker was a Gunnery Division officer.

The ship was to embark eventually on a world cruise to join the 7th Fleet in the Pacific, and Mr. Kiker was one of those in charge of the ship's cruise book, *The 1954 World Cruise of the USS HORNET CVA12*, edited by Gareth Lewis, for which I volunteered to write. Ensign Kiker was happy to accept my services because he had discovered that, although I'd not yet gone to college, I was beginning to publish poetry in the little magazines. For years before that, though, my work had been appearing in Lydia Atkinson's column.

Several years later, in 1961 while I was a Poetry Fellow at Bread Loaf, the classical scholar and poet Dudley Fitts was assigned to me as the critic of my poetry. At one of our sessions he mentioned that when he was teaching at Cheshire Academy he used to read *The Morning Record*. I told him that was my home town paper and I'd first published my poems in Lydia's "Pennons of Pegasus" while I was a high school student. He guffawed and said, "My wife and I used to read that column aloud every Wednesday morning and begin the day with a hearty laugh." I told him I had no idea I'd had such a distinguished audience, and I was pleased he'd been familiar with my work for so long.

In August of 1953 "Two-Face" and "Flip," the first of my poems to be published in a national literary periodical, appeared in *The American Poetry Magazine*, at that time the oldest continuously-published poetry periodical in America. I decided in my hubris to take a subway from Brooklyn to the main branch of the New York Public Library on 42nd Street to see if my work were really circulating in the great world at large.

Dressed in uniform, I approached the periodicals desk and asked for the latest issue. The librarian gave me the once-over and came back with *The American Poultry Farmer*. Flushing furiously and totally mortified, I corrected her and eventually got what I asked for, but it was already too late.

Not yet quite willing to accept that fact, however, I went home for a weekend in September, about a month later. I was carrying around a copy of the magazine when I met downtown on West Main Street near Molloy's Stationers Georgia Bradley, one of my former classmates — at her request I had actually written a poem for her, "To Georgia," and I had published it in Lydia's column. She asked me, "What's new?" I showed her my poems, and she completed the job the New York librarian had begun, for she responded, "Who reads magazines like that?" This time I acknowledged, I think, at least in some dim recess of my consciousness, that I had chosen to follow a path few people in America would respect. At about that same time Lydia Atkinson reprinted "Two Face," the first of my poems that she would recycle from other sources.

In November another classmate, Joyce Rebstock, was killed in an automobile accident. She had been out on a date with Fred Flatow, one of my childhood playmates from Benjamin Franklin Elementary School — I had myself dated her once in high school. A drunken truck driver had demolished the car Fred was driving. Since I was back aboard the *Hornet* by that time, I wrote a letter to Mrs. Atkinson: "Joyce Rebstock was one of my dearest friends. Since I can't be at the funeral to tender my respects, this poem is the only way I can think of to say good-bye." With the letter, Lydia published "In Memory of J. R.," datelined *U.S.S. Hornet*, 26 November.

By the middle of the month of December the newly commissioned *Hornet* was on its shakedown cruise. We put in briefly at Jacksonville, Florida, but we were soon in the Caribbean. It was pretty in Cuba, very warm, and we were delighted to be out of the blizzards we'd left behind. At sea there is very little for an office worker to do, so I found the time to write my first article for Ensign Kiker:

> With voodoo intensity the crew of the Hornet, which was but newly emerged from the cocoon, went to work to develop her sting. Arriving in Guantanamo Bay, Cuba, after having passed her shipyard inspection and sea trials, the *USS Hornet* entered into a new phase of duty: drill, drill, drill. During operating hours, not a spare moment could be wrung from her schedule. Regular ship's work had to be carried out despite Air Defense and General Quarters exercises; Fire and Man Overboard drills; refueling operations; AirOps and the myriad other details of a shakedown cruise. Slowly but inevitably, by dint of much conscientious labor and constant interest, the *Hornet*, ship and crew, underwent a metamorphosis. From a largely inexperienced crew, and as-yet-untested ship, the *Hornet* became an integral fighting unit of the fleet.

But our shakedown cruise was not *all* work. The ship spent many in-port hours, during which the men from the *Hornet* and the other ships which were also in training at "Gitmo," enjoyed liberties and divisional parties on the base. Fishing parties and other activities were organized for those who were interested in participating.

For many of us, Cuba was a distinct change from what we had known previous to embarking aboard the *Hornet*. The nearly tropical climate and the corresponding scenic differences were both interesting and enjoyable. While swimming in the gentian-blue waters of the Caribbean we could see fish and coral growth of seemingly impossible colors and shape. Palms and the brownish hills of Cuba formed sharp contrasts in the landscape. Aboard ship crew members could sit on the forecastle and view lurid sunsets...and think of the folks back home who were, if not downright cold, at least chilly, for it was January!

By this time my work had begun appearing in *Our Navy*, a monthly slick, which soon featured a poetry column. I suspected that I was at least partly responsible for it because, prior to my submitting work, the magazine had not used poetry at all. Other sailors began sending in their own work, and soon the column was a regular feature.

Then came the day we visited Haiti. The ship steamed into the harbor between vast, eroded hills and verdurous shoreside farmlands. Ashore, the market place seemed like a page out of a pirate story. We were offered articles made of mahogany, teakwood, and alligator skin.

Much of the city of Port au Prince hadn't changed since the days of the pirate captain Henry Morgan; much of it was squalid and even sordid — I spent the day with Peter Perkins on Shore Patrol duty and found areas of the city to be unspeakably filthy, but that merely emphasized the truly modern portions: tall buildings of progressive architecture, exotic night clubs and hotels, and spic-and-span living districts. Many American tourists were on hand to greet us.

Back at Guantanamo I spent a very nice day with Rev. Mr. Withey, who came to the Naval Base on orders from my father. I'd had no idea he could pull such strings! The chaplain got me off the ship for the entire day, and I spent it with Dr. Withey, the base chaplain, and two other ministers who came with him. We went into Havana, which no one else had been allowed to do from the *Hornet* because Fidel Castro and Che Guevara were raising Cain in the hills.

In the morning, while I was waiting at the base library for the ministers to arrive (I had been dropped off before the ship sailed for fleet exercises), I read "The Song of Songs" and was transported: the scenery was much like that of the Middle East, I imagined, and I lay down and stared at the fish swimming off the pier: a thousand brilliant colors. It was as though I were gazing into a gigantic, more brilliant version of the aquaria I used to maintain in the sun porch of my father's parsonage on Windsor Avenue in Meriden.

On February 14th we were in Ciudad Trujillo, the Dominican Republic. It was much nicer than Haiti. My friend Perkins and I visited a bordello, my first ever, and his, too. The whores didn't know Perkins understood French — spoke it fluently, in fact. He told me they compared our prowess and I was the consensus winner, which was no doubt a compliment of sorts, but I was surely not very experienced.

A little magazine called *Different* took one of my poems, "Release," but I needed more validation than that after the debacle that had gotten me a berth at sea. I wanted to prove to myself, after my "failure" at the NROTC Prep School, that I could do college-level work, so I took the G.E.D. tests aboard the *Hornet* to see if I were as stupid as the Navy thought I was. When the scores arrived the first week in March of 1954 I thought the news was bad again, for I was summoned to the Education Officer's den and, as I climbed down the ladder into the compartment, the yeomen and personnelmen who worked there looked up at me, stared, and began whispering among themselves. I was plunged into depression as one of them ushered me into the inner sanctum.

I sat down, the officer looked down at the papers in his hands, then looked at me and shook his head. I remember being flooded with anxiety. Then he said, "I've never seen scores like these before."

I started to grow angry — I couldn't possibly be that dumb. I said, "Are they that bad?"

"Bad?" he replied. "They're the highest scores I've ever seen since I've been in the Navy." After a moment of astonishment, I was flooded with elation. From that point, as far as the Navy was concerned, I had one year of college to my credit, and I had the sense that anything was possible.

Lydia was still reprinting my poems in the Meriden *Record*, and on the 5th she used "Guantanamo Bay" which was the dateline as well as the title of the poem. I passed the USAFI course in News Reporting which I had been taking because I hoped to get the Navy to let me switch ratings and become a Journalist, but there didn't seem to be much chance. I persisted anyway and continued writing articles for the *Cruise Book*. On Monday, the 13th of May, the *Hornet* sailed from Newport News, Virginia. Lisbon, Portugal, was to be the first stop, then Naples, Italy.

Lisbon was lovely. Some of us went out on the town and were sitting at a booth in a bar after a full day of sightseeing, talking — as best we could — with a little Portugese boy. We gave him some Navy memento or other. A young man at the bar with a couple of friends called to him, took it from him, and looked it over. We thought he was trying to rip the boy off, so we began to mutter macho things like, "You take the skinny guy and I'll get the fat one." I glared at the young man, pointed at him, then to the boy, and said, "You, no! The boy, yes!"

Although I was no expert, in what I thought sounded like an Oxford accent he replied, "Yes, I understand, it belongs to the boy." Humiliated again. Nevertheless, we struck up a conversation with the young man, and then we all went out on the town together. He took us down narrow cobblestone alleys where lovers were making out in ancient doorways. We went into several fado houses — fado is the national song form of Portugal — listened to the singers, ate olives, and drank wine. We had a wonderful time. Before we said goodnight and farewell we promised to write each other. Although I tried once, he never replied.

The first week in June we passed Stromboli off the coast of Sicily and, cruising through the Straits of Messina, we approached Italy and hove to in the harbor of Naples. I will not discuss what happened when Perkins and I tried to walk from Pompeii to Mount Vesuvius, as that was simply *too* humiliating. While we were in port a train tour to Rome was arranged, and we went there, saw all the monuments and some of the basilicas, the Coliseum, the Roman Forum, which looked unbelievably small.

When we left Italy we passed through the Suez Canal — the reason we were taking this world cruise was because we were too large a ship to fit through the Panama Canal, and our hangar deck doors would be too badly battered if we tried to round the Horn. As we were sailing through the Red Sea I happened to look over the rail and down, and I saw a simply enormous fish — it must have been a whale shark — lying beside us just beneath the surface of the water. The canal was as one would have expected: hot, dry, exotic, with the pyramids far off in the distance and Egyptian soldiers sitting in their gun emplacements on the bank. And then it was all ruined by an immense Coca-Cola sign sitting in the desert.

On June 19th I was informed that I had passed the NavPers course in Armed Forces Newspaper Editorship with a 3.73 average, but I was no closer to becoming a journalist. Doug Kiker and I exchanged books often. He was quite interested in my poetry publishing and very friendly, treating me more often as a colleague than as his subordinate. I wrote my next article for him:

> The sun was hot and bright when the *Hornet* dropped anchor in Singapore Harbor. The city lay like a crescent off our port beam, and myriad islands and ships flying many flags speckled the waters to the horizon.
> For many of us this was the first time we had seen junks. They were a strange sight as their weather-beaten hulls and matted sails wove in and out among Chinese freighters and Dutch liners, South American and island trading ships, and

tankers from the United States, making for the open sea or berths in the harbor.

Singapore is a conglomerate city. Founded by an Englishman, its population composed of Chinese and Indians for the most part, its trading facilities used by nearly every country in the world, it is the hub of commerce for the Orient. As each liberty party went ashore, the crew of the *Hornet* found that Singapore was more than just conglomerate: it was fascinating.

Those of us who took the tour to Johore Bahlu on the Malayan mainland saw much of Singapore through the windows of a bus. We passed native market places and modern department stores, mosques in the traditional Arabian manner and a tremendous Church of England; we walked among blond and auburn-haired Englishwomen and dusky Asiatic girls, all of whom looked perfect to the eyes of sailors who had been at sea for a time.

Johore Bahlu is connected to the island of Singapore by a causeway. As we passed from Singapore into its sister city, we left the Occident and entered the Orient. The Sultan's Palace was huge and golden on our way to the Sultan's Mosque. Its grounds were extensive. Small elephants and peafowl seemed to be the sole inhabitants of its gardens and woods.

The mosque was painted blue and gray and was built of stone. We took off our shoes and went in. Inside, marble pillars and great crystal chandeliers vied for our attention with such modern adornments as microphones and loudspeakers. A brass altar and brass incense burners fringed the rugs which covered almost every square inch of floor space. When we left the mosque, our bus took us back through the gardens and roads which twisted through the outskirts of a zoo. Half the day was gone.

Back in Singapore we took advantage of the two beautiful English military clubs whose services were offered for the use of the crew of the *Hornet*. When we had eaten and were refreshed, we again sallied out into the streets and alleys of Singapore.

Night was falling. Around us the stone buildings and monuments took on the grey tinge of evening. In the harbor, lights were lit aboard the ships and the varicolored flags were furled. The water became dusky, and the ripples stirred up the ever-moving junks; bumboats glinted in the sunlight reflected from the clouds. Silhouettes of ships became black, and then indistinct, fading at last into the darkness. Then we heard the bells of our liberty launch. Our day in Singapore was ended.

On the 24th of June the ship crossed the Equator. Charge 4 of the subpoena I was given to appear at the Court of Neptunus Rex was, "Scribbling poetic doggerel on Navy time." All my hair was shaved off as part of the initiation, and the seadogs made us crawl through parachutes stuffed with offal; they spanked us with paddles as we ran a gamut, gave us a vile concoction to eat, and we graduated from Pollywog status to that of Shellback.

I had completed half of my enlistment by the eighth of July; we were in the South Pacific and had been anchored in Subic Bay, the Philippines, for a day. We sailed out to operate around Corregidor, but shortly we were in Manila harbor. I hadn't been ashore since Singapore. We stayed in the Philippines for about a month, and I tried unsuccessfully to find Chuck Verba, the original bass in our high school barbershop quartet The Sportlanders, who was purportedly stationed in Subic. During the cruise I had had poems accepted by quite a number of magazines.

By the end of the month the *Hornet* was on its way to what was then called "Indo-China," but would later be better known as Vietnam. The French were fighting the war then that the U. S. would agonize over later for a decade. When we got to the China

Sea we began searching for the wreckage of a British airliner the Chinese had shot down on the 23rd. When General Quarters was sounded suddenly I ran to my post on the Gunnery Deck which was located in the ship's island above the Captain's deck; there I stood watch at Gunnery Plot — a plexiglass board behind which I was stationed with earphones on. I was in contact with CIC which gave me the coordinates of our airplanes and any "bogies" in the area.

Planes from our carrier and the *Philippine Sea* were suddenly jumped by two bogies. Our planes engaged them, and then over my phones I heard, "Scratch two bogies!" I peered around the edge of the board and asked Commander Edwards, "What means 'scratch two bogies?'" He said, "They shot 'em down!" I was stunned. Although Douglas Kiker and I couldn't have known it at the time, those were the first shots fired by Americans in the "Vietnam War."

On the 27th of July I was up on the gunnery deck of the island watching air operations. On two other occasions while I had been watching I was filled with the certainty that particular planes would crash; on both occasions those planes did crash. Once Chief Gunner Adams was standing beside me when the landing gear of the plane beneath us collapsed and it skidded into the island just below. Gunner Adams screamed, "Duck, Turk!" and fell to the deck, but I just kept looking over the rail at the spectacle directly under my feet. Adams chewed me out, red-faced, when he got up. "You could have been sprayed with burning gasoline!" he roared. But, of course, so could he.

On the 27th as I was watching I experienced a truly powerful feeling that one plane would crash, and it would be the worst so far. I watched the jet as it came in for a perfect landing, stopped, folded its wings, and taxied toward the port side of the ship to be spotted forward on the flight deck. With great relief I turned to look at the next plane coming in.

And then I heard a rending sound. I turned to look back at the first plane — its jets hadn't cut out; they kept pushing it forward (afterwards I could see the skid-marks curving across the flight deck). I saw it teeter on the edge of the ship, its foregear momentarily resting on a radar housing. I saw the radar operator standing in the middle of the flight deck screaming into his headset microphone, but the wires to the headset were dangling uselessly, torn out of the panel in the radar shack he had suddenly abandoned. The plane tilted nose down, parallel to the side of the ship — I could see its tail sticking straight up — then it disappeared out of my range of sight.

I was later told what had happened next: the plane hit the water nose-first, fell over on its cockpit, trapping the pilot, and then it sank immediately. The pilot, Lt(jg) Thomas Moir Gardiner, was never seen again. Horrified, I resolved nevermore to watch air ops. I didn't know whether I was a jinx or merely unlucky to be watching every time there was a landing accident, but whichever, I never wanted to see another crash as long as I lived. And there were no others.

The last week of July the ship was in Manila Bay when Chuck Verba walked into the office — I had left messages for him everywhere the last time we'd been in port there. I'm not sure whether it was on this occasion that we were chased by a waterspout across Manila Harbor, but during one crossing we heard someone shout, "Look!" Everyone aboard the forty-foot motor launch turned to see the whirlwind tearing up the surf as it made its way toward us. An engineer threw the cowling of the engine up, reached in, and somehow switched off the governor.

It's probably not true or possible that the boat began to plane, but that's what I remember. The spout was coming faster, though. In its path there was the aerial of a ship that had been sunk during World War II — the twister hit it dead on, tore it off, and disappeared as suddenly as it had touched down. Chuck and I spent the evening together and a couple of days knocking around Sangley Navy Base. It felt good to see someone from home, especially an old friend.

Soon the *Hornet* weighed anchor to help guard Formosa — later to be called Taiwan — for a while. The mainland Chinese were shelling the islands of Quemoy and Matsu. When we arrived in Japan for a stopover we felt that we had waited a long time for our liberty, but when we finally got it, it was well worth the delay:

Yokosuka Harbor looked almost like a miniature Portsmouth as we slid alongside Piedmont Pier: the first time we'd been tied up at dockside since Naples. The only incongruous note in the landscape were the tunnels, caves, and dugouts which could be seen in every cliff big enough to house a colony of mice.

The familiar bustle of a naval shipyard swept aboard as soon as the plank was down. The little Japanese yard workmen looked strange wearing the same steel helmets we'd last seen worn in Brooklyn. The same giant cranes towered over the ship like prehistoric reptiles: even the ships scattered throughout the harbor looked like Fleet Landing at Norfolk.

It didn't take the crew long to catch on to the yen situation. At first it was a little confusing using both MPC's and yen, not to mention silver change aboard ship. Usually you'd be able to tell a *Hornet* sailor by going over to the gedunk [the Post Exchange] and watching to see which white hat would haul a handful of change out of his pocket and then turn red as he remembered the "play-money" MPC's in his wallet.

After the first day of liberty the ship took on the look of a bargain basement. The hangar deck was converted into a department store, and the men who returned to the ship after a sortie into Yokosuka were, as a rule, laden with everything from porcelain pipes to bolts of silk.

The Enlisted Men's Club, located off the base in Yokosuka, turned out to be a fabulous place. Every night there was a turnover of bands in its several ballrooms. The big building contained every convenience, including a yen exchange, ship's stores, several tap rooms and a large restaurant.

Some of the crew went to Tokyo and other localities for "R&R" periods. They always found the Japanese people amiable and glad to help in any way they could. In many ways, Japan was more typical, or what you'd expect to be called typical, than any of the other Oriental countries we had visited. In other ways, it was much more modern than would have generally been believed.

The terrain around Tokyo Harbor is very hilly. The Japanese, whose propensity for industry is persistent enough to be a trait, have burrowed tunnels through any hill that happened to stand in their way. Miles and miles of catacomb-like networks can be found burrowed through the rock. Within these hills, hundreds and hundreds of sailors, marines, soldiers, and representatives of every branch of the service can be found. Also, you can find almost anything else you'd care to look for. And nearly everyone did: from good food to knickknacks.

Our stay in Yokosuka was brief, only two weeks. But that was plenty of time for nearly the entire crew to spend their pay. We only hope that next time we pull into Yokosuka, it will be after having spent three or four months at sea where, as every good sailor knows, it's practically impossible to use up all his funds.

I contributed to this article that appeared in the *Cruise Book,* but I don't believe I was the major author. On the 23rd of September we pulled into Manila again after having operated twenty-two days in the Straits of Formosa. While we had been cruising I'd seen an amazing sight one morning when I woke up and went topside. There, from horizon to horizon, were junks and sampans packed in so close that I thought anyone might walk clear to the China coast just by jumping from one gunwale to another. I asked a sailor leaning over the rail, "Are they invading Formosa?"

"Naw," he said, "that's just the Chinese fishing fleet."

We were barely making steerage way in the midst of it. I had a vision of the Chinese tossing grappling hooks over our rail and climbing aboard, and I doubted we could have done anything about it despite our weaponry, including atomic bombs aboard. It was then and there that I realized the complete futility of any Western nation attempting to do battle with Asia, as the French were doing in Indo-China at that very moment. There were simply too many people there. It was overwhelming.

By the time Jean and I decided to be married when my hitch was up, not sooner, I'd had poems accepted or published by numbers of little magazines — nothing spectacular yet — and back in Meriden Lydia Atkinson had continued to reprint most of them in "Pennons." At the end of October my mother wrote that Dad was going to go to Italy now that he had been forced into retirement. I wrote her that I planned to be home for Christmas, after we hit Hong Kong and Manila again, then Hawaii in December, San Francisco, and finally San Diego:

> Hong Kong: what a town! We hauled into the harbor and dropped anchor. Mary Soo, "Garbage Mary," [who made her living by collecting the garbage, which she sold for pig food and other uses, from the ships in the harbor] was there with her girls before the anchor chain had time to get well-soaked. So were the sampans and bumboats. And the water-taxis. Maybe the taxis were lop-sided and couldn't do more than one knot, but they got us ashore. And they got us back aboard, loaded like barges with "Real No-Squeak Young" boots, "Taj Mahal" suits and trousers, bamboo furniture, carved chests and....
>
> Anyway, Hong Kong was a crazy town. Ashore we jostled along through crowds of Chinese, Indians, British troops, American tourists; beleaguered and badgered by rickshaw boys and sidewalk vendors; awed by women in the slinky slit

skirts which have been the fashion thereabouts for millennia, I guess.

Hong Kong: King Kong of the Chinese coast. But it loomed even larger in our eyes for a simple reason: it was nearly the last stop.

Hawaii in December. Waikiki Beach by night was a crescent of white sand ending at Diamond Head to our left. The Royal Hawaiian Hotel was the main feature of the beach, set among its palms. We had seen the sunken battleships at Pearl Harbor and taken part in a ceremony honoring those killed in the Japanese sneak attack of December 7th, 1941 — it was an anomaly to consider what they'd done to us and we'd done to them, and then to recall how good relations were between Americans and Japanese.

On our way across the Pacific we ran into an immense typhoon. I got seasick twice in my Navy career — once was while we were on sea trials, and the next was while we were riding out this big blow. It was the most incredible sight. When General Quarters sounded I went racing up the tower to my station, and as I did so the escalator stairs beneath my feet fell away and I was floating in mid-air. I kept my balance somehow and came out on the Gunnery bridge to see the great ship poised on the lip of a simply gargantuan wave, heading down.

We dived like a porpoise, and when we hit the trough we started up the hill again, but not before the wave crested and broke...halfway along the flight deck! I had seen this happen in gales to destroyers and destroyer escorts which, it seemed to me, were more than half submarines, but I'd never thought to see it happening to an aircraft carrier. Somehow, we rode out the storm, but our hangar-deck doors were a wreck by the time we hit port.

Another mid-Pacific event of note was the transfer of Fairall, the con-man Yeoman. He was into all the Gunnery divisions for money — he'd borrowed from everybody except the office personnel, and he had no hope of ever paying it all back. Some of the gunner's mates and bo'sun's mates were beginning to press him, and it was getting harder to put them off.

One day Fairall carried his duffel bag topside to the hangar deck. I went up to the flight deck to watch the proceedings below me. As I looked, a destroyer appeared on the horizon, slowly approached, and pulled alongside. A line was passed across, secured, and a breeches buoy containing Fairall and his gear was drawn across to the other ship. The line was disengaged, and the destroyer pulled away, disappearing at last into the distance. When word got around that Fairall had escaped in mid-ocean, there were lots of furious sailors aboard the *Hornet*. I imagined that inevitably some of them would run across him.

Eventually we sailed into San Francisco harbor beneath the Golden Gate Bridge, and were berthed near Oakland. In those days the Beat Generation was holding sway over San Francisco. Lawrence Ferlinghetti was publishing what I considered to be trash from his City Lights Bookshop. I spited myself by refusing to set foot in San Francisco for that reason, a decision I have long regretted.

After a brief stay, we traveled down the coast to San Diego. I spent one weekend in January with my paternal cousin Joe and his wife "Big" Josie Sardella in La Mesa, California, and another weekend with another cousin, "Little" Josie Higgins and her daughter Gigi. I had a short story accepted by a magazine and got a letter from the poet John Holmes who said he would help me get into Tufts when I was discharged. I had chosen Tufts in the first place not merely because it had an NROTC program and a journalism major, but because I'd wanted to study with Holmes.

In San Diego I saw a lot of Little Josie and Gigi — Josie had been a Navy nurse. Her uncle, my father, was back from Italy, according to a letter from mom. I would sooner live in Tierra del Fuego than in southern California, I decided. The climate could hardly be called a climate at all — I'd had three sore throats since I'd arrived. It seemed that everyone in the streets, including Josie and Gigi, was coughing, spitting, sneezing, or clearing his or her throat. It was the most miserable land in the world, outside of Oklahoma. And I refused to go down to Tijuana to see what was going on. I felt I knew.

The new Assistant Gunnery Officer, a man named Lieutenant Commander Daniels, was the most nauseating personality I had ever run across, and I didn't know how long I was going to be able to take him. He had the compulsion to do everything by the book. The trouble was that there were more books than one! Whenever he wanted to do something he would have us yeomen break out all the pertinent manuals; then we were required to look up the rules that applied to the project in hand and try to steer a course among the contradictory regulations. Each of these situations was truly a grueling and useless exercise in futility.

I broke out in huge hives and had to go to sickbay. The doctor ran all the tests he could think of to find what it was that I was allergic to, and we finally settled on Daniels. I was hospitalized, things were so bad, and I was in danger of missing my transfer to the East Coast. "Please, Doc," I asked him, "just let me out of bed. I have orders, and that'll cure me." He was good enough to let me go, and as I flew across the Rockies I could feel the monstrous hives on my belly diminish and disappear.

I spent the last year of my enlistment as one of the most fabled creatures in the U. S. Navy: the shore duty yeoman at the Bureau of Naval Personnel in Arlington, Virginia — not the chief of the section, but the sailor actually in charge of the list itself, which consisted of two very large tub files.

I had some leave coming, so I went to spend my first time in Dresden, Maine, visiting Jean's folks at their summer farm. We went over to Pemaquid Beach, a lovely spot, and I wrote a poem about it that I would eventually read at my father-in-law's funeral many years later.

The next summer, on June 16th, 1956, Jean and I were married by my father at 2:00 p.m. in her church, the First Congregational in Meriden. All our high school friends were there and my brother Gene was Best Man. Afterwards, Jean and I drove up Route 1, heading for Dresden where we would spend our brief honeymoon and I would do little except sneeze because I was allergic to the kapok mattresses in the house, which was quite primitive in other ways as well, including the water supply.

I returned after a short leave to Arlington and was released from the Navy a couple of weeks later at the Naval Receiving Station in Washington, D. C. When I got back to Meriden and Jean's folks' house, I began to work building houses for the summer with Jean's dad, John Houdlette, and his next-door neighbor, Jack Conroy, both of whom had been my junior high school shop teachers.

Over a decade later I was watching NBC News when Douglas Kiker came on. Since I had known him he had grown a large wen on his forehead, but he still looked like the amiable southern gentleman from whom I had borrowed a pirated Japanese edition of *Lady Chatterley's Lover* to read in the long Pacific nights. He looked out of the television screen at me and asked, "Why does the American academic world so dislike President Johnson?" He considered several possibilities which, as I recall, he dismissed as unreasonable.

When the program was over I sat down to type him a letter. I asked him if he remembered the young yeoman poet who had written the cruise articles for him while he was aboard the *Hornet*, and I told him I had for a number of years been an academic. I admitted to him that I was one of those who disliked Johnson intensely. My reasons were simple — could he recall those Chinese junks and sampans that stretched from horizon to horizon while we were patrolling the Straits of Formosa? One did not have to be an idealist, or an academic, or even an educated person to realize that the U. S. was not going to win a war against such masses of humanity. The French had finally realized it and gotten out, and we had been fools enough to take their place.

Douglas never answered my letter, if he ever received it, but Lyndon Johnson was forced by the war to refrain from running for a second full term and to withdraw from politics. Nearly twenty years after I had formulated my views of the Vietnam War, and more than ten years after I had participated in the first Poets for Peace reading in Cleveland in 1962, America was finally out from under the shadow of "Indo-China."

Lewis Turco

FRIENDS AT LAST

In January of 1959 I graduated in mid-year from the University of Connecticut and became a graduate assistant and part-time instructor in English teaching Sophomore Composition and Introduction to the Short Story for the spring semester. I vacillated for quite some time about whether to apply to the University of Iowa's Writers' Workshop or stay at UConn the following academic year, but my friends, Alexander Taylor, Jim Scully, and Morton Felix decided things for me.

Jean and I lived in campus housing at Northwood Apartments in Storrs. Sandy Taylor, as editor and publisher of a magazine called *Patterns*, had used some of my poems while I was serving my four-year hitch in the Navy between high school and college. He phoned one day and asked if he could stay with us while he interviewed for a teaching job at the local high school. We were happy to accommodate him. He got the job.

During the summer of 1958, it must have been, Sandy and I decided to go up to crash the University of New Hampshire Writers' Conference so that we could visit some of our friends, including Loring Williams, editor of American Weave Press which, in 1962, would publish my second collection of poems, a chapbook titled *The Sketches*.

We weren't registered for the Conference, of course, so we had to be surreptitious about our presence on campus. Sandy spent the evening getting completely smashed. The next morning when I woke up I was warned that the Campus Security officers were looking for me because I was parking illegally. Immediately I went looking for Sandy. When I found him I was unable to waken him, he was still so drunk. I looked around the room he had used and found a bottle of soda, which I poured over his head while he was still lying in bed. That did the trick. He opened his eyes. "We have to get out of here," I told him.

"Why?"

"The Campus cops are looking for me."

"I'm not going," he said.

"I have to take off, Sandy. I'll have to leave you here."

"Go ahead."

I thought he was rational — he sounded as though he were — so I got in my car and took off for Storrs. I had no idea how he planned to get back.

As it turned out, neither had he, but when he finally managed it he accused me of having ditched him without telling him. I recounted my tale, but he had no recollection of it, and he never believed it. I wondered how he otherwise could explain the soda-soaked bed. That was one grudge he harbored.

Jim Scully was an undergrad with me, but a few years younger. He had been my discovery and protégé; as judge of the poetry contest sponsored by The Connecticut Writers club on campus, I had given him the poetry prize, which he well deserved. A few years later he won the Lamont Award of the Academy of American Poets for his first book. He and I were involved in one major incident while we were fellow students:

I was responsible for bringing writers to campus to read under the aegis of the Student Union Board of Governors. Richard Wilbur was among those my committee asked to visit; others were Donald Hall, with whom I had begun corresponding while I was still in the Navy; George Abbe — who in 1960 would be one of three editors, with Loring Williams and Clarence Farrar, to choose my *First Poems* for publication as a selection of The Book Club for Poetry; John Hollander, Philip Booth, Richard Eberhart — who had taught at Storrs for a few years; E. E. Cummings — whose disciple on campus was my teacher, the poet Norman Friedman; James Wright, and the novelist James T. Farrell.

Wright was on a tour of area colleges when he visited our campus, and he was to go on to Wesleyan after he had read at Storrs. The plan was to deliver him to the bus station in Hartford where he would be picked up by Richard Wilbur and driven to Middletown. Accordingly, Jim Scully and I took Wright to Hartford, dropped him off, and drove back to campus. No sooner had we gotten back, though, than we were given the message that Wilbur was unable to pick Wright up, and he asked us if we wouldn't go back to Hartford, fetch Wright, and drive him to the Wilbur home. Jim and I got back in the car and did as we were asked.

When we got to Middletown and rang the Wilburs' bell we were ushered in and straight up to the master bedroom where Charlee Wilbur was lying in bed experiencing the early stages of labor. Wright, Scully, the Wilburs and I sat together visiting, but Jim and I were very ill at ease, and after a polite interval we excused ourselves, got back into the car and drove to Storrs again. We subsequently learned that Charlee's labor had been a false one. Some while later she gave birth to a son who, unfortunately, was autistic.

Mort Felix was a psychology graduate student who was interested in poetry and began to hang around with us. We four had been talking about founding a magazine together, *The Wormwood Review*, but when the time came to do so I discovered that the others had decided to cut me out. They seemed to resent my publishing regularly in the little magazines, but Taylor especially felt rancor toward me beyond the New Hampshire incident. He had told me sometime during the fall of 1958 that he was applying to Yaddo, the artists' colony in Saratoga Springs, New York. I had never heard of Yaddo, but I thought that sounded like a good idea, and I decided to do the same. As it happened, I was selected, he was not. He seemed to feel that I had taken a place specially reserved for him.

When in the spring I was accepted by the Iowa Writers' Workshop, therefore, I decided to go. I was clearly not welcome in the society of my Storrs friends. Morton Felix and his wife Susan came eventually to visit Jean and me at our summer place in Dresden, Maine, where he apologized for the *Wormwood* incident, but we haven't kept in touch. I have never since heard from Scully or Taylor.

I spent six weeks of the summer as the youngest Yaddo resident, writing a huge amount of material. Afterward Jean and I traveled out to Iowa in August in our little Fiat 600. In September of 1959 I was enrolled in the Graduate Program of the Writers' Workshop of the University of Iowa. Paul Engle and Don Justice were my poetry teachers, and I took a course in modern fiction with Hortense Calisher whose husband, Curtis Harnack, was also around, writing his first novel.

I recognized one face in the Poetry Workshop, that of Ed Skellings who had been a fellow student — one year ahead of me — at Suffield Academy in Connecticut during 1947-49, scene of the Suffield Reader-Writer Conference during the 'fifties, while I was an undergrad. That had been another conference my Storrs friends and I had crashed at the behest of George Abbe, who had been on the staff there but who had for some reason been fired. When we showed up to show our solidarity for him, it appeared that the Conference had been forewarned, because State Police were stationed at the doors. But all we planned to do was attend a public lecture and there was no trouble.

At Iowa I quickly made friends with Morton Marcus, Jim Crenner, Vern Rutsala, and John Gilgun. Robert Mezey didn't seem to like me; his friends were Kim Merker, Raeburn Miller, and Peter Everwine, so there was a distance between his crowd and mine. This coolness was entirely on Mezey's part, because I had wanted to meet him ever since we had published poems together in the national college anthologies *Riverside Poetry 3*, edited by Marianne Moore, Howard Nemerov and Alan Swallow, and *New Campus Writing 3*, edited by Nolan Miller and Judson Jerome. In fact, one of the first things I did when I arrived in Iowa City was to go looking for Mezey, but he had moved from the address I had been given, an apartment outside of which I noticed rather a large stack of chapbooks titled, as I recall, *Berg Goodman Mezey*, published in Philadelphia in 1957.

When the new bookstore The Paper Place opened nearby, I

recalled those evidently discarded booklets, and I went back to see if they were still there in the hall of the apartment building. They were. I gathered them up, carried them over to The Paper Place, and donated them. Many years later I learned that when the bookshop burned down most of those booklets were destroyed in the fire. I didn't keep one for myself, for some reason, and I wish I had.

For two years in a row Mezey had won the Academy of American Poets Prize at Iowa. Unknown to me, he had been barred from entering the contest a third time. Everyone else in the Poetry Workshop entered, of course. The judges, E. L. Mayo and Ralph Salisbury, awarded my poems the prize, and Mezey was quite disdainful. Evidently he felt that it was a sure thing that he would have won had he been allowed to enter.

Perhaps it was so, for I began to have some insight into how things were done at Iowa. I overheard a conversation between Mezey and Harry Duncan, the famous fine editions printer and publisher of The Cummington Press in Iowa City. Harry told Mezey that Engle was going to be one of the judges for the next Lamont Award of the Academy of American Poets, at that time one of the two most prestigious first poetry book awards in the country. Only publishers could enter a book in the contest, so he suggested that Mezey give him a manuscript, which he would accept and then submit to the contest. If it won, and he was pretty sure it would, he would then publish the book in one of his famous limited editions and also in a trade edition. And that's what happened with Mezey's *The Lovemaker* (1961). Don Justice's first book, *The Summer Anniversaries*, was published a year earlier and also won the Lamont Award.

I have remained friends with Marcus, Justice, Rutsala, and Gilgun for many years. Though Engle and I had our differences, we made them up before he died, and I have written about him in two reference books and the Iowa history, *A Community of Writers*, edited by Robert Dana. Don Justice and I still correspond heavily, and we have visited each other often. Howard Nemerov was a good friend until he died, and Judson Jerome later published his first book of poetry from the same publisher, Golden Quill, that issued my *First Poems* in 1960, while I was still at Iowa. Norman Friedman and I have always been friends and correspondents, and when his first collection of poetry was published, a chapbook titled *The Magic Badge: Poems 1953-1984*, I reviewed it favorably in my annual essay, "The Year in Poetry" for *The Dictionary of Literary Biography Yearbook 1984*.

The oddest thing, though, is the fact that Curtis Harnack became Director of Yaddo where I spent a second summer in 1978. Mezey spent a semester in Cleveland where I taught for four years, and the summer of 1996 he came to Gardiner, Maine, for a Robinson Festival; I had retired that year to Dresden, Maine, eight miles away. In 1999 Mezey published a *Selected Poems of Edwin Arlington Robinson* and sent me a copy. I wrote him to say that I thought the life of Robinson he wrote for his book was the best short biography I'd read in a very long time. He replied that my opinion meant a lot to him, and when I sent him a copy of my book *The Green Maces of Autumn: Voices in an Old Maine House* (2002), he wrote me a letter that ended with, "The writing is awfully good throughout and sometimes rises to an eloquence that silences everything else in the world." That's got to mean we're friends at last.

Engle's Workshop

I.

On Friday the 23rd of May, 1986, Jean and I drove from Oswego, New York, to Hancock Airport in Syracuse, forty miles away, in time for me to catch my flight to Chicago at about a quarter past eleven in the morning. I was on my way back to Iowa City for the first time in twenty-six years to attend the Golden Jubilee celebration of the Writers' Workshop, the world's oldest and most famous graduate program in writing arts. I pondered the unsettling thought that when I'd left Iowa in 1960 the Workshop had been about to celebrate its silver anniversary with publication of a volume edited by its early director, Paul Engle. Now, returning, I was more than half as old as the program I had attended! As I flew west it seemed to me that I was in some true sense returning in time as well.

In 1959 I had transferred to the Iowa Workshop from the University of Connecticut Graduate School. During the fall of 1958, while I was an undergraduate at UConn, I had applied to the Workshop, and on January 21st of the following year Paul Engle had written to ask me to see that the letters about me from my teachers John Malcolm Brinnin and Kenneth Spaulding, and from

Tom Ahern, Manager of the Student Union, for whom I had run the *Fine Arts Festival* magazine and the literary reading series, be sent to him "as soon as possible." He'd also wanted copies of my published poems and my best work for his own records. At the end of March W. F. Loehwing, Dean of the Graduate College at Iowa, had written to tell me that I had been awarded a Graduate Fellowship for the academic year 1959-60 in the amount of $530.00. On the 4th of April Paul wrote to offer me a teaching assistantship of $1,300 instead of the fellowship, which was worth only half as much. He also wanted me to submit poems to be considered for publication in the Workshop's silver anniversary anthology which was to be titled *Midland: Twenty-five Years of Fiction and Poetry from the Iowa Writers' Workshop.*

I'd written back to say I'd rather not teach as I wanted to get my degree as quickly as possible. Paul replied, telling me about the differences between the English M. A. and the M. F. A., which took longer. I decided to go for the M. A., as I still had a year left on the Korean G. I. Bill and could transfer my six UConn graduate credits to Iowa, thus in effect finishing my class work at Iowa in a year.

I'd spent the spring semester at UConn as a graduate assistant and part-time instructor of English taking two graduate courses and teaching an introduction to the short story / composition course to sophomores, then several weeks during the summer as the youngest resident of Yaddo, the artists' colony at Saratoga Springs, experimenting with writing unrhymed quantitative syllabic poems.

In the fall I'd transferred to the Workshop. The graduate fellowship was an honor, but the stipend was quite small. Jean and I were pretty strapped, so Paul, even though it was against the rules to give me both a fellowship and an assistantship, arranged for me to become Editorial Assistant to the Workshop in order to bring me back up to the financial level of the teaching assistantship I had foregone. I was to help Paul with correspondence and with the permissions work for both the Random House *Midland* and the Hallmark *Poetry for Pleasure*, to be published by Doubleday. Jean found a full-time job in the Bureau of Labor and Management.

I'd wanted to attend Iowa's Writers' Workshop, not so much because it would be beneficial to sit in a classroom to learn about writing — I'd been publishing for six years, after all — but to associate with other young writers. My teachers would eventually have their effects on me and my work, particularly Donald Justice, but mainly I wanted to rub elbows and ideas with my contemporaries.

By the 24th of August, 1959, Jean and I were settling into our new apartment on the second floor of Mrs. Keith's farmhouse outside of town. I was to dump the garbage into a ravine, blow snow out of the driveway, and so forth, as part of our rent. Our landlady kept a few sheep, one of which was a ram who inhabited the field I had to cross to the ravine. I was always careful to keep an eye on him and one of the garbage cans between us in case he decided to attack, but he never did. By October Jean was pregnant; her morning sickness was lasting all day, every day, and she was pretty unhappy. This was the first time she had been away from her family for any extended period of time.

Curtis Harnack was on campus with his wife, my fiction professor Hortense Calisher, and Verlin Cassill labored away in the Quonset hut where the Poetry Workshop was held. Hortense liked to take baths in the tub there because there were only showers available in the apartments where she and Curt lived. Paul Engle and Donald Justice shared the duties of the Workshop. At that time Don, a Floridian who had recently taken his Ph.D. from Iowa, had not published his first book.

Paul, a native Iowan, had been born in Cedar Rapids in 1908. He had studied for the Methodist ministry and preached at Stumptown church at the edge of town, but he'd heard no call and had instead taken an M.A. from Iowa in 1932. In that same year he'd published what may have been the first creative thesis ever submitted anywhere for a graduate degree, *Worn Earth*, which had appeared as a volume in the prestigious Yale Series of Younger Poets. Subsequently, he had studied at Columbia and then traveled to Oxford on a Rhodes Scholarship, taking another set of degrees there.

In 1937 Engle had returned to the University of Iowa as a faculty member and had eventually become director of the Workshop. Under his leadership the Workshop, by the time I'd joined it, had become world-famous as a training ground for young writers. On that first day of class in 1959 Paul asked us how many were from the state of Iowa. Not a single person raised a hand. Paul said, "I'm embarrassed. This is the first time such a thing has happened." I looked around and saw what seemed to me to be a familiar face, and indeed it was — it turned out to be Ed Skellings, with whom I had gone to prep school at Suffield Academy in Connecticut from 1947-1949. Some of my other fellow workshop students were George Keithley, Robert Mezey, Vern Rutsala, Morton Marcus, Raeburn Miller, and Kim Merker. Walter Tevis, John Gardner, and Jerry Bumpus were members of the Fiction Workshop.

Paul's and Don's styles were completely different. Paul was the feisty, funny, slippery-tongued pepperpot, and Don the practical critic who knew just how to approach each particular poem. Paul never got angry, but Don could sometimes be peevish, especially when he thought he was wasting his time on a poem that had not been carefully worked over before it was submitted for the worksheets.

When I had arrived in Iowa City, I'd been surprised to learn how literally the poets rubbed elbows in all kinds of competitions, including most particularly physical competitions. From this distance in time, it seems as though nearly every day of the semester some of us spent a couple of hours at least in the ping-pong room at the Iowa Memorial Union viciously pasting a bouncing ball over a net. It was almost as though some kind of literary superiority depended upon our whipping Don Justice. Many of us tried, but most of us failed. In fact, I can't recall Don's ever losing a game, though I suppose he must have. I'm sure I never beat him.

His technique was maddening. No matter how hard you hit the ball, Don would stand way back and let the ball drop over the edge of the table, out of sight. There, underneath, he would give the ball some kind of gentle, satanic slice, and back it would come, floating over the net. It would kiss the table, but where it would go from there was anybody's guess.

Ed Skellings had the same kind of style, and he was pretty good too, but not in the same league with Don. I recall those Justice-Skellings tournaments vividly: they were evil. Somehow, when Don played Ed, he got really mean, and inevitably Skellings would go down to ignominious defeat, calling for a rematch on the last point. Since I left Iowa before he did, I wonder sometimes whether Ed ever managed to put together a genius game and win one.

Seeing Don's prowess on the ping-pong table, I never dared sit in on the weekly poker games some of the poets — Bob Mezey, Kim Merker and others — engaged in, but I hear they were marathon. In the spring ping-pong would give way to softball, but poker went on forever.

I was the only member of the workshop turning in syllabic poems, some of them those I'd written at Yaddo the previous summer. At one point Don said to me, "Lew, you're cheating. Your poems don't rhyme." Dylan Thomas and Marianne Moore had been writing rhymed syllabics, but no one other than haikuists had been writing just plain syllabics. I considered that Don's remark in this case was ignorable, and I went on writing my rhymeless syllabics, as I've done ever since. A few years later I couldn't help noticing that Don's second full poetry collection, *Night Light*, consisted of unrhymed syllabic poems.

Robert Mezey was anticipating the coming year when he was to attend Stanford as a Fellow under the latter-day Messiah of the neo-classical poets, Yvor Winters, of whom Mezey was a professed admirer. As things were to occur, however, they would have a falling-out even before Mezey arrived on campus, and the younger man would become one of the fringe Beats rather than the formalist poet he had been during his years at Iowa and, earlier, at Kenyon College under the Fugitive poet John Crowe Ransom.

Like Mezey, I had always been interested in the traditional forms of poetry — I was born a formalist, and I wanted a reference book that contained the whole range of them, but I'd never been able to find such a book other than those that contained merely the standard sorts of things: the sonnet, the villanelle, the haiku and tanka, the sestina — mainly the medieval Italian and Provençal forms plus a few others.

But what else was there? Perhaps there weren't enough forms to fill a short book. Then, one day while I was browsing through the bargain bin of Iowa Book and Supply on Clinton Street, I ran across a book of poems by Rolfe Humphries titled *Green Armor on Green Ground*. Humphries had laid out "the twenty-four official meters" of the Welsh bards, and he had written a poem in each of these complicated syllabic forms. I bought the volume, of course — I think I paid a quarter for it, or maybe a dollar — and I took it home. After I'd looked it over a while I got to wondering whether, with such forms as these, I might not be able to gather enough material for a book, particularly if I filled it out with examples of poems written in the forms and with schematic diagrams of the forms, which I had never seen in any other book. I discovered, incredibly, that no one in the history of English literature had ever put together a compendium of all the traditional forms, and I asked Don Justice whether he thought such a volume would be useful. He encouraged me, and I began working on the project.

That period of time when I began putting together what would eventually become, first, *The Book of Forms: A Handbook of Poetics*, two intermediary texts, *Creative Writing in Poetry* and *Poetry: An Introduction through Writing*, then *The New Book of Forms*, and finally The Third Edition of *The Book of Forms*, was not auspicious for such projects. The so-called "Beat Generation" was in the process of consolidating its anti-intellectual stranglehold on a generation, and the self-righteous, self-indulgent decade of the 1960s loomed ahead. Christopher Wiseman, a Workshop poet from England, one day submitted to the worksheets a parody of the work of the Beat poet Allen Ginsberg. Mezey, however, did not see the humor in it, only the threat, and he reacted by writing, and the next week submitting to the Workshop, his response, "A Coffee-House Lecture."

Interesting things were happening off campus as well as on. The Paper Place, one of the first paperback bookstores in the country and certainly the first in Iowa, was being tacked together by graduate students. Upstairs the Renaissance II Coffee House was also taking form, and it was over coffee that Steve Tudor and his friends were starting the anti-establishment student newspaper, *The Iowa Defender*, which was to stand against the philistinism of *The Daily Iowan*. Across the street Kenney's Fine Beers was another hangout for the writers. In all three places we got together for talk and socializing, but at Kenney's, things were generally more boisterous.

Before The Paper Place could open, of course, it had to be built. One day when Mike and Marlene Fine and the rest of the group of grad students who founded it were putting up shelves, I dropped in to watch. They had the frames for the shelves up. One person would lift a shelf up to the frame, and someone else would scribe it about a half-foot in at each end. After a while I said, "Can I ask you a question, Mike?"

"Sure," he replied.

"Instead of cutting six inches off each end of the board, why don't you just cut twelve off one end?" There was a tableau and silence for a while, and then everyone began to blush. But the shelves stood until The Paper Place burned down a decade or so later, long after the Fines had left to return to Manhattan and Mike got involved in publishing with Simon and Schuster.

One evening, after a group of us had left Kenney's, we walked across the street to see in the window of the bookshop a display of the manuscript drafts of his novel *The Hustler* and the contract that Walter Tevis had signed, for which he had received a $10,000 advance. One of us asked him, "What the hell are you doing at Iowa?" "Learning how to write," he replied.

It was at the Renaissance II upstairs that the first student readings ever organized at Iowa took place. John Gilgun was the entrepreneur. Vern Rutsala and I and one or two others had the honor of inaugurating the series. Others who read that year were, as I recall, Kim Merker, Peter Everwine, Jim Crenner, Morton Marcus, and Bob Mezey who read his reply to Wiseman, "A Coffee House Lecture." He later included the piece in his first book, *The Lovemaker*, which won the Lamont Award of the Academy of American Poets in 1960 — Paul was one of the three judges. That same year two other books would come out of the Workshop, Don Justice's *The Summer Anniversaries*, which had won the Lamont Award for the previous year, and my own *First Poems*, which was published as a selection of The Book Club for Poetry during the summer.

At the coffee house, too, Steve Tudor approached me about serving as poetry editor for his *Iowa Defender*, which I agreed to do; however, my service was short because Tudor chose to put poems into his pages — very bad poems, embarrassing to me — without asking for my opinion. I resigned and wrote a furious letter to *The Daily Iowan* about it. The fight raged back and forth for a few weeks in the two papers, getting personal at times. Other people entered the fray, Mort Marcus for one, who got wrought up about a slur that Tudor attempted — he'd wanted to write that I was "weak-chinned," but it got set in type as "weak-chained," which was true enough, it seemed to me, so I just thought it was funny. Despite our disagreements, however, the *I.D.* was a lively and interesting underground venture while it lasted. It would be replicated often nationwide during the impending 1960s.

I met Jerry Bumpus at Kenney's early in the autumn. Whether it was on that occasion or another soon after, for some reason we got into a discussion about words that described places where particular kinds of creatures were kept. I said that a herpetarium held snakes, an aquarium held fish, and an aviary was for the birds. Jerry nodded his head amiably and drank his 3.2 beer. "And an apiary is a place where apes are kept."

"Right," Jerry said.

"Wrong," I said. "An apiary is a place for bees."

"Bull," he said, or words to that effect.

"How much do you want to bet?"

He checked his pockets and found that he had three dollars. So did I, so that was the wager. I went to the bar and asked for Irene Kenney's tattered dictionary, brought it back to the table, showed Jerry the entry, and asked him to pay up. "You set me up," he said, and wouldn't come through with the three bucks.

What happened next is apocryphal because I don't recollect it. In 1976 Steve Wilbers, who was researching his history of the Workshop, wrote me a letter and asked in a postscript, "By the way, is it true that when you met Jerry Bumpus you poured a glass of beer over his head while talking backwards? He claims you're the only person he ever knew who could do that."

Whether Wilbers meant pour a glass of beer on Bumpus, talk backwards, or do both simultaneously, I'm not sure. In any case, I wrote back to say I had no specific remembrance of the beer-pouring, but not only can I talk backwards (for some reason), but I can write backwards as well — when I was at sea aboard the *Hornet* in the early 1950s, my battle station was behind a Plexiglas plotting board on which I had to write so that the officers on the other side could read it, thus the incident may have occurred as Jerry remembers it. If so, I was getting even for his welshing on our bet, and what I said to him amphisbaenically was without doubt insulting.

The *Esquire* symposium was held at Iowa that year, and a lot of famous writers and editors were present, including, as I recall, Dwight Macdonald and Norman Mailer. I remember a cocktail party — was it at the Engles' or the Justices'? — where I saw Mailer pinned in a corner by Ed Skellings who was gesticulating earnestly and jabbering at him at a great rate. It was there, too, where I exercised another of my abstruse and exotic talents, the ability to clap with one hand by making the fingers flap against the palm of my hand — not snap, a true *clap*.

I'd been wandering across the room and happened to be passing a circle of people who were listening to a philosopher explaining the zen "koan," or unanswerable question. "The best known koan," he was saying, "is probably, 'What is the sound of one hand clapping?'" I stuck my arm into the center of the circle and did my bit, then withdrew and kept on walking. I looked back over my shoulder to see the group staring in silence at the spot where my hand had been. I don't know what happened to them after that.

There was an active social life among the writers. Jean and I were invited to have Thanksgiving dinner with Paul and Mary Engle, and we were very glad to accept, for it would be the first celebration of the feast that my wife had spent unclasped in the bosom of her family. It was there where, among many others, we first met Ben Santos, the Philippino novelist, and his wife. She and Jean got on as though they were old friends, and Ben and I struck up the same sort of conversation. Paul had been involved for years in bringing foreign writers to the Workshop.

There were parties at the homes of Don and Jean Justice and Mort and Wilma Marcus, and on New Year's Eve we went to a gathering at the apartment of the Gregory FitzGeralds; Greg would review my *First Poems* for *The Iowa Defender* the following year and later become a colleague at Brockport, one of the S.U.N.Y. branches. Toward the end of January Jean and I went out for dinner with Vern & Joan Rutsala to The Carousel, a "sophisticated" Iowa eatery. For dessert Joan ordered a "Flower Pot" and I ordered a "Vesuvius Fountain." She got a clay flowerpot filled with ice cream, and I got a tall soda glass with some fruit cocktail in the bottom and a mound of sugar soaked in brandy flaming on top. It was rather bizarre. Joan and I cracked up, and the *maitre-de* threatened to kick us all out. The other patrons were scandalized by our behavior.

There was one big trip to Chicago that year to hear a reading by T. S. Eliot, sponsored by *Poetry*. Several cars full of Workshoppers drove up from Iowa City, and Paul got some of us invited after the reading to a reception and cocktail party on Lakeshore Drive at the home of Thomas Lannan, the largest patron of the magazine. I remember the cavernous modern apartment as being wall-to-wall carpets and floor-to-ceiling works of art. I knew that Eliot was present somewhere, so I wandered through the rooms one by one, looking for him, stumbling over famous writers everywhere, but he was well-hidden, and I never laid eyes, let alone a hand, on the great man.

Another *Poetry*-related incident I recall from earlier in the year. One day I received a letter from the editor, Henry Rago, accepting a poem titled "Like a Fleet Thief." I was stunned — I recalled having written no such poem. I fell to my knees before the couch in our living room with the letter on the cushion before me, held my head in my hands, stared at the acceptance, and thought, "Oh, no! I've been trying for years to get into *Poetry*, and now they've taken a poem by someone else that they think is by me!"

I don't know how long I knelt there, my mind whirling frantically. But then some dim shadow of recall began to encroach upon my memory, and I got up and went into the bedroom where there was a large stack of my manuscripts sitting on the floor beside the door. I began sifting through the pile, despair growing ever stronger until, at last, at the very bottom, I found an onionskin carbon copy of the forgotten poem titled "Like a Fleet Thief." I had thought so little of it, I had not recalled having written it, let alone submitting it to *Poetry*.

My despair was not alleviated, for I didn't want such a poem to appear on my permanent literary record. I pondered and mulled. At last I came up with what seemed like a fair solution: I rewrote the poem, turning it into what I felt to be a good effort, a companion-piece for my Yaddo poem titled "Raceway," which was to be reprinted in *Midland*, and I titled the draft "House and Shutter." However, I didn't dare to send the new version to *Poetry* for fear that Rago would turn it down, so I wrote him and asked if he wouldn't be so kind as to change the title of the poem he had to "House and Shutter." He did so. Paul had asked me to choose one of my poems to put into *Poetry for Pleasure*, and I'd not yet gotten around to it, so I inserted the new poem into the manuscript, wrote Rago for per mission to reprint, and I had both my initial publication in the June issue of *Poetry* and a decent version of the poem on the record.

It was time, I felt, to do some weeding of that pile of poems on the floor. Mort Marcus volunteered to help me. He came out to the farmhouse one day and we sat in the livingroom of the apartment while I read the first few lines of poem after poem. If he liked the sound of the beginning of a poem, Mort would give me the thumbs up; if not, the thumbs down, and I would crumple the sheets up and toss them on the floor. By the time we were through, the floor was completely covered with wadded balls of paper.

The first week in February Mrs. Daniel B. Green, Awards Chairman of the YM/YWHA of Philadelphia Arts Council, wrote to tell me that my play, "An Onyx Dream," later to be retitled "The Dark Man," had won honorable mention in the 1959 Waldo Bellow Memorial Award Contest. This same play at UConn had been performed in the Little Theatre and won the Undergraduate Play Contest.

Bob Mezey had won the Academy of American Poets Prize at Iowa the two previous years, so Paul and Don had barred him from entering, and possibly winning, a third year in a row. I was unaware of this fact and, with everyone else in the Workshop, submitted poems to the contest. The judges were to be E. L. Mayo and Ralph Salisbury, whom I had not previously met. They selected my work for the prize that year, which made Bob sneer.

The third thing that happened in which I took some pride was an acceptance by W. H. Auden of "Raceway" for publication in what I took to be a new magazine, *The Mid-Century*. However, one of the Workshoppers approached me one day and asked how I had managed to have a poem published in an issue of the monthly bulletin of The Mid-Century Book Club, a new venture whose books were selected by Jacques Barzun, W. H. Auden, and Lionel Trilling. My classmate was a member, and he had just received the newest bulletin; my piece was, I believe, the only poem ever published in one of them.

When spring arrived in Iowa City, the softball games began. I recall a contest between Philosophy, I think it was, or Poli-Sci, and the Poetry Workshop. Don Justice was playing first base. A huge philosopher, weighing easily three hundred pounds, came to the plate and took a couple of swings, one of which hit the pitched ball into the infield. It was an easy throw to Don at the bag: the philosopher was trudging up the baseline in slow motion.

Tall, thin, stretchy Don — built like the perfect first baseman — caught the throw and held out his mitt to touch the runner as he came pondering up. At last the meeting took place. The runner — give him the benefit of the doubt — could not readily slow down. He hit Don's extended arm, and the ball went flying. Don began saying things, and the philosopher turned the error into a double before anybody retrieved the ball.

Don bided his time. A couple of innings later the heavy thinker came to bat again and hit the ball so far and hard, it was an obvious homer. Don jumped up and down screaming, "Throw the ball! Throw the ball!" But there was no ball to be thrown. Don could take it no longer. As the philosopher rounded first the poet launched himself at the ponderous ponderer who paid no attention whatsoever, continuing on his way home — it was like a gibbon attacking a hippopotomas. The image left in my mind is of an enormous marshmallow with a walking stick insect stuck all over it. I mentioned this event to Don some years later, but he disclaimed all memory of the event. I couldn't have imagined anything so funny.

I discovered, rather too late, that there was a good deal of ill-feeling on the part of the English Department's scholars toward those Workshop students, such as myself, who were trying to get a straight M.A. in English without taking the "proper" courses in 20th-century literature. The hostility manifested itself on the M. A. exams through unfair questions. On my exam, for instance, one of the questions was, "Name <u>the</u> ten greatest prose works of the 20th century." If one hadn't taken the course from the teacher who wrote the question, one had little hope of answering correctly, since what was meant was, <u>the</u> ten greatest works in the teacher's opinion, not the student's. I recall that two of the answers were supposed to be *Shadows on the Rock*, by Willa Cather and *The Seven Pillars of Wisdom* by T. E. Lawrence.

Running out of money, and with a wife who could no longer work because she was about to give birth, I left without taking my degree, but my publication record was strong enough to land me a job at what was then Fenn College in Cleveland, later to be

Cleveland State University. In 1961 I founded the Cleveland Poetry Center at Fenn, after spending two weeks in Middlebury, Vermont, as a Bread Loaf Fellow with John Ciardi and Dudley Fitts, and in 1962 I returned to Iowa briefly to finish my master's degree in company with Mark Strand, whom I had met at The Festival on the Green in New Haven where he and I had read our poems to a sparsely populated meadow during the summer of 1959.

If these on-campus events are vivid, so are scenes like the one that took place at an M.L.A. convention in Chicago a few years later when, after the annual Iowa get-together, a bunch of the poets from various eras adjourned to my room for an all-night one-upmanship word-game marathon — Don was there, and Bob Dana, Steve Parker I think, and several others. Toward morning, Justice, who was lying on the bed — or, rather, dripping half off it — whenever a particularly good *bon mot* was passed, grunted feebly in a gesture of humor appreciated. I believe we kept it up so long largely to see if we could elicit just one more grunt of approval from Don Justice.

For me, at least, the Iowa experience in terms of the Poetry workshop was largely Don. One of my books, *Awaken, Bells Falling: Poems 1958-1967*, is dedicated to two great teachers: John Brinnin at Connecticut, and Don Justice at Iowa. In many ways, he is a diffident and self-effacing man. I don't think he realizes what effect he had on the minds of many af his students. One of his phrases could set you off. I've already mentioned how *The Book of Forms:* was conceived. Again, when my sequence of "free verse" poem-portraits, *The Sketches*, came out as a chapbook in 1962, Don said, "You ought to try writing prose poems." I did, and eventually my sequence *The Inhabitant* appeared. "The Study," one of the poems included in the series, in fact, was written in Don's living room in Syracuse where he was teaching at the time. I'd penned it on the spot to illustrate the system of grammatical prose parallels in which the poetry of the Bible is written.

I could give more examples of the kind in which a word from Justice went a long way toward getting one of his students into a project, or simply to raising our self-esteem. But Paul Engle had his effect, too, and it was at least as large. It was Paul, too, who stood in the line of fire to take the hits, for the Iowa Workshop has always elicited a fair amount of criticism, a good deal of it of the sour grapes variety. In his essay titled "A Poet of the Ordinary," Frank H. Thompson, Jr., wrote in the fall 1964 issue of *Prairie Schooner*, "The early work of [W. D. Snodgrass and Philip Legler], as represented in *Heart's Needle* and *A Change of View*, shows how easily they could have remained the technically adept, empty poets that Paul Engle so complacently turns out." I felt constrained to reply in an essay titled "The Iowa Workshop: An Assenting View," in the spring 1965 issue of the same periodical:

> Readers of the country's literary periodicals are used to this sort of remark concerning the Writers' Workshop at the State University of Iowa. In my view, the hostility displayed by various writers who have never been to Iowa, and by some few, such as Robert Lowell, who have resided there, is remarkable and largely unwarranted.
>
> First, in defense of Iowa, I would like to point out the simple truth that Paul Engle does not "turn out" poets. Rather, what he does is encourage them to go to Iowa. In this encouragement he is successful, because Iowa has earned a reputation as a gathering place for young writers, and for *would-be* writers who may never make it — but how can one tell until they are given their chance?
>
> It seems to me that very few young people go to Iowa expecting to be "turned out" as accomplished writers. Rather, they go there in order to be with other young people who are also interested in writing — to talk with them, to fight with them, to be excited by the atmosphere generated in one of the very few communities of the United States where the art of writing is treated as a serious subject.
>
> That any number of mediocre talents seem to come out of Iowa can be explained simply: any number of mediocre talents are *attracted* to Iowa. In any given year it would be remarkable if the law of averages permitted more than two or three potentially excellent writers to be enrolled in the

Workshop. The rest, as in any other kind of specialized gathering, must range from good through average to poor. Thus, the appearance every now and then of a Snodgrass, or a Legler, or a Justice, or a Mezey, or a Sward, is to be expected and applauded, as Mr. Thompson rightly applauded the first two in this list.

But why must all the rest, by the same token, be deplored — worse, vilified? The purpose of a school is to develop the excellent, certainly. But it is also to develop, to the limits of their capabilities, the rest as well. If all our schools were to restrict their enrollments only to the potentially supreme, we would have no society, or an unworkable society at best.

On this basis, I would like to suggest that Iowa's Workshop does its work quite well. It encourages an interest in writing; it provides an atmosphere in which various levels of talent may develop; it provides competition for the ambitious and talented, and it provides a certain level of excellence which the less talented writer can try to attain. Even in the case of the totally untalented writer, Iowa's efforts are not wasted: hopefully at least, the writer who fails will be a more responsive and aware reader of poetry — Mr. Snodgrass and Mr. Legler, I feel sure, will not scorn an intelligent reader of their work, a reader as informed, perhaps, as Mr. Thompson himself seems to be.

Last, but not least by any means, Iowa is an exciting place for the young writer; at times, indeed, it may be a bit too exciting and hothouse, but these are conditions which any intense place must hazard from time to time if it is to proceed towards accomplishing its goals. Regardless of stereotypes to the contrary, Iowa is an essentially unacademic place. Most of the learning process takes place, not in the classroom, but in the private bull session at the Union or at Kenney's bar perhaps; in the library and books stores where students introduce themselves and each other to all kinds of writing, from the *avant garde* to the conservative.

The measure of Iowa should not, I would argue, be taken by the unreasonable yardstick that it does not "produce" uniformly excellent writers, but by the rule that it encourages the young person to write seriously, to develop to one's best capacity, to learn something about the art and the craft of writing. And to fight like hell for one's own point of view and kind of expression, if one has them.

If one has no point of view, and if one wants to run with a herd, so be it. Pay no attention. But do applaud the real artist who manages to rise above the ordinary, and do give Iowa the credit it deserves for providing a serious first forum for the person with a true voice.

On November 22nd, 1964, Paul wrote, "Dear Lew, Thanks for attacking the Philistine Thompson, whom I don't know. The only thing I wish you had also said is that I couldn't possibly be 'complacent' about mediocre poets. They pain me as much as anyone, and often more, because I have put time in on bringing them, on criticizing them, and it is sad to see little come of it. This is an annual assault and I'm hardened! As for Lowell, I feel he is not quite fair. We saved him, in a sense, by being the first place in the USA to give him a job, to help him develop confidence after the shattering sequence of psychopathic hospital and federal prison. Only Iowa would take a chance on him; others did, after we made the initial risk. It gave Cal security and a hope; both the Dept. Head and the President took a hard look at the risks involved, and decided to hire him because I said he was the best poet."

II.

Many of these recollections passed through my mind as the plane passed between Syracuse and Chicago where I changed planes to arrive in Cedar Rapids at 2:31 p.m. I caught the chartered bus to

Iowa City, and it was in that vehicle where I met the first of my fellow Golden Jubileers — Eugene Cantalupe, of an older generation, and David Lunde from the College at Fredonia whom I'd first met at the S.U.N.Y. Festival held at Brockport seven or eight years earlier. Also on the bus was Scott Heller, a young journalist who had attended Iowa, but not the Workshop — he was back to cover the story.

I was the only one on the bus who had signed up to stay at a dorm rather than at the Iowa House or the Holiday Inn, so the driver let me out at Burge Hall where I picked up my keys and walked across the street to Daum Hall. I had room 5404, on the fourth floor. It was air conditioned, but it didn't need to be, as the weather, unlike the soggy mess in the East, was a bit cloudy but very fine, the temperature perfect, around 70 degrees Fahrenheit.

As soon as I got unpacked I went to the Iowa Memorial Union at the foot of the hill to attend registration, which was at 4:00. I noticed that my old friend and classmate John Gilgun was among the first to have put his name on the sign-up sheet for the marathon reading that was to take place that night. While I stood there I met Joe Nigg, now a Coloradan and editor of company publications of Re/Max in Englewood. He and I, it turned out, were across the hall from one another in Daum, and Gilgun was next door to him. We also met Sam Hamod, who swore he had met me somewhere, but we couldn't figure out where.

Sam gave Joe and me a ride to the Prairie Lights Bookstore where, Sharon Arnone of the University of Arkansas Press had written me on May 7th, my just-published book of literary criticism, *Visions and Revisions of American Poetry*, was to be found. She was as good as her word, and I was delighted to find my collection of poems, *The Compleat Melancholick*, published the year before by the Bieler Press, sitting next to it. Another Bieler book, cheek-by-jowl with mine, was *Everything That Has Been Shall Be Again: The Reincarnation Fables of John Gilgun*. I was finding John's tracks everywhere, but he himself was nowhere in sight.

After we left Prairie Lights our next stop was across the Iowa River that flows through the center of campus — the cocktail party and buffet held at the Iowa Museum of Art at 6:00 p.m. It was here that we began to meet the people we'd come to see. One of the first new faces was that of Nick Crome, like Joe a Coloradan. It was Nick who had made overtures in 1965 for me to go to Colorado State University at Fort Collins as visiting poet-in-residence, though we had never met. I'd not been able to swing it, however, and now we were face to face for the first time.

Scott Heller took me aside for an interview, and while we stood on the terrace by the wall of the museum I spotted Paul Engle and went to talk with him. Seeing him under these circumstances filled me with delight. Paul introduced me to his second wife, Hualing, whom I'd not previously met, and told me he'd received the announcement of *Visions and Revisions*, ordered a copy of the book from Prairie Lights, and then gotten the copy I'd sent him by first class mail, together with my 1981 *American Still Lifes*.

"Now that's what I call class, Lew," he said. "Knowing you were going to see me in a day or two anyway, you sent me a copy by priority mail. I told Hualing, 'That's a class act!'" Then he said that the first chapter he'd read was the one on Eliot. "That's first rate work, first rate!" He had an ulcerated foot which was going to prevent him the following week from accompanying his wife to China. "I've been reading a chapter a day and three poems while I soak my foot," he said. "There's just enough time for me to do that." On the last day he added, "The poison flows out of my foot and the balm flows into my eyes."

I laughed and asked him, "Can I get a blurb from you that says my book is a pedicure as well as a book of literary criticism?"

"Sure," he replied, "and you can say it's an eyewash too."

Donald Petersen was there, another colleague from Oneonta, a branch of the S.U.N.Y. system. Don Justice arrived and I hugged him, a sort of demonstration of affection he's not used to. I saw Mark Strand and Kim Merker, by then poet and fine editions printer for the University. I tracked down John Leggett, director of the Workshop for the past sixteen years, and met him for the first time. I told him of the progress of Leigh Allison Wilson, a recent Iowa M.F.A. and my colleague at Oswego. He asked me to find James McPherson and tell him about Leigh too, which I did, but it turned out that he had talked with her just a day or two before on the phone.

At last I ran across John Cilgun, and another classmate, Greg Fitzgerald, was on hand as well, but I'd seen him on and off over the years at various S.U.N.Y. events. He said he'd just retired from the faculty at Brockport. I met Henri Coulette for the first time, Phil Levine likewise. Mike and Marlene Fine were present, and we exchanged reminiscenses of The Paper Place with John Gilgun. However, as one searched among the faces for old friends, it became evident that there were quite a few people missing. Of these, a considerable percentage had evidently boycotted the Jubilee on principle. As Vern Rutsala put it when he was asked whether he would attend, "I didn't see my name or the names of any of my friends on the program, so I guess I'll pass." John Gilgun later wrote in a letter, "...this is the same point I made in 1959 — that the clique system, the star system is nonsense." Many didn't attend owing to circumstances of various sorts. Hortense Calisher and Curt Harnack, the outgoing director of Yaddo, were among these. So was John Irving, who was back in Vienna, scene of episodes in several of his novels. David Duer, a young man who edits a little magazine called *Luna Tack* in West Branch, a town fifteen miles distant, was perhaps over-familiar with the Iowa City scene, and he had family responsibilities that prevented his attendance as well. John Gilgun said of Duer, "He's the kind of person this Jubilee is all about," the unsung laborer in the literary vineyards. Leigh had said Iowa was too recent an experience for her.

After we'd socialized awhile and had a couple of free drinks we ate at the buffet, and then Don, Mark and I toured the museum. Paul was doing the same, so I talked with him some more. He told me that over the years my books had been arriving with "alarming frequency." It was at the cocktail party that a division among the participants became noticeable: there was an older "Engle crowd," and a younger "post-Engle group." Although the two intermingled physically, there was remarkably little interaction between them. The two groups remained spiritually and conversationally discrete. This situation was formalized later on at the "Decade Parties" that took place beginning at 9:00 p,m. in a tent in the field across from the entrance to the Iowa House, the hotel and conference center that had been built as a wing of the Memorial Union.

In the Union at the same time the Marathon Reading was taking place. It was mostly the young people who were participating, but John Gilgun had signed up and he talked me into doing likewise; Harold Bond, whom I'd first met the previous fall at the New England Poets' Conference at Harvard, also enlisted and we three, being last, closed the show. Harold and I are formal poets, and even Gilgun's prose poems are chant-like. There had been one or two earlier readers who had read rhymed and metered pieces as well. Afterward John and I went back to the decade party where a young woman who had heard us read said to me, "The poets of your generation do that formal sort of thing so well, but we never learned how."

While I was talking to her I mentioned *Strong Measures*, the newly published anthology of "Contemporary American Poetry in Traditional Forms," edited by Phil Dacey and David Jauss. As I turned away, Dacey walked up and introduced himself — he said he'd heard somebody mentioning his book and came over to see who it was. We got into an argument about the relative merits of Walt Whitman, whom he likes. I told him I kicked old Walt around a fair amount in *Visions and Revisions*. He said, "You've got a lot to answer for," but he thought he'd use the book as a text anyway, just to stir up his students, not that they'd believe me. I told him not to bet on it.

At the continental breakfast next morning in the Terrace Lounge I managed to say hello to Mike Curtis of *The Atlantic*, whom I'd met in the spring of 1965 while I was teaching at Hillsdale College in Michigan. Dan Menaker of *The New Yorker*, who had for years been rejecting my stories with friendly notes, came over and sat with me while he ate. We talked for a long while before he had to participate in the 9:30 panel on the "Care & Nurture of New Writers" in the Main Lounge of the Iowa Memorial Union. Curtis and Theodore Solotaroff, whom I'd met at Brockport, were the other panelists. I took the microphone during the question period to say that I felt the Iowa Workshop had spawned too many replications of itself in the form of graduate programs over the years, and that undergraduate programs that trained young people for jobs other than college-level teaching positions would have been of greater service and would have provided many more teaching positions for graduates of M.F.A. programs than currently exist, for there are innumerably more undergraduate colleges than graduate schools. Oswego, where I taught, was an example of a large undergraduate program that employs seven writers.

Looking among all these people and discovering who they were gave one the sense that Iowa had done a bit better than all right. I was meeting and remeeting many old friends, correspondents, and people with whom I've been sharing publishing space for years: Kent Baker had graduated from UConn a year after I did; he lives in Canada now. Scott Weeden, my former student at Oswego, was sitting almost directly in front of me a couple of rows down during the panel — he and I got together briefly after it was over. James Baker Hall said hello and chatted awhile. He introduced me to Dan Marder. Bob Dana didn't remember the marathon word-game session we'd held in Chicago many years earlier, but Don Justice did and mentioned it first. Joe David Bellamy said hello and we recalled the joint reading we'd done at Canton Ag & Tech several years earlier. Edwin C. Cohen, Frank Conroy, Gerald Freund, and Kenneth Hope gave a panel on "Grants & Arts Colonies" at 10:35, and at 11:40 there was one on the "University as Patron" with the President of Iowa, James Freedman; the novelist Doris Grumbach; my old acquaintance, the poet Michael Harper; John Leggett, and Paul Engle. But it wasn't much of a "panel," for the opening statements of each participant took up all the time allotted.

When he took the stand at last Engle was reborn. No longer a seventy-eight-year-old retiree, he suddenly was transformed into the person one recollected from the Poetry Workshop sessions of the past. He was absolutely at the top of his form. Most of the people present were transported, amazed, and delighted. It was certainly the high spot of the Jubilee to that point for me, and later on I told him so.

The noon-day barbecue was another fine meal. Everyone talked about how cheaply and yet elegantly the Iowa Foundation had managed the program. I sat with Don Justice, Henri Coulette, Phil Levine, and several others at lunch — I taught them some new word-games: the con-game, puns on prisoners beginning with the prefix *con*: (What did the warden ask Lawrence the turnkey when Lawrence had been knifed by a prisoner? ans., "Con stab you,

Larry?" This was Don's favorite); the humanoid little furry creature game (puns beginning with *ob* — what do you call a segment of a film made by a little furry creature? ans., "An ob scene."), the divorcee game (prefix *ex*), and the golfer game (prefix *pro*). Paul came over to talk, pursued by the omnipresent photographers and a television crew. One cameraman wanted to get him in a "candid" shot walking down the street with a bunch of his friends. He tried to recruit several of us, including the poet Jane Cooper, the Dons Petersen and Justice, Mike Harper and the word-game gang, but the session turned into a free-for-all snapshot-fest, and it was many minutes before we were walking down the street, talking and laughing self-consciously while the lenses blinked and the sound crew dangled the mike boom over our heads.

At 2:00 p.m. there was a panel on "The Writing of the 80's" with Russell Banks, Tess Gallagher, Levine, Strand, Charles Simic, and Hilma Wolitzer, but I found time to carry some of the books I'd brought along up to The Prairie Lights Bookstore and add them to the pile on the Iowa Workshop table. I also dropped in on Iowa Book and Supply and the Iowa Memorial Union Bookstore; both places said they'd order *The New Book of Forms* when it came out in August.

The 3:05 panel was "Renaissance in the Short Story" with T. Coraghessan Boyle, Ray Carver, James McPherson, Bob Schacochis, and Stephanie Vaughn. It appeared that Syracuse University, where Carver and Tobias Wolff taught, was the trendsetter, or at least that was the impression left by some of the panel. Boyle would publish a novel in 1990, *East is East*, in which he named a character "Lewis Turco." Before he attended Iowa Boyle had been an undergraduate at S.U.N.Y. Potsdam, graduating in the spring of 1968 where, the following fall, the real Lewis Turco was Visiting Professor for the year. When I wrote to him to ask why he had so named one of his *personae*, Boyle claimed to have made the name up!

No one was going to every session because we were beginning to show signs of fatigue. For my part, I was exhausted and went back to my room for a nap. I got up in time to attend the 4:10 panel, "Trends in Poetry: New Directions for the 90's." James Tate, the moderator, wasn't serious and did a fair amount of clowning around, but Jorie Graham was interesting. The rest of them —

A Sheaf of Leaves: Literary Memoirs

Marvin Bell, Daniel Halpern, Michael Palmer, and Charles Wright — seemed not to agree on where the literary scene was going.

The Presidential Reception took place at Dr. Freedman's house at 102 Church Street at 6:00 p.m. If I had remembered how close the mansion was to the campus I'd have walked, but I took the shuttle bus and sat with Doris Grumbach on the way over and back. It turned out that she runs Wayward Books in Washington. I told her about my summer Mathom Bookshop in Dresden, Maine, and we had a fine chat about that and about how sorry we were over the death of John Ciardi, her National Public Radio colleague that spring.

I had been searching for George Keithley, my classmate in 1959-60, since the first day, and I finally ran into him at the reception. I said hello to Tess Gallagher, who taught at Syracuse University where my daughter, Melora, had been a teaching assistant in the English department during the past year, and I chatted with Tess' husband Ray Carver a while — he hadn't heard that John O'Brien, a colleague of mine who had brought Ray to Oswego to read three years back, had been institutionalized in West Virginia.

At the 7:30 Jubilee Dinner — chicken cordon bleu, asparagus, chocolate cake — the tables were reserved by decades. I sat in the 60s with the Fines, Gilgun, Joe Nigg, Kent Baker, and George Keithley. Waiting at our places were copies of *Seems Like Old Times*, an anthology of reminiscences of the Workshop edited evidently at breakneck speed by Ed Dinger. Masters-of-ceremony were John Leggett, Doris Grumbach, and Galway Kinnell. Pres. Freedman gave the welcome.

The members of John Berryman's class read poems: Jane Cooper, Coulette, Bob Dana, Bill Dickey, Ronald DiLorenzo, Shirley Eliason, Don Justice, Melvin Walker LaFollette, Phil Levine, Don Petersen, Paul Petrie. Henri read a poem sent by De Snodgrass who, when he tried to come from his Mexico vacation, was stopped at the border because of an irregularity in his visa. By the time the State Department had straightened things out he had driven 600 miles back to the spot where he had been vacationing, but he'd managed to get the poem into the mail, and it had arrived in time.

There were also "A Half-Century of Reminiscences" given aloud: Deborah Digges for the 80s, Allan Gurganus for the 70s,

John Irving's for the 60's read by Ray Carver, for Irving was back in Vienna. Jim Hall and Oakley Hall covered the 50s, and Kay Burford read Ray West's for the 40s. Paul was presented with a chair with a plaque on it by John Leggett, who also announced that there would be Fellowships and a faculty chair established by the Iowa Foundation in Paul's name.

Then Paul got up to speak. Unfortunately, he got carried away and went on at great length. The younger people at the tables in the far end of the IMU Ballroom began to get rather noisy, and Paul's partisans were by turn annoyed with them and embarrassed for Paul. The event had to be anticlimactic for Paul at any rate, for it would have been unreasonable for anyone to expect him to transcend, or even reach again, the peak of performance he'd attained at the morning panel.

At last it was over, however, and everyone drifted off, many to the Jubilee Ball across the river again at the new Theatre Building where two bands, the Max Lyon Quartet and The Rhythm Rockers, were playing. John Gilgun and I sat at a table listening and watching for a while, but then we left and went to walk the streets of Iowa City into the dark hours. We managed to find Iowa Book and Supply, which was still on its corner of Clinton Street, though it was a totally new shop. Nearby was a familiar bar, The Airliner, exactly as we had left it, even to the old neon sign. The next corner, where Whetstone's Drugstore had been, was a hair styling salon. There was a new brick mall next to the spot where The Paper Place had stood and later burned, and across the street where Kenney's Fine Beers had stood, there was a shoestore named, only too ironically, Kinney's. At last Gilgun and I got tired of walking the midnight malls of the city that had been made much prettier than we remembered. We'd come down and calmed down enough to go back to Daum and go to sleep.

On Sunday morning John and I went out walking again to try to find somewhere to eat because brunch wasn't scheduled until 10:30 a.m. We got to the Holiday Inn where we discovered the restaurant open. We had breakfast and afterwards went back past the Prairie Lights Bookstore where we'd noticed stacks of the Sunday edition of *The New York Times* — in the old days the *Times* used to arrive on Tuesday. I took one, slipped money under the door of the closed store, and we went back to the dorm where I began to do the crossword puzzle in the Magazine section, never noticing the big article on the Jubilee we were at that moment attending.

John and I went over to the Union before things got going and discovered that we could have eaten in the cafeteria there if we had only realized it. We sat down and had coffee with Don Justice, Jim Tate, and several others. At 10:30 a fair number of people went to the final panel, "Regional and Fine Press Publishing" with Edwina Evers, David Hamilton, Kim Merker, and Robley Wilson. Paul Zimmer, director of the University of Iowa Press, was also listed — I'd written him I was looking forward to meeting him, but for some reason he wasn't present.

The last meal was the Brunch Buffet in the tent — blintzes and sausage. I ate it with Sven and Kathleen Armens. Sven had been one of the English professors who, twenty-six years earlier, had played softball with the Workshop poets. I had known him rather well in those soft spring days, and it was a delight to have a chance to visit with him again. Everyone was saying their last farewells, taking their last pictures. Paul invited me to a gathering of "the old crowd" at his house at 4:00 p.m., and I had regretfully to tell him my limousine left Daum at that time to take me back to Cedar Rapids to catch my plane. He said he bet it was my private limousine, but I had to disillusion him yet again.

Gilgun, who had been regaling me in the interstices of action, carousing, and conversation for a day and parts of two others with what I began calling his "tatterdemalion tragedies," invited me to go with him to West Branch, a town fifteen miles distant, to visit briefly with David Duer. He thought it would be a particularly appropriate way to end the weekend. And, of course we got lost in the cornfields. We drove back and forth, asking farmers and neighbors the way for the better part of an hour. We were about to give up when finally we found the house. David's wife was in the bath, and his arms were full of children. The wind was picking up and blowing over the greening fields — it came on cold enough for John to put on a sweater, and I redonned my jacket. Before we left he gave us copies of his periodical, *Luna Tack*.

Joe Nigg, Dan Marder and I shared the limousine to the Cedar Rapids airport. When we got there Joe and I went into the tiny bar for drinks. We were talking when Ted Solotaroff, Galway Kinnell, and two others came past grinning and looking at me in an odd way. I didn't understand why, when they sat down at a table nearby, they kept smiling and looking at me. It wasn't till later that I realized they must have overheard me say to Joe, who was talking about my books, that "I'm the most widely published unknown writer in America." It's not a smiling matter.

Joe and I eventually took off in different directions. On my plane I found myself sitting next to a very attractive young woman named Marsha Shultz, a personnel representative of Rockwell International's Avionics Group. We got into a conversation and, of course, it turned out that she writes poetry on the sly. I gave her the last copy of the books I'd brought with me, my 1973 chapbook, *The Weed Garden*. She had two children who were spread out in age almost as much as my two are — a thirteen-year old daughter and a three-year-old son. I promised to send her a copy of the children's picture-storybook, *Murqatroyd and Mabel*, that I'd written a few years back under my anagram pseudonym, "Wesli Court," to read to the little one.

Jean and my son Chris were waiting for me back in Syracuse when my plane landed on time at 11:00 p.m. On our trip home we stopped at Pizza Hut for a pepperoni pizza. The Golden Jubilee was over. I had not spoken with one single person who had attended who hadn't thought it was an utter marvel of enjoyment. That is remarkable. No, it's a miracle, a bona fide miracle. I doubt I will ever again see the day when one-hundred percent of the writers at a literary gathering maintain against all likelihood and all hope that they had, one and all, the time of their life in celebrating the best and the worst times of their lives when they were students in that Camelot Erewhon, the Writers' Workshop of the University of Iowa.

IDEOLOGIES: THE CHRONICLE OF A CONFLICT

Our enmity began in 1960 when each of us published a first collection of poems: James Dickey's *Into the Stone* was one of three collections contained in Volume VII of the *Poets of Today* series edited by John Hall Wheelock; my *First Poems* appeared as a selection of The Book Club for Poetry from the Golden Quill Press. I was asked by Loring Williams, editor of the original *American Weave* magazine and one of the trio of editors who had chosen my collection for the Club, to review *Poets of Today VII*.

I wrote in my critique that Dickey reminded me of the composer Carl Orff. I thought part of the reason for this association lay in Dickey's technique of stating and restating the minor and major themes in each of his poems. In between these demi-refrains the language was controlled, the ideas were concise, and the emotion — like the emotion of "Carmina Burana," for instance — was less explicit than implicit. I said, further, that Dickey's emotion was stylized, which didn't make it bad; in fact, I liked it: style is style.

Another impression I had was that many of Dickey's poems reminded me, even more than of Orff, of Theodore Roethke cerebralized, made less basic, for the images of *Into the Stone* were not so startling and sensual as those of Roethke. Poems such as "Sleeping Out at Easter" and "The Cell" made me uneasy. They did not take the chance that Roethke's took of becoming tiring eventually — but then, they didn't take the chance.

At the time of that review I had no clear idea of what Roethke was doing rhythmically in his poems, but later, when I understood the principles of "podic" meters such as dipodics and heard Roethke talk about such meters on a tape, *Conversations on the Craft of Poetry* (1961), it became clear to me that Dickey in his first book had been trying to imitate Roethke's prosody as well as his imagery. But Dickey hadn't understood podics; therefore, he had substituted for this accentual verse with its falling rhythms an accentual-syllabic system of trochees and dactyls which was more monotonous than Roethke's work.

I did not, however, talk about metrics in that first review — probably just as well, for a few months later Dickey, in *The Sewanee Review*, tore apart my *First Poems*. He hated traditional verse and formalism. Perhaps this condition had something to do with his having attended Vanderbilt University and growing up under the New Critics who taught there.

In a short-lived little magazine, *The Mad River Review* for Spring-Summer 1965, I undertook to examine James Dickey's first book of his collected reviews, *The Suspect in Poetry* (1964). In an essay titled "The Suspect in Criticism" I said that, in opening the cover of the book, I opened the door of the gallery and beheld both the shattered Formalist and Beat idols lying fallen in their legions. There, in frosty ruins, lay the Yvor Winters of our discontent: Donald Drummond, an icicle piercing his breast; Ellen Kay, her remains caught in a gigantic snowball of criticism. In one corner lay Allen Ginsberg shattered beyond salvage. Thom Gunn's bust, clad in the rags of what had once been an impeccably tailored black leather jacket, took up another corner, and about the room lay scattered the many-splendored beads and gewgaws that once had encrusted the Aztec statue of Ned O'Gorman. There were others in the gallery — all, all destroyed: Robert Mezey, Charles Olson, Anne Sexton, Philip Booth....

Why these particular poets? What sensibility or system had informed this destruction? Baffled, I read on, and then, as though I had fallen through a secret panel, I found Dickey's "system" of criticism. In the section of the book titled "The Grove Press *New American Poets* (1960)" Dickey set up his criteria:

> There are four or five main ways of reacting to poems, and they all matter. In ascending order of importance they are (a) "This probably isn't so, and even if it were I couldn't care less"; (b) "This may be true enough as far as it goes, but, well...so what?" (c) "This is true, or at least convincing, and therefore I respond to it differently than I do to poems in the first two categories," and (d) "This is true with a kind of truth at which I could never have arrived by myself, but its truth is better than the one I believed." The first two classifications are useful because they are what we feel about bad poems, very bad ones in (a) and half-bad or unsuccessfully realized ones in (b). In (c) are most of the poems we like well enough to call "good" in reviews and to which we may want to return occasionally, and in (d) are those we continue to call great when conversing only with ourselves, and which we would hope to die hearing or remembering. Almost all writers of verse aspire simply to reside in (c), and many a solid reputation — such as that of Robert Graves — has been founded on just such a semi-permanent residence, which is by no means as easy of attainment as I may make it seem. Even those whom we call "major" poets catch only a few glimpses of the world I have designated (d), or at most stand for a handful of moments in that bewildering light, in the certainty that they are bringing about an entirely new kind of human communication compounded of about equal parts of the commonality of all mankind and the unique particularity of the poet's vision and his language. The achievement of even a small but steadily authentic flame is immensely difficult, as we all know, and requires, as well as a great deal of luck, a lifelong attention to those means by which we might best hope to feed it.

By the time *The Suspect in Criticism* appeared James Dickey had already established a reputation as a critic through the reviews he had published in prestigious magazines. In fact, this book was not much more than a collection of those reviews. It seemed reasonable to me, therefore, that one might question Dickey's critical assumptions, including the first one, the "reaction" Dickey maintained is the best reaction one can have to a poem: "(d) 'This is true with a kind of truth at which I could never have arrived by myself, but its truth is better than the one I had believed.'" One might begin with a definition of the word "reaction" which, according to one dictionary, the Merriam-Webster, means "the act or process of an instance of reacting." The dictionary uses the gerund in its definition of the noun; therefore, one must refer to the verb "react" which means, "1: to exert a reciprocal or counteracting force or influence — often used with **on** or **upon**; 2: to respond to a stimulus; 3: to act in opposition to a force or influence — usually used with **against**; 4: to move or tend in a reverse direction; 5: to undergo a chemical reaction." Since the only one of these definitions that makes any sense if applied to Dickey's statement is number 2, one can assume that that is what he meant.

Now another word has to be defined, "stimulus": "1. something that rouses or incites to activity." I take it that, if one is to react to a poem, one must respond to...something that rouses or incites to activity. It follows that what Dickey described as a "reaction" is not a reaction at all. Rather, it is a mental process of some kind, a process which in some way evaluates something that Dickey called "truth."

What does the critic mean by truth? It is an abstract word, and it may therefore be variously defined. In order for the reader to understand it, Dickey must somehow anchor it, make it concrete. In his description of a "reaction," the implicit relationship of "truth" is with "This probably isn't so, but I couldn't care less." "This probably isn't so" is a reference to a fact of some kind — "A thing is so, or it isn't so" might be a reasonable, if fuzzy, synonym for *soness* or *not-soness*, for "fact and non-fact." As nearly as it is possible to determine, in Dickey's equation truth equals fact.

One may proceed to step (b) in Dickey's ascending hierarchy of "reactions" to poems. Here the relationship of "truth" is again with fact (true enough," *i.e.*, one has the facts straight, perhaps), but even if one hasn't, at least one has made the reader believe one has. This "reaction" is suspect. In (b) the poet as a minimum had the data in order, trivial though they may have been. Thus, one had at least been "truthful." Now, in (c), one may or may not be truthful — Dickey appeared to be unsure which — but at least one is "convincing," and that apparently counts for something, even though one's "response" may be to a clever lie.

One at last arrives back at (d), the top rung in the ladder of the critic's "responses," and the reader is to respond by evaluating the "truth" of what the poet has said. Furthermore, this "truth" is "a better one than the one [Dickey] had believed." The first question that comes to mind at this point is, how can one "truth" be better than another? All truths are absolutes. Is the implication here that it makes no difference as long as the critic is "convinced" that one is better than the other? That is to say, is one set of facts less trivial than another set? If so, how so? If the facts of the lesser "truth" are straight, may they be supplanted by a more convincing set of non-facts?

However, to get back to the main point, the reader is to "respond," but one's responses have been called into question by (c). If one cannot be sure that the poet had the "facts" straight, even though the reader had been so "convinced"; and if, as it would seem, "facts" equal "truth,"

1) How is it possible for one to evaluate the "truth," uncertain as one may be that the "truth" is the truth?
2) How can one "react" by "evaluating" to begin with, inasmuch as an evaluation is not a reaction?

Now that the critic's premises have been called into question, is there any further enlightenment to be found in the remainder of Dickey's argument? Perhaps so. The next major statement he made is this: "Even those whom we call 'major' poets catch only a few glimpses of the world I have designated (d), or at most stand for a handful of moments in that bewildering light, in the certainty that they are bringing about an entirely new kind of human communication compounded of about equal parts of the commonality of all mankind and the unique particularity of the poet's vision and his language."

My "response" is, What bewildering light? No "world" was mentioned in (d); what was mentioned is "truth." Is "truth" to equal "facts" to equal "world" to equal "bewildering light"? Or, since the authenticity of the facts has been called into question, is "truth" to equal "facts" possibly, but perhaps non-facts (depending upon the poet's ability to "convince" the reader) to equal a "world" based either upon facts or non-facts? And is this tantamount to "bewildering light"?

As to that "communication" which, one supposes, is the poem itself — can one conclude that a poem may be defined as "The communication of a world of facts or convincing non-facts"? And, since the critic has defined "communication," can one say that "A poem is a bewildering compound of "about equal parts" of the commonality of all mankind and the unique particularity of the poet's vision and his language with respect to a world of facts or convincing non-facts"?

One might, if one wished, carry this Jesuitical close analysis through many more pages of Dickey's criticism and arrive eventually at a much more complicated, but equally absurd, conclusion. I prefer to believe that a poem is an artifice of language and let it go at that or, at worst, to resort to "Turco's Instant Critical System":

A poet I used to know who was given to overwriting pronounced the word *poem* as though it were spelled *poyme*. Unfortunately, not everyone can pull off just writing a *poem*, and they wind up underwriting a *pome*. Rather a large number of people, poetasters they are called, can't even rise to that level, and they write a *peom*. Still others have no conception of what a *poem* actually is, and they write *somep'n else*. Those are the categories of my Instant Critical System:

Poyme

Poem

Pome

Peom

Somep'n Else

This system is instantly apprehensible, and everyone may now read any poem and place it at its correct level.

But that is disingenuous. To be accurate, I had developed my own critical system when, in 1959, Harold Vinal began to ask me to review books for his magazine *Voices*. I felt I ought to tell his readers how I was judging books; therefore, in my second review, published in 1960 and titled "The Poet's Court," I wrote that I approached poems by "levels," of which there were, in my opinion, five.

The first level was the "visible" or *typographical* — how does the poem appear on the page? Is it stanzaic, strophic, or irregular? Does it use printed shape in unusual ways? Do indentations indicate rhyme patterns, syllabic line counts, or other formal elements?

The second was the *sonic* level. Is the poem written in the mode of prose (unmetered language) or the mode of verse (metered language)? Does it utilize rhyme, assonance, consonance, alliteration, and other echoic effects?

The third level was that of the *sensory*. What sorts of images are used — descriptions, comparisons and contrasts, allegories, rhetorical tropes? Does the poem appeal to the senses or the emotions?

The *ideational* level was the fourth. What is the subject of the poem, the theme? How does it proceed — logically or intuitively, discursively or impressionistically?

And, last, there was the *fusional* level. How well does the poet utilize and blend the four lower levels? Does he or she use all of them — is there a balance? Or does the poet emphasize one or some of the levels and not others? Readers comparing Dickey's method with mine — if any ever did — would immediately be able to tell why we were at loggerheads, for one is a formal, objective approach, while the other is an emotive, subjective "system."

I must confess that, writing in 1964 of Dickey's *The Suspect in Poetry*, I was perhaps overly logical, too didactic. But in the same review, published in *The Mad River Review* for spring-summer 1965, I also took on his newly published collection of poems *Helmets* (1964) and, rather emotionally myself, dismissed it as page after page of darkly mysterious, subterranean murmuring, of snakes and frogs and flowers bogging along mumbling runic legends into the poet's monotonous dactylic ear. It seemed to me that, sure enough, James Dickey was Theodore Roethke reborn as a tame black swan — no mean feat, since Roethke was only recently deceased.

There the matter lay until 1968 when three books were published that were to reopen both the feud and the ideological conflict and, oddly enough, sow the seeds for an eventual truce; the first was James Dickey's *Babel to Byzantium*; the second was Hyatt H. Waggoner's *American Poets from the Puritans to the Present*, and the third was my own *The Book of Forms: A Handbook of Poetics*. Dickey's book had a "Preface" that began with these words:

> A book such as this one seems to be obligated to carry with it the notion that the critic has a System of Evaluation that he can defend not only in its practical and local instances but in its broader theoretical and philosophical implications as well. If the critic is myself, he knows that any reasonably good teacher of aesthetics could tear his "ideas" apart with no trouble; he lives in constant dread of falling into the hands of the neighborhood community college's Socrates. But even should this not befall him, he is still inordinately bothered by the number of quite obvious contradictions that occur throughout the book, some of them on the same page. He certainly cannot claim consistency, although he secretly thinks he has it, in some intuitive, mysterious, and perhaps subliminal way. Nevertheless, despite all his misgivings, he has at one time or another had these opinions. And now he has collected them, and is consequently obliged to believe that there is some value in doing so.
>
> Though I have been made aware by my whole education of the necessity of internally consistent thinking and judgment, it appears to me that, where poetry is concerned, there are more important things than judgment involved, and that foremost among these is participation.

Having thus dismissed systematic criticism and logical systems; having himself used the words "intuitive," "mysterious," and "subliminal" to describe his aesthetics, rather than drop his hierarchy of "reactions" he moved it to first place in *Babel* from its original place deeper in the pages of *The Suspect*, no doubt feeling he had erected sufficient defenses in the "Preface" of the new book to forestall the attacks of more logical thinkers.

Babel was largely a rearrangement and expansion of *The Suspect*. I had felt free to review the earlier book because Dickey had not included in it his review of my *First Poems*. In the new volume, however, he resurrected the eight-year-old piece, and I therefore did not review it because such an item would have appeared self-serving. Nevertheless, I was considerably disturbed, for Dickey's notice of my book had been the only adverse review it had received, and now I could be sure it would be the only one most people remembered.

On a more abstract and theoretical level, however, another book published the same year, Hyatt H. Waggoner's critical history *American Poets from the Puritans to the Present* provided me with many crucial insights into, among others, the roots of James Dickey's criticism and poetic philosophy. Waggoner said that Dickey currently "is restating in contemporary language some of Emerson's leading ideas about poetry." If this is true, as I believe it is, then Emerson's ghost wandered through the pages of *Babel to Byzantium*. The unity of Dickey's *The Suspect in Poetry*, Waggoner said, "...springs from Dickey's conviction that poems that seem to lack personal passion and personal vision, poems that resemble autonomous verbal engines, artifacts cleverly designed to stir our emotions without giving us any new perception, any 'fresh glimpse of the world,' are 'suspect.' We do and should resist them, Dickey argues, since we do not want to be manipulated by poets any more than by advertisers." And Dickey would know, for he began making a living originally as an advertising executive.

In the war between Emersonian criticism and The New Criticism's dominance, at that time, of American literary theory, Waggoner was not a neutral. "The surprising, the 'radical' thing about James Dickey's criticism," Waggoner wrote, "is the poet's unabashed use of 'truth' where the modern masters have taught us to expect 'myth' or 'fictive music.' Reading Dickey's words we might almost imaging we were listening to Frost in his old age, when his guard was down, talking about what he really cared about in poetry and hoped the young men [and women, one hopes] would care about. As for the reference to the poet's 'vision'..., talk about 'vision' has been taboo among poets, and even more among critics, since Pound omitted it from his requirements for good poetry.

"But of course 'vision,' as Dickey uses it here stops short of being fully Emersonian, or transcendental and religious, in its implication."

This, it appeared to me, was the crux of the problem in Dickey's work, both in his poetry and in his criticism, just as it is the problem of anyone who wants to bypass craft and get right down to the nitty-gritty of mystical experience, for Dickey straddled a chasm and seemed incapable of bringing his feet together, either on one side of the gulf or on the other. Even further beyond his capacity, judging from the later *Babel*, is what he would like to do: bring the two faces of the chasm together in a fusion of vision and art. It is the problem of our time, and of any other, as perhaps even Waggoner would have admitted, for when he criticized a poet it was as often for a lack of craft as for a lack of insight. But if there was a certain sense of ambiguity in some of Waggoner's judgments, this sense was even more acute in Dickey's.

Read a bit carelessly, Dickey's criticism might have seemed to be written intelligently, an illusion that confused the issue, because a good many of his primary observations were at root puerile. How to react to adolescent yearnings couched in adult language — and wasn't this Emerson's problem too? Dickey had an aversion to rhymed poetry, for instance. In his essay titled "The Poet Turns on Himself" in *Babel* he said,

> I had in the beginning a strong dislike of rhyming poems, for the element of artificiality is one of the characteristics of poetry I most distrust, and I have always had trouble distinguishing between artificiality and the traditional modes and methods of verse; for a time I was convinced that craft and artifice were the same thing. At the same time I also had a secret suspicion that Whitman, Lawrence, the Imagists and others were cheating, absolving themselves from the standing problems and difficulties of verse.

Dickey was a victim of the Anglo-American traditional confusion that poetry equals verse, but poetry has often been written in the mode of prose as well. His troubles were just beginning, though, for he continued,

> But I found, unlike so many others, that the qualities of poems which seemed to me poetic — essentially poetic — were not in the least dependent on whether or not they occurred in poems which rhymed. I also discovered that the restrictions imposed by rhyme led me away from what I had intended to say. Other writers have since told me — citing Valéry and others — that significant discoveries are made through the attempt to satisfy such restrictions and that as often as not one ends up as a result with a better poem than one anticipated. Doubtless this is true, and it is also true that certain poets, certain kinds of creative minds, are helped enormously by the support they receive from such sources. Nevertheless, such a practice did not seem right for me; I felt continually carried past my subject, carried around it, sometimes close to it but never in it in the way I wished to be in it.

Having thus been defeated by the exigencies of rhyme, Dickey had to consider what other element of craft he would jettison. Would it be meter? Not quite:

> Although I didn't care for rhyme and the "packaged" quality which it gives even the best poems, I did care very much for meter, or at least rhythm.... Most of the material I read on metrics concluded that the systematic use of anapests and dactyls tends to monotony, and I accepted this judgment on faith and continued to try to work with the customary English iambic line.

But the iamb would work no better for Dickey than would rhyme. Fortunately, however, he "found that the anapest was as capable of interesting variation as any other kind of line; in fact, as the iamb itself." He found, further, that what he "really wanted to do was to make effective statements." So he began, in his earlier work — the poems that appeared in *Into the Stone* — to use anapests, dactyls, and "a kind of refrain technique that, so far as I know, I invented for the occasion. In this, the last or refrain lines of the stanzas unite to make, themselves, a last stanza which sums up the attitude and action of the poem."

Dickey, setting out to invent poetry all over again, had not discovered that his "invention" is at least as old as medieval Provençal verse forms such as the villanelle and the triolet which do the same thing, or the English carol, for that matter, though they rhyme as well. Or was Dickey being entirely truthful at this point? In his later book, *Self-Interviews* (1970), the poet James Dickey seemed to be saying something quite different than the critic James Dickey:

> While I was writing *Into the Stone*, I was very much interested in experimenting with verse forms. I've always been a great admirer of Hardy and tried to take a lesson from him in inventing. He seemed to get a good deal of enjoyment from inventing forms. You can look through Hardy's *Collected Poems* and see forms that you never see in any other poets. He has poems which have a very long line — hexameter or even longer than that sometimes — and then a very short line that rhymes with the first one. The physical difference between them is so great you hardly know they rhyme. Hardy's interest in inventing forms is something that I thought I might appropriate, because I have a similar interest. So I invented some new stanza forms. I had some poems in a semi-couplet form, like "The Underground Stream." Another form was based on a relatively simple rhyming quatrain followed by a refrain line. There are a number of these stanzas, and finally their refrain lines make a separate stanza which serves as a summation or coda.

When I read these words I was fascinated for two reasons. First, when I reviewed Dickey's first collection I identified these same forms, which I called "demi-refrains." More fascinating still, however, was the fact that Dickey, in his review of my first book was outraged as much by Donald Justice's "introduction" as by my poems. He said, in the *Sewanee Review* and in *Babel*,

> In his introduction, Donald Justice speaks of Lewis Turco's playfulness and his penchant for difficult exercise poems, like "a gifted musician practicing scales, arpeggios,

and the sonatas of Clementi." I must say that I don't feel this is a promising sign in Mr. Turco's work. As a game it is all right, I suppose, but why play games with Mr. Turco when one can be reading real poetry? Skillful Mr. Turco may be, but his is the most ordinary of all kinds of skill, and shuts off more of the potentialities of poetry than it opens.

Dickey not only chastised me for doing in *First Poems* what he himself says he was doing in *Into the Stone*, he also chastised Justice for saying things like this:

> There is a good deal here of what some people call versifying, meaning something unpleasant, perhaps. It is as if the poet had come across a handbook on versification and set himself to working out the problems there, as the student of mathematics might do, a process sure to appall the tender-minded. The models to be found in such handbooks are, to be sure, appalling enough, clever at best and very soft. But Mr. Turco is not soft and he is very clever. One is reminded less of the H. C. Bunners of this world than of someone like Hardy, that great versifier who was also, at times, a great poet. There is something of Hardy's approach to poetry here, not that of the gloomy philosopher, but of the poet who set himself repeatedly the most trying technical problems and in solving them took and gave pleasure both.

Not only were Dickey and I doing similar things in our first books, a third party saw that we derived at least partially from the same source, though Dickey's admission of this fact was not forthcoming for a decade. However, to return to *Babel* and the technical revelations therein, the reader might well have been wondering at the amount of time a "Transcendentalist" was spending worrying about craft. Why not get going on Vision and let the necessary argument choose its own form, create its own meter, as Emerson counseled? But Dickey instead

>...discovered that the simple declarative sentence, under certain circumstances and in certain contexts, had exactly the qualities I wanted my lines of poetry to have. As I wrote more poems of this kind, I was increasingly aware of two things. The first was that I liked poems which had a basis of narrative.

Thus, the visionary added two more techniques to his arsenal — grammatical parallels and narrative. And another, stream-of-consciousness, although Dickey didn't use the term:

> I also discovered that I worked most fruitfully in cases in which there was no clear-cut distinction between what was actually happening and what was happening in the mind of a character in the poem. I meant to try to get a fusion of inner and outer states, of dream, fantasy, and illusion where everything partakes of the protagonist's mental processes and creates a single impression.

Many of the terms he was using at that point were from the discipline of fiction: "Character," "illusion," "protagonist." And, with all of these things, there was the technical fusion at last:

> My second book, *Drowning with Others*, is made up of poems written in this manner: poems with a predominantly anapestic rhythm and dealing often with dream, hallucination, fantasy, the interaction of illusion and reality. My third book, *Helmets*, employed many of these same themes and approaches, but was less pronouncedly rhythmical and less hallucinatory. By this time I had begun to grow a little restive at the limitations of my method and was beginning also to dislike the way I had been handling the narrative elements. All my old reservations about the vitiating effects of artifice began to trouble me once more; I was afraid that I had simply substituted another set of conventions — of artifices — for those I had congratulated myself on discarding earlier.

A Sheaf of Leaves: Literary Memoirs

The sympathetic reader no doubt sits stunned before this epiphany: the mystic had again failed to avoid using language and its conventions. But Dickey was not above trying yet another time:

> I began to conceive of something I called — doubtless misleading — the "open" poem: a poem which would have none of the neatness of most of those poems we call "works of Art" but would have the capacity to involve the reader in it, in all its imperfections and impurities, rather than offering him a (supposedly) perfected and perfect work for contemplation, judgment, and evaluation. I was interested most of all in getting an optimum "presentational immediacy," a compulsiveness in the presentation of the matter of the poem that would cause the reader to forget literary judgments entirely and simply experience. I experimented with short lines some more and, eventually, with putting several of these together on the same physical plane to make up what I called the "split line," in which spaces between the word groups take the place of punctuation.

Dickey had invented a good deal of jargon to explain his discoveries — the "open poem " (not to be confused with Charles Olson's "open verse" or "projective verse," which Dickey demolished earlier in *Babel* but which, if one looked closely enough, appeared to be exactly the same thing as Dickey's "split line." (Question: did Dickey resent it when other poets seemed to be doing what he himself was doing?), "presentational immediacy," and so forth. But such jargon isn't necessary, for words exist to cover what he was talking about: grammatical parallelism, lineation (or line-phrasing) of prose, caesura, empathy; or even William Carlos Williams' "breath pause" and "variable foot." But these terms were suspect, of course, because if one used them one must be talking about traditional techniques, and if one avoided traditional techniques somehow, Vision might ensue.

James Dickey wanted to be a visionary poet, evidently — a purely visionary poet, as he made amply clear in many of those passages where he praised certain contemporary poets. When he talked about Theodore Weiss, for instance, Dickey said, "Many of his passages seem to me to be nothing more or less than visionary, with the vision-seeing that only the poet's truest and most personal language can attain, with 'the world / lit up as by a golden school.'"

It is as though Dickey wanted to sink into vision, into Emerson's Transcendental Oversoul, allowing words no demands of their own. He said of the poems of his master Roethke that "They are simple, tragic, profound, and unutterably joyful. They are, and will be, permanent parts of our perception of reality, and one feels guilty of an unjust act, of a dislocation of nature, in referring to them as 'literature' at all." Dickey wrote in a later essay on Roethke, "What matters to me is not so much the form the poems took as the sensibility that lived in them, the superior quality of observation that made them possible: the presence of insight, of vision."

In short, Dickey wanted very much to be an American poet of what I sometimes think of as the "Druidic School," but which Hyatt H. Waggoner called the "Emersonian mainstream." Language is to be used only as an instrument of "vision," or "insight" and "revelation," not for "literary" purposes; language is not to be tolerated as an element, in and of itself, of American poetry. There is, in fact, to be no such thing as "literature" at all, only "higher consciousness."

Yet the Word would intrude, artifice kept getting in the way, and Dickey now and then stumbled over it on his Fourfold Path to Vision, as in this passage from the essay on Hayden Carruth:

> "On a Certain Engagement South of Seoul" is as fine a poem as an American has ever written about the ex-soldier's feelings, and that takes in a lot of territory. It is only after the inevitable has clamped us by the back of the neck that we go back and look carefully at the poem, and see that it is written in terza rima. And so, hushed and awed, we learn something about the power of poetic form, and the way in which it can both concentrate and release meaning, when meaning is present.

But Dickey didn't learn very well or retain what he had learned for very long, because he arbitrarily eschewed rhyme, external form, and iambs, which he could not handle, but he found himself forced to substitute refrains, statement, anapests, dactyls, until it occurred to him that he was still struggling with craft. Thereupon he substituted another prosody based on grammatics, stream-of-consciousness, phrasing, and narrative...the "un-well-made poem," in his own words, but "prose fiction" in almost anybody else's.

Many years ago I picked up a copy of *The Saturday Evening Post* and turned to the table of contents. There, under the heading "Fiction," I discovered Dickey's name. I hadn't known James Dickey wrote fiction — his novel, *Deliverance*, had not yet been published — and when I turned to the piece I found it wasn't a story, but a poem. Then I read it and discovered it wasn't a poem, but a story in verse. Not a vision at all, nor a poem, but a work of fiction in his new grammatical, "split-line," open versification. Dickey had reinvented the medieval fabliau, a short verse narrative that takes its material from the middle classes.

I thought to myself, We have come to this — full circle from the fabliau; through John Lyly and his *Euphues*, the novel-born-of-poem; through James Joyce and his epic *Ulysses*, the poem-born-of-novel. Now we are back to the fabliau. And still nobody can see what's going on, we're so hypnotized by stereotypes of the nature of poetry. We still think on the one hand that anyone who writes in verse is a poet, and on the other we suspect traditional verse techniques because we're good American Transcendentalists and don't want to be identified with decadent old Europe.

We therefore redefine poetry, with Emerson and Whitman, not in the classical, "masculine" tradition of mind; not in the mainstream, balanced tradition of mind and feeling, but in the only alternative left open to us: the romantic, "feminine" tradition of heart: the American poet must be someone with "soul, " if one prefers today's idiom, or "Oversoul," if one prefers last century's term. The simple solution never occurs to us: a poet is both mind and heart, both objective and subjective, both masculine and feminine, both craftsman and visionary...but that's European too, and we want our own national personality as artists. We want something different, overtly different. Just being Americans writing poetry in America is not enough. We must have a National Program for Doing Our Own Thing. Emerson said it, and Whitman did it — by reading the Bible and adapting the techniques he found there, techniques that began with the ancient Sumerians 7000 or more years ago; ignorance is bliss, for Whitman as for Dickey — as long as we don't know what we are doing, we must not be doing it.

In 1968, the year that *The Book of Forms* was published without fanfare beside Dickey's and Waggoner's books of criticism, I wrote some of these things down in a talk, which I delivered at Bread Loaf Writer's Conference late in August. Later on I published the talk as an article, "Confession, Vision, and Artifice," in *The New England Review* for July-August 1969. It is now many years since that last arrow was fired, but even by then the feud was over, as I see it in retrospect; it was over — or it should have been — by 1963 when Theodore Roethke died, because on that unhappy occasion (I, too, greatly admire Roethke, as well as Hardy) Dickey published in the pages of *Poetry* a eulogy in which he acknowledged Roethke as his master, just as I had perceived in my original review of *Into the Stone*. Dickey reprinted the eulogy in *Babel*, and I ought to have felt vindicated and let it go at that.

Perhaps I would have, except that Hyatt Waggoner's book gave me to see that, though the personal feud was nothing, the battle of ideologies among American poets is a continuing war, and Dickey and I were involved in it on opposite sides, and if his criticism has had its effect on contemporary poets, so has *The Book of Forms* which, for sixteen years held the formalist fort.

But I would not have the reader feel that I do not believe in mysteries myself, for in 1965, five years after Justice wrote his "Introduction" to my first poems, I came to live in Oswego, New York, which I was astonished to discover was the birthplace of H. C. Bunner, the other poet besides Hardy that Justice had mentioned. And in 1977, while I was writing some notes for this essay, a curious thought occurred to me: I was sitting in the Tower Room of Yaddo mansion in Saratoga Springs; it used to be Theodore Roethke's room.

In 1981, when my book *American Still Lifes* was published, the first person to order a copy of the book was James Dickey. Not long after it had been sent to him, I received a letter from him which was astonishing to me — he asked to bury the hatchet. It is one of the most magnanimous letters I have ever received, and for a while I was perplexed as to what response I should make, for what he said was that he not only liked the book very much, but that he thought I was a fine writer.

After pondering a while, I replied in a series of notes — a sort of thinking in process — to the effect that I was a bit reluctant to do as he suggested because the end of a conflict which had lasted twenty years was going to leave a big hole in my life. With what was I to fill it? But the biggest surprise was yet to come. Five years later, in 1986, when I received my first copies of *The New Book of Forms*, I was astonished, without forewarning, to read this blurb printed on the front cover:

"Belongs in the hands of every poet, student, and teacher, for the greater good of the art. — James Dickey."

Lewis Turco

Meters and Missiles

The Fenn College (now Cleveland State University) Poetry Center was established on April 14, 1962, and I was named founding director. My only collaborator at the school was the late David French, director of audio-visual education at the college and an amateur poet who later went on to take a Ph.D. in history from Western Reserve University and to pursue an academic and administrative career at Lake Erie College. David and I immediately began to line up and record poets for the Fenn Series of Contemporary Authors, an audio archive. Dave also planned to record the poets and writers who came to perform at the Poetry Center in the future.

The Center's first official guest that spring was William Golding, the British author of a novel, *The Lord of the Flies*, that was an enormous hit in the United States. I had discovered at Bread Loaf the previous year that he was to be in America, and I managed to sign him by offering him our entire first-year budget: $100.00.

Following Golding that spring there was a Jazz-Poetry Festival featuring Eddy Halas reading his poem "The Odyssey of Jazz" to a background of music played by the Bobby Brack Trio. Capping the academic year, the National Federation of State Poetry Societies at the end of June held its convention on the Fenn campus, and John Crowe Ransom was the featured speaker on Saturday, June 30th. Ransom, a central figure among the so-called "*Fugitive* Poets" — named after the periodical that he had founded with others including his colleague at Vanderbilt University, Robert Penn Warren, and his student Allen Tate — had thirty years earlier stopped writing poetry and dedicated the intervening decades to criticism. At the convention he read the first poem he had finished writing after all that time, "Prelude to an Evening," and it was clear that the hiatus had not been good for Ransom as a poet.

All of these programs were free; the jazz reading was a charity event, and all we did for the Federation was allow them to use our facilities. Nevertheless, the first few offerings in the Poetry Center program were so successful that our budget was doubled for the succeeding academic year: We had $200.00 to play with.

On August 22nd Richard Frost arrived in Cleveland with his wife and children. They were billeted at Fenn downtown, but ate with my family out in Euclid. Dick and I had met at Bread Loaf where I had introduced him to his namesake, Robert Frost, and where we had become quick friends. Dick read at the Center on August 24th; he was followed on October 5th by another Bread Loafer, Robert Huff.

Loring Williams, who with George Abbe and Clarence Farrar had chosen my *First Poems* as a selection of The Book Club for Poetry in 1960, before I knew I was moving to Cleveland from Iowa City, and who single-handedly published *The Sketches of Lewis Turco and Livevil: A Mask* as the American Weave Award Chapbook that same spring of '62, began leading the weekly Poetry Forums, workshops that were immediately popular and still are so in 2002. Dave French and Al Cahen succeeded to the editorship of Loring's poetry periodical *American Weave* when, several years later, after the death of his wife, he left Cleveland to return to his native South Berwick, Maine.

Besides Dave and Al, d.a. levy (he liked to use all small letters *a la* e. e. cummings), Russell Atkins, Bill McLaughlin, Alberta Turner, the Oberlin student Sam Hudson, and Julie Suk were among those attending the Forums. My student Russell Salamon attended as well, and he became close friends with levy. Many years later he wrote an epic about his relationship with levy and about levy's suicide, *Descent into Cleveland* (Orange: Words & Pictures, 1994). Louis Albion Williams was the focus of Poetry Forum I on October 19th.

However, by Tuesday, October 9th, Loring and I were making plans to attend the National Poetry Festival at the Library of Congress in Washington, D.C., for five days from October 22-24. We had both been invited, but Loring dodn't drive and I was broke. Loring offered to pay all expenses if I would drive, which I was happy to do.

Unfortunately, the public would never hear about the Festival, certainly the greatest gathering of poets in the history of the U. S. if not, indeed, the world, because it coincided exactly with the Cuban Missile Crisis. To this day it remains a non-event, with not even a mention of it on the Internet where everything is mentioned. The only documents to record the Festival were the official "Program" and the *Proceedings* of the *National Poetry Festival Held in the Library of Congress, October 22-24, 1962* (Washington: U. S. Government Printing Office), published in 1964, two years after the event and by then already long forgotten.

Louis Untermeyer, while he has Consultant in Poetry to the Library of Congress from 1961 to 1963, wrote the "Foreword" to the *Proceedings*. He said in part, "When the Library of Congress first envisioned the 3-day activities of the National Poetry Festival, it was hoped that the program would bring together representative poets from all parts of the United States. It was recognized from the outset, of course, that some of the poets invited to appear on the program would be obliged to decline because of previous commitments or for other reasons. Several distinguished poets were indeed unable to take part, but their proportionate number was fortunately small.

"In addition to the speakers, many other writers (mainly poets who have recorded their works on tape for the Library of Congress) and individuals who have contributed to the development of poetic expression in this country were invited to attend and to participate in informal discussions. The public was also admitted to all sessions of the 3-day meeting." (PNPF 1-2)

Although I was only twenty-eight years old in 1962, I had been publishing in the little magazines since 1953, and I had recorded my poems for the Archive of Recorded Poetry and Literature of The Library of Congress in 1959 at the invitation of Richard Eberhart, Poetry Consultant at that time, whom I had met at the University of Connecticut where, as an undergraduate from 1956 to 1959, after my Navy enlistment from 1952-1956, I had been director of the Student Union's visiting writers series of literary readings.

On that occasion there had been a party at the home of L. F. Dean, chair of the English Department. Before the poet had arrived, we had written Eberhart to ask if he would let us have a poem for the undergraduate periodical, *The Connecticut Writer*, and he had agreed. At the party I reminded him of his promise. He invited me into the bedroom where he and his wife, Betty, were staying, and he showed me a notebook full of typewritten poems — dozens if not scores of them. "These are all unpublished," he said, "pick one." I stared at the notebook, began to riffle through it. I didn't have time to read them all, so I read a few and finally, in desperation, chose one that I liked at first glance.

At about the same time I had met Untermeyer as well, at the Suffield Reader-Writer Conference at Suffield Academy in Connecticut where I had been a student in the eighth and ninth grades. On that occasion, or perhaps a later one, Untermeyer addressed a roomful of people on the subject of poetry and made some sort of comment that I knew to be erroneous. I rose to correct him. When I finished he hesitated for a moment as though to gather his thoughts for a rebuttal; instead, he looked around the room and said, "The trouble with Mr. Turco is that he knows too damn much."

Loring and I drove down the Pennsylvania Turnpike from Cleveland and checked into our hotel on Sunday, October 21, 1962. The last time I had been in Washington was in 1955-56 when I was stationed at Arlington Barracks across the Potomac and worked at the Bureau of Naval Personnel (BuPers) as shore duty yeoman. Loring and I were up and about early the next morning to attend the first session of the Festival at 9:45 a.m. It began with "Greetings" by L. Quincy Mumford, Librarian of Congress, who said,

"This is a great occasion. It is an honor as well as a pleasure to have a part in it. Although there have been other festivals at other times and at other places, this is the first National Poetry Festival to be sponsored by an agency of the United States Government. With its historic interest in American culture and with its pattern of active participation in the field of poetry, the Library of Congress has a natural role in fostering this event. The Bollingen Foundation has provided a grant which enables us to make the Festival a reality. With other officers of the Library of Congress, I extend a hearty welcome to this unprecedented event, a 3-day National Poetry Festival. It celebrates 50 years of the craft of poetry in these United States and, by a happy coincidence, also marks the 50th anniversary of the founding of *Poetry*. This magazine of verse, the first issue of which appeared in October 1912, had a distinguished founder in Harriet Monroe, who was herself succeeded by able editors many of whom are here with us today.

"It is now my pleasure to turn this meeting over to the present editor, who will serve as chairman of this session, Mr. Henry Rago." (PNPF 13)

Henry had been very welcoming to my work since my graduate school days at Iowa in 1959-60, and he would remain so during the remainder of his tenure as editor. The first discussion, which he moderated, was "The Role of the Poetry Journal"; the panel consisted of Louise Bogan, Stanley Kunitz, and Morton Dauwen Zabel who had succeeded Harriet Monroe as editor of *Poetry* after her death in 1936.

Mr. Zabel, who was the first panelist to speak, said among other things that, "We are meeting and talking here in October 1962. The 'Fifty Years of American Poetry' which this Festival celebrates are an accomplished fact, and without any doubt they have been, beyond any 'golden day' or earlier phase in the native literature, the richest, most productive, most energetic and resourceful chapter in the records of American verse. It would have taken a prophet bold to the point of recklessness back in 1900 or 1905 or 1910 to believe that such an accomplishment lay in the immediate future of poetry in this country, as any glance at the standard anthologies or conventional magazine verse of that stagnant and indifferent period in American writing will testify." (PNPF 20)

Basically, Zabel and Bogan discussed the history of *Poetry* and what had gone before. It was not until Stanley Kunitz spoke that I heard something not only that I knew and agreed with, but that was not part of the received opinion of the period. Kunitz said, "When a poet in a democracy strives for popularity through a public style — deliberately aiming at the mass ear — he soon loses himself in endless and shapeless vulgarity. Whitman may be offered as a refutation of this thesis, but the common man preferred to listen to Longfellow; it was primarily other poets and intellectuals who welcomed Whitman." This is a point I have reiterated since in many of my essays and books, but it is a point that has not been taken by many. The common man would still rather read rhymed and metered verse poetry rather than maundering prose poetry, including that of Kunitz and of Whitman.

During the general discussion that followed, Marian Taft said that "At present the poet and his public are largely isolated. People are not reading poetry. They don't get a chance to, much, from the newspapers or the channels they would normally hope to find it in. They are not reading poetry magazines, except in isolated pockets. What we need is poetry today, but we are not getting the people and poetry together." (PNPF 39)

Various people, including the panelists, demurred. Kunitz said, "I think one way for the poet to find an audience is to live long enough, and I seriously recommend that to all my fellow poets." (PNPF 39) He has followed, and continues to follow his own advice, forty years later. Untermeyer said, "I should like to add that there has never been so wide an audience for poetry in America." (PNPF 40) As one of the two most widely published anthologists of poetry of the period, he knew what he was talking about. The other editor of popular poetry anthologies, also present, was Oscar Williams.

Someone asked Rago how many poems were submitted to *Poetry* in a year. Henry said, "…we receive, by our last count, 70,000 poems a year."

I added, "I'm Director of the Fenn College Poetry Center, and we put on two kinds of programs. First, we have poets come and read; and, second, we have a thing called the Poetry Forum, which is a kind of workshop. I have found that one of the reasons why so few people read poetry is the fact that they're all writing it, and they're not interested in anybody's work but their own. We had Robert Huff come to read in October, and I think we had 20 people there. The other day we had our first Poetry Forum, at which we requested the public to bring their own material, and we had a hundred people, all clamoring to read." (PNPF 41)

Another audience member said, "I'd like to have reconciled for me, if someone can do it, these two statements: nearly every poet who comes to the Library of Congress says that there has never been such an audience before and that people are coming in busloads to hear readings at various colleges, that poetry is simply the biggest thing on the market; and yet, at the same time, everyone says, 'isn't it unfortunate that books of poetry only sell 26 copies and are then remaindered?' I wonder how these things go together."

Kunitz replied, "The answer is quite simple there. The people in the colleges read anthologies." (PNPF 42) Kenneth Rexroth, John Berryman, Randall Jarrell, A. R. Ammons — whom I also had met at Bread Loaf the previous year, Judson Jerome — who was an early anthologist of my work in *New Campus Writing 3* in 1959, and William Meredith all got into the discussion.

At noon we broke for lunch and then, before the afternoon session, gathered in a room with a large table and many chairs that served as a lounge. The great names in American poetry sat around the table, and the rest of us spread out along the peripheries in the folding chairs. One of the poets at the table was Richard Wilbur, someone with whom I had been acquainted for several years. He had begun to teach at Wesleyan University in 1957, while I was a student at the University of Connecticut at Storrs. Wesleyan is located in Middletown, Connecticut, about ten miles from my home town, Meriden. When my wife and I traveled from Storrs to Meriden the back way we would go through Middletown, and as soon as I found out that Wilbur was there I took to visiting him from time to time. Wilbur had been among those poets my Student Union committee had asked to visit UConn.

On May 24th 1963, while I was still teaching at Fenn College, I would again host Richard Wilbur, this time for the Cleveland Poetry Center. Although no one was a more formal poet than Wilbur, he held the curious but prevalent notion of poets at the time that somehow the poet isn't responsible for what he writes, and while we were driving along Euclid Avenue Dick said, in so many words, that "the poem chooses its own form."

Unfortunately, I have a tendency to be sarcastic (I trust only when sarcasm is called for, although my friends tell me this is a forlorn hope). I replied, "Oh? And how did Moliere's *Tartuffe* come to inform you it wanted to be translated into heroic couplets?" There was a chill in the car for a little while, and a frosty rime settled over our conversation.

Back at the National Poetry Festival a year earlier, however, Dick was sitting at the lions' table when Oscar Williams came in, looked for a place with them and, finding none, spotted Loring Williams and me and came over to sit with us. I was not a great fan of Williams. While I had been a student at Iowa we had both attended the *Poetry* Day party at the Chicago home of Thomas Lannan where I had seen Williams sitting like a garden gnome on a piano bench with a poetess perched on either knee, and we had a year or two later locked horns at an Oberlin College literary event.

I remember our sitting in a coffee house that was part of an art gallery in Oberlin and Williams saying, "If you're going to be a poet you need to get a loft apartment in Greenwich Village where you can look out the window over the people in the streets and write your poems. Don't you agree, Mr. Turco?"

I thought his idea was fatuous. "No," I said, "I don't."

"Then what do you think?"

I replied that I thought the would-be poet should arm himself with as much knowledge about poetry as possible, and then sit down to write his poems on whatever subject he chose with whatever techniques he needed for his particular project.

"Oh, Mr. Turco," Williams said, "it sounds as though you should be an insurance man rather than a poet."

I was, of course, furious on the instant. "To the contrary, Mr. Williams," I said, "you're the insurance man, not me."

"How so?" he inquired.

"Well, you spend much of your time anthologizing the work of poets so that it doesn't die. That's a form of literary insurance, isn't it?"

Williams blanched, and the Oberlin students flanking him on both sides of the long bench where he sat turned on me just as though I hadn't been the first to be insulted.

Now, here was Oscar again at the Festival. "Well, hello again, Mr. Turco," he said as he sat down. "And how is my reputation in Cleveland?"

"I don't know, Mr. Williams," I replied. "The subject hasn't come up."

While Loring and I had been sitting there listening to the conversation at the lions' table I had been scribbling an epigram on a piece of paper. Williams said, "May I see what you're doing?"

I handed the sheet over to him. He read it. "I like it," he said. "If you'll make a change or two in it, I'll publish it in one of my books." He told me what he thought ought to be changed.

"No thanks, Mr. Williams," I said. "I like it the way it is." And I believe that was the end of the conversation.

By the time that the Festival resumed at 2:00 p.m. the word was out that President Kennedy would address the nation that evening. The mood of the Festival became more and more apprehensive and charged with tension as the afternoon wore on and rumors spread wave on wave among the participants.

The readers for the afternoon, introduced by Roy P. Basler, Director of the Reference Department of the Library of Congress, were Leonie Adams, William Meredith, Howard Nemerov, John Crowe Ransom, Muriel Rukeyser, Delmore Schwartz, Karl Shapiro and Mark Van Doren. Two other poets on the program, Peter Viereck and Robert Penn Warren, were scratched. When John Crowe Ransom read, he said, "It's been such a long time since I have been creative in making verse that I finally decided that about the best thing I might do would be to create a diversion, which consists in reading an old poem, written about 30 years ago, which was a little bit inconclusive, and adding four stanzas, which I've done in the recent few weeks, retouching it every time I came across it. It's about the homecoming of a man, not just from his daily work but from a long journey. He is talking to his wife in her absence long before he has reached his home and begging that he won't spend the evening sitting with the children at their lessons. He nearly persuades her of another policy, or thinks he does; and there the original poem stopped. It consisted of eight stanzas, quatrains of four-beat unrhymed lines. The four that I have added make a different ending and indeed a happy ending. I don't know whether it will be received or not." (PNPF 69-71)

Ransom's poem was the same "Prelude to an Evening" that he had first read at Fenn. He paused to inform the audience of the point at which the original version had been abandoned thirty years earlier, and after he had read the four new stanzas he spent some little time discussing the now completed piece. Both Shapiro and Van Doren, who followed Ransom, evidently took their cue from him and did more exegesis and background of their work than reading of it.

Dr. Basler rose and said, "Ladies and Gentlemen, at this point I should like to announce that Mr. Peter Viereck, who was scheduled to read this afternoon, was unable to get back from Europe, and Mr. Robert Penn Warren is in the hospital, for a short time, we hope. In order to balance the program perhaps I should say unbalance it we are asking Louis Untermeyer to change his scheduled reading from tomorrow afternoon to this afternoon, as the final poet on the program. Louis."

"The unbalanced Mr. Untermeyer," he said as he came to the podium, "will begin by reading a poem which was the aftermath of a competition sponsored by a Midwestern college a few years ago. The contestants had been taught, or they had assumed, that the best way to be poetic was to be exotic. I had been chosen to award the prize — a rather awkward position. And all I got out of it was this poem." Its title was "Song Tournament: New Style." (PNPF 96)

The evening session was scheduled to begin at 8:30, after President Kennedy's television broadcast. Everyone was extremely apprehensive. "De" (W. D.) Snodgrass suggested to me that instead of listening to it we go out and get drunk. I demurred, so he went alone. At seven everyone gathered in the television lounge to hear President Kennedy announce Doomsday.

Nikita Khrushchev, who in 1960 was the Soviet Premier, began to implement his plan to install in Cuba ballistic missiles capable of reaching the United States. He evidently believed that the U. S. would acquiesce, and whenever he was asked he denied publicly that the U.S.S.R. was taking any such action. However, by the summer of 1962 American U-2 spy planes had taken photographs of the construction sites and had actually documented the installation of the first missile on the 14th of October.

On the 16th of October President Kennedy had been shown photos of the first missile itself and, according to *The New York Times* (Sunday, October 13, 2002, WK 7), "Defense Secretary Robert S. McNamara advised the president: 'We need to have two things ready: A government for Cuba, because we're going to need one...[and] plans for how to respond to the Soviet Union.... It will be an eye for an eye.'"

However, Kennedy instead chose to order a naval and air blockade of Cuba to prevent Soviet ships from delivering offensive weapons and equipment to Castro. It was this announcement that the gathered poets in the Library of Congress watched on a black-and-white television screen. I sat toward the back of the room and looked at the President between the heads of the famous poets gathered there: Robert Frost, Sir Herbert Read, Eberhart, Ransom, Delmore Schwartz (who was escorting a tall and spectacular redhead during the Festival), and many others. It was an eerie scene, full of gloom and foreboding. Nuclear war impended for the first time since the end of the Second World War.

"Good evening, my fellow citizens," President Kennedy said. "This Government, as promised, has maintained the closest surveillance of the Soviet military build-up on the island of Cuba. Within the past week, unmistakable evidence has established the fact that a series of offensive missile sites is now in preparation on that imprisoned island. The purpose of these bases can be none other than to provide a nuclear strike capability against the Western Hemisphere. Upon receiving the first preliminary hard information of this nature last Tuesday morning at 9 a.m., I directed that our surveillance be stepped up. And having now confirmed and completed our evaluation of the evidence and our decision on a course of action, this Government feels obliged to report this new crisis to you in full detail."

President Kennedy proceeded to lay out in detail the facts as our government had been able to establish them, and to make the case for taking immediate steps to prevent the arming of Cuba; these steps were seven:

First "...a strict quarantine on all offensive military equipment under shipment to Cuba is being initiated."

Second, "...the continued and increased close surveillance of Cuba and its military build-up."

Third, "...to regard any nuclear missile launched from Cuba against any nation in the Western Hemisphere as an attack by the Soviet Union on the United States requiring a full retaliatory response upon the Soviet Union."

Fourth, "...I have reinforced our base at Guantanamo, evacuated today the dependents of our personnel there and ordered additional military units to stand by on an alert basis." I remembered Guantanamo from my days aboard the *Hornet*. It was the only place I could think of to be at that moment that might be more terrifying than Washington, D. C.

Fifth, Kennedy continued, "...an immediate meeting of the Organ of Consultation under the Organization of American States, to consider this threat to hemispheric security and to invoke Articles 6 and 8 of the Rio Treaty in support of all necessary action."

Sixth, "Under the Charter of the United Nations, we are asking tonight that an emergency meeting of the Security Council be convoked without delay to take action against this latest Soviet threat to world peace. Our Resolution will call for the prompt dismantling and withdrawal of all offensive weapons in Cuba, under the supervision of UN observers, before the quarantine can be lifted.

"Seventh and finally: I call upon Chairman Khrushchev to halt and eliminate this clandestine, reckless and provocative threat to world peace and to stable relations between our two nations. I call upon him further to abandon this course of world domination, and to join in an historic effort to end the perilous arms race and transform the history of man. He has an opportunity now to move the world back from the abyss of destruction — by returning to his government's own words that it had no need to station missiles outside its own territory, and withdrawing these weapons from Cuba — by refraining from any action which will widen or deepen the present crisis — and then by participating in a search for peaceful and permanent solutions." (*Microsoft Encarta 98 Encyclopedia*)

At 8:30 p.m. the evening session of the Festival continued, just as though nothing had occurred outside the walls of the Library of Congress. Mr. Mumford introduced August Heckscher, Special Consultant on the Arts to the President of the United States: "In this official capacity, he embodies the increasing recognition that our literature and our arts must enjoy the active support and encouragement of the Government if they are to flourish and are to continue to enrich our cultural heritage." (PNPF 105) I and, I assume, others experienced a certain sense of irony as Hecksher took the podium.

The one thing Mr. Heckscher said that I wholly agreed with was this: "I could make a plea…for a more deliberate effort to teach children and young people the craft of versemaking. Let them not be under the illusion that they are, or are about to be, poets. It is enough if, through versemaking, they rise to an understanding of the higher muse, forming the audiences which tomorrow will sit at the poet's feet." (PNPF 108) Well, I agreed with everything except the part about the feet, and I, for one, was already embarked upon just such a lifetime enterprise. The only hint he made to the events of the earlier evening was, "But I know you are not looking for answers tonight. You are listening for the word; you are watching for the deed that is done when words are truly wrought. May I only wish you much pleasure in these days, and say what a very great distinction — an almost unprecedented distinction — it is for the city of Washington to have this convocation in its midst." (PNPF 109) One might have added, a distinction that is already lost to the city and the world.

Mumford then introduced the poet-critic Randall Jarrell who delivered an address titled, "Fifty Years of American Poetry." Toward the end of his talk Jarrell attacked the so-called "academic poets" of the period, many of whom were present and among whom Jarrell himself would certainly have been numbered by nearly everyone present:

"There is another larger group of poets who, so to speak, come out of Richard Wilbur's overcoat. The work of these academic, tea-party, creative-writing-class poets rather tamely satisfies the rules or standards of technique implicit in what they consider the 'best modern practice,' so that they are very close to one another, very craftsman-like, never take chances, and produce (extraordinarily) a pretty or correctly beautiful poem and (ordinarily) magazine verse. Their poems are without personal force — come out of poems, not out of life; are, at bottom, social behavior calculated to satisfy a small social group of academic readers, editors, and foundation executives." (PNPF 135)

Jarrell was a turncoat in a war that had already been lost by the academic poets. Their hosts were, even as he spoke, being swiftly depleted by teachers everywhere who had since the 1950s been dropping any pretensions of teaching technique in their courses and were rapidly joining the hosts of the anti-intellectuals — the Beats, the Black Mountaineers, the San Francisco and New York Schools (who were, in fact, taking over the creative writing courses).

It would be decades before, in the 'nineties, there would be a counter-movement called The New Formalists. Among those who were, besides Jarrell, listed in the Festival program and wanted their students to know that they were not part of the so-called conservative "military-industrial complex" that would shortly, beginning in that very year of 1962, purportedly sponsor the U. S.'s replacement of the French in the "Indo-Chinese War" (*aka* "The Vietnam War) were Karl Shapiro and a poet who would be scratched the next day, Robert Lowell. Both had made their reputations as formal poets, but Lowell had in the 'fifties abandoned metrical verse for prose egopoems and founded the "Confessional School," and Shapiro had become a neo-Beat who proselytized openly for the prose poem.

During the Second World War, long before his formal transmogrification, Lowell had been a conscientious objector, and he had spent prison time paying for it. But one didn't need to be a poet of a particular metrical persuasion to be against war, for as early as the summer of 1962 people were becoming aware that President Kennedy was pulling America into the undeclared "War" in Vietnam when he sent "military advisors" there. The original "Poets for Peace" reading took place in Cleveland at University Circle in front of the art museum with Mac Hammond, P. K. Saha, Leonard Silver, myself and others reading poems written for the occasion.

Roy Basler the next morning, on October 23rd, acknowledged that something had happened. In his introduction to the panel "The Poet and the Public" he said, "We did not know when we scheduled this Poetry Festival that we would arrange to have an international crisis along with it to give excitement." It was an exceedingly feeble attempt to undercut the tension, because the Navy and Air Force were stalking the shores of Cuba, and Soviet vessels en route there began to avoid the blockade rather than try to run it. Khrushchev and Kennedy were communicating through diplomatic channels, and it was not long before the former began to waver in his position.

Meanwhile, Basler informed us that "We have had our chairman of the morning fall by the wayside. Mr. Robert Penn Warren sent us a telegram that he is in the hospital, and I have asked Mr. Richard Wilbur to pinch-hit for Mr. Warren as chairman this morning." (PNPF 141)

Wilbur, who had so many poets in his overcoat, introduced the panelists, Babette Deutsch, Howard Nemerov, and Karl Shapiro. Miss Deutsch was first, and when she took the podium she said, quite accurately, "The speech from the White House last night would seem to obliterate every other matter for consideration. Yet while time for thought remains to us" [and one wondered what exactly were the implications of that remark], possibly the topic of this morning's discussion has some relevance to our situation. That it engages the minds of those present is apparent from the fact that it cropped up so often in the course of yesterday's talks, thanks largely to Mr. Kunitz' contribution, and it was touched upon obliquely in Mr. Jarrell's lively speech last night."

Later in her talk she said, "As for the other poets just mentioned [in her talk, including Li Po and Chaucer], I fancy that more than one of those names would be spoken 12 centuries hence, should men and books survive the threat that hangs over us at this moment.

"In a much more recent poem published in *Partisan Review*, Karl Shapiro touches upon this threat. The poem is different in tone and form from that at which we just glanced, although it, too, deals with the poet, specifically with "The Bourgeois Poet" [which would two years later, in 1964, lend its title to a book full of prose poems]. This means practically all of us, since among the nearly 40 poets participating in this Festival only one, Sir Herbert Read, is a person of rank, and there is no member of the late and largely unlamented 'Beats,' who included one or two men capable of writing poetry but who ceased to be 'beat' when they achieved success." This statement was more wishful thinking than accurate, for the Beats had not disappeared, and would not do so for many years; further, Kenneth Rexroth was present at the Festival, and he was the Grandaddy of the Beats.

Miss Deutsch continued by quoting Shapiro's prose poem which included the phrases, "century of the turning-point of time, the human wolf-pack and the killing light." She said, "I read the last phrase as a pun. 'The killing light' is the light of knowledge; we know how to split the atom. It is also the physical light that we set ablaze in Hiroshima and Nagasaki and that may yet blaze in the capitals of Europe, in New York, Chicago, Washington." (PNPF 145-151)

On this cautionary note Wilbur next introduced Howard Nemerov who, with Marianne Moore and Alan Swallow, had early anthologized two of my poems in a college collection, *Riverside Poetry 3* (New York: Twayne, 1958). His opening paragraph was typical, and it went a fair distance toward easing the moment. He said, "Talking to fellow union members has its possibly embarrassing side: one doesn't want to go all mouthy before an audience professionally concerned with mouthing. But it also makes possible a certain brevity; we needn't spell everything out." (PNPF 53) He hewed to the subject of the panel, and when he was finished Wilbur introduced Karl Shapiro. As one expected, the gist of his comments had to do with justifying his new literary religion.

In the discussion that followed I rose to say, "I want to speak to Mr. Shapiro's talk. I've read a couple of times in various periodicals about how the Canadians are terribly upset because they can't find their culture, they can't find their voice. They're worrying about what kind of poetry they should be writing, and they're being inundated by American writers and by this and that and the other thing; and here I come down to the Library of Congress, and we're saying the same thing: 'What is true American poetry?' I would like to propose a motion, since I think we probably have here a quorum of poets in the country, that all writers, critics, and others who are interested in the question of what is real American poetry be banished to Kokomo, there to fight it out among themselves and leave the rest of the poets, who simply want to write poetry, to the craft of their art." I would expand upon these remarks the following year in a short polemical essay titled "For Poets in Search of Poetry Prose Wise." (*Shenandoah*, xv:1, Autumn 1963, pp. 67-69)

My mentor and former teacher at Iowa, Paul Engle, spoke next. He said, "I want to make a comment about the fact that the word 'academic' has been used here as if it were a naughty word. There are too many poets in colleges teaching for the same reason that there are too many poets working at jobs which are not writing poetry. We'd all quit tonight if the Library of Congress said, 'Look, here's a small hundred thousand dollar bill. You do what you please with it.' We would wire our resignations at once." (PNPF 175) He said many other intelligent things, even though he was almost single-handedly responsible, through the Iowa Writers' Workshop which he directed, for the explosion of teaching writers and writing programs in the United States, including me and the Cleveland Poetry Center.

Then Untermeyer called upon Ogden Nash to say something as perhaps the only poet present other than Robert Frost who had actually made a good living as a poet for three decades and more: not only that, but as a prose-poet who had invented a kind of writing — rhymed colloquial prose — that was as original and as American as anybody could possibly wish, and that antedated the Beats by at least two decades.

For the Tuesday afternoon poetry readings Mr. Basler first introduced John Berryman who read some of his "Dream Songs." Louise Bogan followed, and then Gwendolyn Brooks who, introducing her third selection, said, "After reading yesterday's headlines, I decided to read this last sonnet from a series of soldier sonnets, which was published in 1945. It's called 'The Progress.'" It ended with this sestet: "But inward grows a soberness, an awe, / A fear, a deepening hollow through the cold. / For even if we come out standing up / How shall we smile, congratulate: and how / Settle in chairs? Listen, listen. The step / Of iron feet again.   And again   wild."

The fourth poet was J. V. Cunningham, and Eberhart followed. Cunningham was quite brief, but Eberhart went on at some length. Then it was Engle's turn. Robert Lowell was not present, so Engle was followed by Henry Rago who had moved up a notch.

De Snodgrass was next, the youngest poet to read in the Festival. As an undergraduate I had written a poem for him, "Letter to W. D. S." (*Wormwood Review*, i:2, 1960), after I had read his book *Heart's Needle* and reviewed it for Harold Vinal's magazine *Voices* (171, 1960) in an essay, "The Poet's Court." This review laid out the critical premises for what would eight years later become my *The Book of Forms: A Handbook of Poetics* (New York: E. P. Dutton, 1968).

Allen Tate was introduced and began by reading "The Wolves," then followed — and ended! — with his famous "The Swimmers," about a lynching in the South. It was a brave and shocking poem then, and it still is.

Before the evening session began at 8:30 there was a strange interlude. Delmore Schwarz's spectacular redhead showed up harried and weeping, with a black eye. Richard Wilbur disappeared with one or two others, and then reappeared after an interval with a disheveled Schwarz: his hair looked like a fright wig, his shirt hung partly out of his trousers, he was wild-eyed and obviously not in control of himself. He had evidently beaten his girl friend at their hotel, been arrested, and thrown in jail. Wilbur had gone down to bail him out, but why the police had let Schwarz go in the condition he exhibited was problematic. Wilbur must have called in some big guns to pull it off.

Louis Untermeyer introduced Robert Frost for the evening session. All of us present recalled vividly Frost's reading at President Kennedy's inauguration. I had met him at Bread Loaf in 1961and had spent the evening talking with him, and he was now in the penultimate year of his life, though of course no one could have known that. Untermeyer's introduction was lengthy, but he made some good points. "It is easy for us to smile at the hesitancy to recognize Frost for what he was and is," Untermeyer said. "We forget that 50 years ago his casual lyrics and his colloquial monologues came as a distinct shock; many of the arbiters of what was considered 'good style' resented Frost's peculiar insistence that 'all poetry is the reproduction of the tones of actual speech.'"

Robert Frost had been the first American or British poet to bring off the 19th century Romantics' call to reproduce common speech in poetry without tossing out either meter or sonic devices. It was a huge accomplishment, and it remains so. Very few others have duplicated it as late as today. Even Whitman, who has been given credit for having first done so, never achieved this feat, for his diction is nothing if not artificial in the manner of Longfellow and Wordsworth. One cannot reproduce here much of what Frost said at the Festival, but his talk / reading ought not to remain buried among the *Proceedings*.

While we had been meeting the world had been busy with other things. It was beginning to appear as though nothing immediate was going to happen to bring life on earth to a sudden end. I can't say the poets of the Festival were yet relieved, but we were at least a bit less apprehensive.

On Wednesday, October 24th John Crowe Ransom introduced the panelists for "The Problem of Form," but first he laid out the perimeters of the discussion. The formalists had it all their own way, for Ransom's former student and fellow "Fugitive" Allen Tate was the first to speak, then Leonie Adams, and at last that arch-formalist J. V. Cunningham who represented the neoclassical school of Yvor Winters, for some reason not himself present at the Festival, though his views certainly were.

The afternoon readings began with R. P. Blackmur who was much better known as an influential critic than as a poet. He had taken the place of the scratched John Hall Wheelock, who was ill. Katherine Garrison Chapin was next: as a poet she has followed Blackmur into obscurity as well. Babette Deutsch, too, who read next, is today little known, although some people continue to use her handbook of poetry.

Then Langston Hughes took the microphone and gave an interesting and provocative performance. Jarrell and Kunitz followed, then Ogden Nash who read by far the most entertaining and humorous poems. Kenneth Rexroth was next, but the poems he read were hardly revolutionary, as one might have expected, though several were prose poems. Richard Wilbur was moved up to take the place of Wheelock, and his reading was fine. Unfortunately, he was followed by Oscar Williams who put the quietus to the Festival readings.

In the evening Sir Herbert Read, who was introduced by Eberhart, lectured the gathering on "American Bards and British Reviewers," and then Eberhart took the podium once more to close the Festival and bid us farewell. The next morning Loring and I got into my car and drove back to Cleveland through the autumn landscape of Pennsylvania and Ohio. Two days later, on October 26th, Premier Khrushchev capitulated to President Kennedy's demands that he remove all the missiles that had been installed in Cuba.

The next day Khruschev attempted to negotiate different terms, but Kennedy responded only to the first missive, and by the 28th the Soviets caved in completely, offering on-site inspections and requesting only that the U. S. agree not to invade Cuba if all the missiles were dismantled and removed. Kennedy agreed, and the blockade was halted. A furious Castro refused to allow the inspections, but U-2 spy planes were able to verify the removal of the weapons, and by 1964 Nikita Khruschev was himself removed from power by his government.

The Cherub

In Albrecht Dürer's engraving "Melencolia I," executed in 1514, Melancholy sits staring into space, her head leaning on her left fist, her left elbow resting on her knee. Her right hand, lying in her lap, holds a pair of compasses. Her face is dark, in shadow, the whites of her eyes showing starkly. About her head is a laurel wreath, so she is not sad, as the observer might believe; rather, she is lost in thought — a poet, perhaps. She appears to be blonde. At her left shoulder a bird with a long tail is perched.

Her gown is long — only her bare toes show beneath it. At her feet there is a plane, a rule, some nails and other tools of the artisan, cast aside. A large white ball is before her on the floor as well, perhaps a crystal ball, and a censer — or is it an ink pot? Between it and her right leg a starved hound is curled up: it is the emblem of the physical body for the moment forgotten. Behind the dog there is a large polyhedron, and behind that a ladder stretching up a column and out of sight overhead. It is the ladder of Jacob, the ladder of aspiration. On the column there is a set of scales hanging, an hour glass, and a bell suspended over a square on which are graven numerals and cabalistic symbols.

In the background there is a body of water, parts of a coastline, and on the horizon, shining out of a black sky, a sunburst beneath a rainbow. The only other figure of significance in the engraving is a cherub sitting on what looks like a smooth stone with a round hole struck through it.

In the early 1960s I was teaching at Fenn College, at that time a private, downtown engineering school located in Cleveland, Ohio; it has since become Cleveland State University. The instructorship in English was my first job after finishing graduate work in the Writer's Workshop of the University of Iowa, and it was at Fenn where I first met a colleague in my department whom people called "The Cherub," because of his surname, Cherubini. He was anything but. Tall and thin, with a saturnine face, he was clearly a votary of Melancholy. He became my familiar.

People assume, perhaps, that melancholy is the state of the depressive personality, and to a degree this is true, but it's also the state of creation. In the Dürer print Melancholy is in what used to be called "a brown study." Her trance is caused, not by dejection, but by contemplation, the condition of the artist or philosopher. Her eyes are focused not outward, but into herself where she sees the condition of mankind, of the world lost in the vacant regions of the universe.

As the occult philosopher Agrippa saw it, the humor melancholicus, when it takes possession of a soul, creates the *furor poeticus* which leads to revelation and wisdom, in particular when the influence of Saturn combines with it. The melancholy humor attracts demons which enable the possessed person to prophesy or create. The force of melancholy takes three forms. When it is concentrated in the imagination, its possessor will be a poet; when it is epitomized in the reason, he or she will be a philosopher; in the intellect, a prophet.

Artists of all kinds are generally what we call today "manic depressives," but those terms ought to be reversed, for the "depression" or melancholy comes first — the inward gazing, the contemplation. Then the physical act of creation takes over, and the artist puts visions on canvas or paper, or works it in stone or some other substance; hence, the tools lying unused, for the moment, at Melancholy's feet.

I've been contemplating The Cherub for more than a quarter-century now, and I feel the time has come to put him into words, yet I still don't know at this moment exactly what it is I have to say about him, nor why he has for so long inhabited my imagination, for he wasn't a major portion of my life in those old days, yet he is today much more vivid to me than most of my other colleagues at that college.

The Cherub had a particularly trenchant way of putting things into words himself, but when I quote him to myself I realize that it was not so much his words as the manner in which he delivered them that made them memorable. For instance, one day we were talking about someone we both knew who was in the hospital, as I recall, and I was venting the standard platitudes. The Cherub, who was tall and sallow, hovered over me and said, "Life gets us all." He didn't smile, but the phrase stuck vividly in my head all day, and I had the distinct impression that he took pleasure in the thought.

On another occasion he told me that his wife, whom I do not recall ever having met, had recently had to have a hysterectomy. Again I commiserated. He merely shrugged and said, "They leave everything that's interesting." I believe The Cherub wanted to be a poet himself, a condition that all my life I'd known was to be mine. He had half of what he needed, the contemplative half, but he lacked the physical portion, the ability to sit down and put the words on paper. I think I must have fascinated him as much as he did me. He was for me a mirror.

Looking at him, I could see one part, the foreview, of Melancholy. He could see me in the round, both front and back, as though I were a hologram. I could walk forward and touch the surface of the mirror, and it would be solid, if flat, but when he walked around me and reached out to touch my three-dimensional image suspended in the air, his hand went through it. He couldn't grasp it. All he could do was apprehend it with his eyes. The creative act was insubstantial for him.

Perhaps what he lacked was a sense of humor, though he certainly didn't lack a sense of the cynical. There was a story about him among the faculty that was hilarious. It was not apocryphal, however, as one day I dared to ask him whether it were true. It pained him to admit it, but he couldn't lie, for the cynic must see and say things as they are, unvarnished by romance or any other ameliorating quality.

Fenn College was essentially three buildings — a skyscraper, a smaller building beside it on Euclid Avenue, and a block-long building across 24th Street. Beside Fenn Tower there was a parking lot facing the long building — formerly an automobile showroom — where most of the classes were held. The Cherub, like all of us except the few students who lived in the tower dorm rooms, would drive to school in the morning, park, walk through the lot, cross the street and go to his first class. One particular morning he got out of his car and went to class as usual.

The Cherub had a routine he followed in class. When he got into the room he would take the chair out from behind the desk, place it to one side, sit down, cross his legs, and teeter back precariously. He would begin to teach, and as he did so he would wiggle the toe of the leg that crossed. As he sat there lecturing on this particular occasion an unease began to manifest itself in the room. The Cherub noticed students' faces turning red with suppressed laughter, or going white with shock. Titters rippled through his audience, and then guffaws.

"All right," he said, "what's going on?" No one answered, but the disturbance continued. "Then we'll sit here until someone tells me what the joke is." A truly painful silence ensued, but The Cherub had decided to see it through, and the atmosphere became tenser and denser as people tried without success to smother their laughter. Finally, one person could take it no longer. He got up, walked to the front of the room, and bent down to whisper in The Cherub's ear, "Professor, there's a condom stuck to your toe."

The Cherub's foot stopped twitching. He looked down. The class erupted. Suddenly, he got up and raced from the room, the condom slapping the floor with each step, leaving the uproar seething behind him. He didn't return to class that day.

At the next session he came in through the door grimly, stood behind the desk, and said, "The first person who refers to the situation the other day in any way will be ejected from this class with a grade of F." He sat down and began to teach. The incident entered into the mythology of the school.

I was younger than most beginning instructors because, having finished the coursework for my M. A., I had decided not to work toward a Ph.D. At my interview I had told 'Dolph, the chairman who was considering hiring me, that I was a publishing writer and that I wanted to do my own work rather than some academic advisor's pet graduate project. I had thought that this would lose me the job, but I didn't at the time realize that 'Dolph had himself taken thirty years to get his Ph.D. and was a missionary in the Great Cause of Postgraduate Education. He evidently thought he saw in me someone whom he could eventually persuade to do the right thing, at least to make a start. 'Dolph gave me the job, and when I arrived on campus I found that the department was half full of people who had been "working on" their terminal degrees for considerable lengths of time. "In my case it would truly be terminal," I told The Cherub.

"He wants to save your soul," he replied. "He won't be satisfied unless he does."

I was, however, adamant. Furthermore, I hated teaching the "socially conscious" novels we had to read in the third quarter of freshman composition: *McTeague, Bleak House, Tess of the D'Urbervilles, Maggie, a Girl of the Streets*. I had nothing against social consciousness, for I was reading James Baldwin's *The Fire Next Time* to my classes as it was being serialized in *The New Yorker*. I simply felt we ought to be engaging students with material that they recognized as applying to their lives and times, not The Great Depression of their parents.

The novels had been chosen by 'Dolph himself, without consultation with his faculty upon whom he looked as "sons" — I suppose there must have been a woman or two on the staff, but I don't recall any. I wasn't alone in my loathing of these works by Lewis, Dreiser, Hardy and Dickens, but I was the only one who dared to speak up about it.

The second year I taught at Fenn 'Dolph had some sort of stroke and was hospitalized for nearly the entire year. The Department got together while he was gone and reorganized the composition course. The bad novels were out. When 'Dolph returned the third year, the books were back in. He couldn't believe that his little family of scholars would do something like this to him, so, irrationally, he blamed me for it. He never accused me in so many words; therefore, I couldn't explain to him that I wasn't a majority of the department in and of myself and could not have voted the old curriculum out unilaterally. I was even slow to realize what was in his mind.

His position became apparent, however, when I began my fourth year. The school had a rule that an instructor had, at the end of that year, to be promoted to assistant professor or be let go. There were no rules about one's having to work on a doctorate in order to be promoted, but there was a section that said one could be let go for "lack of professional development." I felt that this could not be invoked against me because I had finished work on my M. A. at Iowa, and I had been successful in publishing a book and a chapbook of poems, not to mention many poems, stories, reviews and essays in journals. I had garnered a Bread Loaf poetry fellowship and, while my chairman was in the hospital, I had founded at Fenn College the Poetry Center of Cleveland, an institution that subsequently celebrated its twenty-fifth anniversary in 1986.

Yet 'Dolph did invoke the rule when I asked him at mid-year what he was going to do, as I had to make plans for the following year if I were not going to be retained. His decision raised a furor among my colleagues and the students. My office mate that same year had washed out of his Ph.D. program for the second and final time, but at least he had tried, so the chairman retained him.

The students wanted to stage a protest in my behalf, but I talked them out of it. "I don't want to stay here if they don't want a writer," I told them, "and a protest would only make it harder for me to find another job." Still, they wanted to do something, especially Russell Salamon, the student editor of the undergraduate magazine, of which I was faculty advisor. The Cherub hovered over my shoulder during the hubbub, clearly sorry to be losing his hologram of Melancholy, but perhaps enjoying the spectacle of my fall from grace.

As events unfolded themselves, the *furor poeticus* asserted itself in me, and I wrote two poems. One of them was titled "Scarecrow," a satire against 'Dolph who was seen in the poem as a scarecrow lording it over a field full of pumpkins, my colleagues in the English Department. The other poem, "Pocoangelini 15," was specifically about my fellow faculty in the College who were symbolized collectively as a rabbit in a desert full of desks into which surrealistically the rabbit begins to be pressed by the blackboard. The rabbit, his hide and ears caught in the cactus plants of the desert, starts to fall apart. His brain is exposed as a system of "wheels, tappets and cogs, catches." His skin cracks, and out of his split paunch "a cloud of beautiful moths blooms and / dies in the desert air, like dry fire / among the desks."

Russ Salamon saw both poems one day lying on my desk. I was busy with another student, so he read them while he sat waiting to speak with me. When I turned to him he said, "May I use these in the next issue of the magazine?" I was reluctant to agree, but he was importunate, so I at last consented to compromise by letting him publish the diatribe against the faculty, but not the one against 'Dolph.

On the day that the magazine was ready at the printer's I was sitting in my office. Russ came in and said, "I have the magazines."

"Okay," I said, "give me a stack and distribute the rest." He went out, and I sat back to look over the issue. Russell went across the street to distribute the magazines in the lobby in front of the large room that was the snack bar.

It was at the moment he set up shop that an ambulance pulled to a stop in front of the skyscraper. The medics took an elevator up to my chairman's office and removed him on a stretcher — it appeared that he had had another stroke. Later that day I went to the snack bar for lunch where I sat at a table with The Cherub, and it was there that I found out what had happened, as the incident was the talk of the school. Everyone also had a copy of the magazine and had been reading it.

As we were sitting discussing both the chairman's stroke and the magazine Joe Ink, a member of the history faculty, walked by with a tray of food. "Congratulations," he said. "You got him."

"I got him?" I asked. "Who?"

"Oh, don't give me that," he said, "I read the poem about 'Dolph"

"You mean the poem in the magazine?"

"Of course."

"That's not about 'Dolph, it's about all of you rabbits," I said, for the local A. A. U. P. chapter had conducted an investigation and issued a report in triplicate saying that I ought to have been renewed; one copy had gone to me, one to 'Dolph, and the third had gone into the A. A. U. P. files. No one else ever saw it.

"Oh, sure, sure," he said. "But he's in the hospital, isn't he?" He turned and began walking away.

Furious, I shouted after him, "I thought historians were supposed to deal in facts!"

I faced back to The Cherub. "What in the hell is he talking about?"

"He thinks your poem caused 'Dolph's stroke."

"'Dolph never even saw the poem!"

The Cherub looked at me, shrugged his shoulders, and leered like a satyr. He said nothing. The import of the situation began to blossom in me like a spray of belladonna. I stared back. "But that's witchcraft," I said. "He's accusing me of witchcraft!" The Cherub merely continued to smile at me, his teeth beginning to show and his eyes to darken. His black hair fell forward over his brow.

And that was when I understood that we haven't changed. It's still the Middle Ages, even — perhaps especially — in academe. Science hasn't ousted magic from the throne of Melancholy, and the poet is still the priest who knows the secret Names of things, the formulae that will invoke the powers of darkness, even when he doesn't know he's doing it, even when he believes he's doing something else. Auden's remark that "Poetry makes nothing happen" is merely lip-service to reason.

If The Cherub had no sense of humor, the Fates do, or perhaps it's the God of Melancholy, a being whom I imagine squats over the world passing winds for us to breathe and chortling uproariously at our discomfiture, for during the next few days, after batteries of tests at the hospital, nothing wrong could be found with 'Dolph. He hadn't suffered a stroke. No one could figure out what, if anything, was the matter with him.

I left Fenn not long afterward to take another position at Hillsdale College, deeper in the Middle West, at what I hoped would be a better school but was not. It was there that I discovered that the poet is supposed to be not merely a warlock but a rallying point for revolution as well — but that's another story, though it has its features in common with 'Dolph's belief that it was I who had led the forces of evil against socially-conscious freshman composition. The Cherub would have loved it had he followed me which, in a way, he may have done, for I wrote an epistolary memoir of the events of the ensuing year, "The Hillsdale Epistles," that I sent to another colleague in the Fenn English department, Arnold Tew, and he may have shared them with The Cherub.

The thing I took with me most substantially was the look The Cherub gave me that day in the snack bar. I began to imagine then that I too, like Melancholy, had a gargoyle-faced bird perched on my shoulder. I think of the bird as my personal muse, whom I have named Jascha, whose feathers I stroke before the act of creation, for who am I to fight the irrational beliefs of the ages, the myths, the folkways and the traditions? I'm not really fool enough to believe in them — no more than Joe Ink was, or you are, dear reader.

Lewis Turco

MUSING ABOUT STUDENTS

For nearly four decades I taught writing arts. Some people — even teachers! — maintain that "creative writing" cannot be taught. I would agree that it is impossible to teach anyone *talent*; however, I can teach anyone who can read, and who wants to learn, the *techniques* of writing. That is no small favor to do for someone. I know there are teachers who feel that their main job is to encourage students in their writing and little more. But many of the students I have taught, if not most of them, have jobs in the field of writing, one way and another: advertising, public relations, journalism, broadcasting, editing, publishing, free-lancing, teaching. Some have even become well-known professional novelists (Alice McDermott, Robert O'Connor), poets (Christian Nguyen Langworthy, Ben Doyle) and nonfiction writers (Lawrence Abbott, Mary Doll, Stephen Murabito). I helped give them the tools with which to make a living at something they like to do.

One of the first things I learned is this: A teacher should *never* tell a student he or she has no chance to become a writer, for one will be sure to be wrong every time. I've seen the light go on in students' eyes at every point from the first week of the first freshman semester to the year a businessman retires and goes back to school — I remember clearly the moment the light went on in Larry Abbott's eyes.

Nevertheless, teaching undergraduates how to write poetry can be a lot like trekking across a great plain. Now and then something unusual occurs to break the routine of the journey. When one has done this sort of thing for three decades and more, one can look back and discern some unusually interesting features of the landscape. Some of those features for me were the undergraduate student-poets Russell Salamon, De Villo Sloan, P. J. O'Brien, and Judith Phillips; the non-traditional graduate student Charlie Davis, and the Fenn College Poetry Forum attendee D. A. Levy.

Russell Salamon was an undergraduate student at Fenn College — now Cleveland State University — during the early 1960s when he developed the grammatic prosody called "parenthetics." His showcase for these poems, a chapbook titled *Parent[hetical Pop]pies* appeared in 1964, the year of his graduation, from the Renegade Press of Cleveland. The publisher was a young man, "d. a. levy" [*sic*], who, though not a student at any college, attended Fenn's Cleveland Poetry Center Forums which were conducted by yet another Cleveland poet and publisher, Loring Williams of American Weave Press and Magazine. Levy — as one can tell, perhaps, by the uncapitalized name — was influenced by E. E. Cummings, as in

BOP FOR KIDDIES
i watermeloned down the lawn
and summersalts in season
a red balloon
a blue—a green
an orange one all
floating skyward
with childrens dreams tied

Though I'm sure he wouldn't have known the term, Levy here used the schema called anthimeria, substitution of one part of speech for another, as in "watermeloned down the lawn," where a noun is substituted for the verb. A similar thing happens in line two, where somersaults is perhaps, though not necessarily, deliberately misspelled. D. A. published many interesting poets and poems before he took his own life. He is a legend now, in Cleveland and the underground culture a quarter-century later.

When my student and D. A.'s friend Russ Salamon came into the office in Fenn Tower and showed me how his parenthetical system worked, I told Russ I thought it was ingenious, but that it was too complicated to become a popular prosody. I was partly wrong, for although one can't strictly call it popular, I have seen other poems written in the system since, by more than one poet, and I have introduced it to many people in many situations, most recently at the Philadelphia Writers' Conference in June of 1993. Many find it challenging and interesting.

In his poem "She," Salamon began by taking *parentheses* themselves as his center:

    ().

He then took a sentence, "my hands cup her cup," broke it after the subject, and inserted the set of parens into the break:

    my hands () cup her cup.

This is a metaphor: my hands are a set of parentheses. Next, a second sentence: "all parentheses in which I am warm drizzle-rain inside her," thus:

    All parentheses in which I am
    [my hands () cup her cup]
    warm drizzle-rain inside her.

And a third, "sizzling on snowscapes of her skin, her face, her arms, her thighs, forests full of soundless flowers waited once unseen, translucid; she carries rain constellations to fill flute basins where" with some changed punctuation and a bit of typographical dispersion, appears this way:

sizzling on snowscapes of her skin.
Her face, her arms, her thighs,
all parentheses in which I am
[my hands () cup her cup]
warm drizzle-rain inside her.
Forests full of soundless flowers
waited once unseen, translucid.
She carries rain constellations
to fill flute basins where

And finally, "My finger touch dis[s]olves into a shiverlong echo of rains; we wash our morning faces off":

My finger touch dissolves
into a shiverlong echo of rains/
sizzling on snowscapes of her skin.
(Her face, her arms, her thighs,
all parentheses in which I am
[my hands () cup her cup]
warm drizzle-rain inside her.
Forests full of soundless flowers
waited once unseen, translucid.
She carries rain constellations
to fill f lute basins where
/we wash our morning faces off

The split between f and lute in the penultimate line appears as it was originally printed in *Parent[hetical Pop]pies*; it may or may not be a typographical error. Others have written parenthetics since, and made other parenthetical experiments.

De Villo Sloan was an undergraduate student at S.U.N.Y. at Potsdam when he wrote "A Portrait of the Day." Although I had taught at Potsdam in 1968-69, my acquaintance with Sloan was of a later period, and, though we met and corresponded, he was not one of my students. I did, however, critique this poem in Alberta Turner's *Poets Teaching* (see the notes for this chapter, below). The primary technique he used was *prolepsis*, the expansion of a general statement, particularizing it and giving further information regarding it. This is how the poet began his portrait:

> Morning, afternoon, and evening
> A portrait of the day should be simple.

Simple, like the opening statement. The reader has too little information yet, on the typographical level, to know whether this is going to be a prose mode or verse mode poem — what appears on the page, however, looks like a couplet; moreover, it seems to scan loosely. The second strophe helps to a degree:

> Green morning, brown afternoon, and black evening
> A portrait of the day should be simple.

Sloan's method begins to come clear — he has added a few adjectives to modify the nouns in his initial sequence. He is going to modify and amplify. It is also possible to begin to see this will not be a metrical poem. Some might call it "free verse" at this stage, but as ought by now to be apparent, free verse is merely a mask-term for prose, though in strophe three it still appears that Sloan is using a couplet unit:

> With morning's green, afternoon's brown, and evening's
>   black,
> a portrait of the day should be very simple.

But Sloan has dropped the conventional capital A of his second line now, and what the reader has is clearly prose:

> With morning's green painted on the edges of the
> day, afternoon's brown set in the foreground, and evening's
> black dispersed across the colors, a portrait of the day, with
> a suitable frame, should be very simple.

Another technique Sloan used was incremental repetition; that is, changing a repeating unit slightly each time it appears: grammatically, each strophe was one sentence. There was line-phrasing in the first three stanzas, but the reader was not confused when it was dropped because at this point the poem was so frankly a prose poem, and the phrases were so long, that there was no sense of a premise abandoned, especially since the poem's rhythms did not derive from phrasing, but from repetitions and parallel *structures*:

> With morning's green painted around the edges of the day, creating the impression of sunlight through curtained windows and clothes on hardwood floors, afternoon's brown set in the foreground, intermixing on the edges with green, turning the morning face to brownsad afternoon, and evening's black dispersed across the colors, reminding the observer that the absence of light will prevail, a portrait of the day, with a suitable frame to complement its wild design, should be very simple.

This poem is a clear example of the premise that subject and *form* cannot be divorced from one another, nor can one be ignored except at the expense of the other. The two things are one thing — language *is* the poem, and Sloan evidently learned the lesson young. Here is the last stanza of "A Portrait of the Day":

> With morning's green painted around the edges of the day, creating an impression of sunlight through curtained windows and clothes on hardwood floors, that digresses into hues of minutes and hours, through lacquered halls and coffee, through artbooks and palettes searching for colors and symbols, afternoon's brown set in the foreground, intermixing on the edges with green, turning the morning face to brownsad afternoon, trying to find the spot where green ends and brown begins, following in the footsteps of one who went before, through tea and conversation, throwing flowers at a singer's feet, beginning to see that this job is not so easy, and evening's black dispersed across the colors reminding the observer that the absence of light will prevail, that sees the day changing in

degrees like the colors of the spectrum from radiating green to blackdeath, a portrait of the day, with a suitable frame, carved in a way that would complement such a wild piece, that would firmly transfix the images of a day upon the wall for all to see, should be very simple.

Successful prose poems like this one derive their cadences from grammatic *structures* — line-by-line phrasing, such as Sloan began with; sentences in parallel construction, as throughout this poem; strophic paragraphs, and so on. "A Portrait of the Day" is uniquely structured; Sloan invented his own *grammatic prosody*, but that prosodic *structure* is clear. So is the poem; therefore, it is dense and rich.

The critic can merely quibble with "A Portrait of the Day." Only here and there, in single words and an occasional phrase that slips from one *level of diction* to another, can one point to flaws. For instance, the clause in strophe 6, "this job is not so easy," and the word *wild* in "such a wild piece," are not in keeping with the sophisticated level of diction of the rest of the poem. The same might be said of the *epithetic compound* "blackdeath," which seems too theatrical for the meditative air of this piece.

It is not necessary, however, for student poets to invent a new prosody or formal structure in order to come up, sometimes, with something original and fine. P. J. O'Brien was a pupil in a writing arts class at the State University of New York College at Oswego when he wrote "Cartoon Show," which I published in a college textbook in 1973. The assignment was to write a series of related poems on a particular subject. O'Brien took as his model a Saturday morning children's television cartoon show such as most Americans will recall from their or their offsprings' youth. The first poem in the set was "The Old Skipper," the local host of the show, who spoke the prologue:

> I announced every episode of
> your lives,
> knowing just what would happen;
> that you would love, lust,

fight, go mad and a thousand other
meaningless passions.
And I sat on my film with my fake beard
looking like Zeus and feeling like an
oldtimer in a Greek chorus.

The mode of the poem is clearly prose, not verse, and all that O'Brien did was to disperse the prose lines according to phrases, one phrase to a line. Some people like to call this method "free verse." I call it "line-phrasing," and others call it "lineating."

The second poem in the set, "Brutus" — later called "Bluto" — moves us directly into the cartoon:

In my lumbering ox obscurity
I lusted over you, Olive Oyl.
With my thick lipped bearded mouth
I wanted your flesh, to take it by
force and never let it go.
I had not the strength of vegetables
nor white clothes and noble ideals,
only the desire of animals.
With the cunning of beasts
I tracked you until, each time,
that runt kicked me silly, and
running with my tail between my legs
my hatred filled the land like poison.
Why couldn't that bastard have left his
spinach at home just once?

Although we recognize the character and the situation, we have never heard this language from the cartoon itself. This is a "confessional" poem spoken by Brutus, and we detect a serious purpose behind the lines, even though we smile or even guffaw while we read. The next character to enter is "Popeye":

I have tasted the spinach of victory,
transforming matter with my bare fists

> turning bulls into packaged meat
> and alligators into shoes and purses.
> I have fought every creation of man and God
> on every battleground from Alaska to Mars
> to prove my love, Olive Oyl.
> But still you questioned it,
> flirting with that lummox
> with the "nyah nyah" in your voice,
> the challenge in your eyes.
> And yes to protect your chastity
> after you had aroused the animal,
> I swallowed my spinach and became
> your white knight again and again.
> Each time hoping I would lose,
> to escape your prison.
> But when films flashed in my biceps
> and tattoos danced across my chest;
> I loved you more than the sea,
> I loved you more than spinach.

And "Olive Oyl," the object of contention, who turns out to be a human being also:

> I am Helen of Troy.
> I am Deirdre.
> I am all the women men
> have died for.
> I am all the women men
> have made fools of themselves over.
> But I asked to be no Goddess,
> and I asked to be no object.
> All I simply asked for was
> a mayun.

One of the overtones that O'Brien worked with was created from simple allusion — to the Greek chorus in a classical tragedy, to Zeus, to Helen of Troy and Deirdre. Although this is a humorous poem, it takes a solemn dimension from such epic and tragic referents.

"Sweet Pea" provides an element of mystery and unease:

> My parentage was never explained.
> Continually crawling in my
> Doctor Dentons, a doubt.
> A doubt that kept me young,
> never dreaming of puberty or
> responsibility, cut off from
> the forbidden vegetable,
> I wanted your breast, mother.
> I wanted your piggyback, father.
> So I continued to creep away
> from those strange sailors and
> their lady friend, looking for
> answers in circuses and construction yards,
> missing lions' jaws and
> iron girders by inches. "Saved"
> *ad nauseam* by the muttering bowlegged
> warden with green teeth.

"Alice the Goon" is the spurned woman, the pariah:

> I have been fed on the dog-food of despair
> and in my raging bitterness I saw your
> foolishness, my lungs filling with hysterics,
> my mouth rabid with foam.
> And because you could not understand
> my madness you thought yourselves sane
> and ran from my outstretched arms,
> trying to impress that wench Olive Oyl.
> Because I am tired of screaming alone,
> tired of crying in the hills,
> I will ask you why?
> Why, in a world of ugliness, was mine so
> repulsive, my flesh so leprous?

"Wimpy" comes bringing up the rear, as he always did. He provides the poem with an architectural symmetry, for he speaks the epilogue as "The Old Skipper" spoke the prologue. Both are observers more than participants:

> I'm not bitter, nosireebob.
> While you have talked of love and lust
> I have devoured the hamburgers of fulfillment,
> tasted the cheeseburgers of tranquility
> and supped off the fat of the land.
> You who laughed at Alice the Goon,
> You who laughed at me, the roly-poly sponge,
> I have watched your petty wars
> waged for the smile of the ugliest
> woman in the world.
> I have watched you all chew your loco weeds.
> And carrying my omniscience quite unobtrusively
> I watched the cartoon roll by,
> picking my teeth with celluloid
> and farting noisily (Turco, *Poetry*, 328-331).

O'Brien's poem does something remarkable: it satirizes *satire* — the Popeye cartoon show is already parody — and, in satirizing satire the poet achieved a basic seriousness. O'Brien mythicized the characters of the cartoon show so that they no longer stand merely for parodies of humankind, they stand for humanity itself. They become symbols of being, and at the heart of the symbology is a paradox — life is both ineffably comic and tragically serious. The poem is inclusive, not exclusive; both possibilities exist and, in fact, *are*, so the poem does what life does: it holds both.

It also holds people, and O'Brien let the people speak for themselves. In their voices we can hear each individual comic tragedy, and as a group they represent this world; we can see types and prototypes in the characters. We can even see ourselves in them. One never knows what a student is going to do next. O'Brien turned to music and produced an album titled *Starship Beer — Nut Music as Free as the Squirrels* (1979).

At SUNY Oswego five main genres are taught: fiction, drama, poetry, nonfiction, and journalism. In each of these, except in journalism, there are three tiered courses: basic "Nature of..." courses; "Creative Writing in..." workshops, and "Advanced Writing in..." major project courses (in journalism the last course is an internship). Back in the early 1980s Judith Phillips had taken the first two classes in the poetry series without distinguishing herself. In the advanced course there are one-on-one sessions with each student the first half of the semester instead of classes. At the second of these each student comes in with three ideas for a series of related poems or a long poem. Judith's first idea had to do with some sort of princess and a prince or a dragon, or both, but I told her that I didn't teach children's writing — another teacher did. I don't recall what her second idea was. For her third, she told me that she had her great-grandmother's diary which chronicled her trip across the prairies in a covered wagon, and perhaps Judith could do something with that.

I stared at her a moment, and then I said, "You've got your great-grandmother's diary, and you want to write a poem about a princess?" We eventually agreed that what she would do was turn her grandmother's diary into a set of poems. I told Judith that, since the diary had gaps and hiatuses in it, her biggest problem would be to invent incidents and put them into words that the reader could not distinguish from those of the grandmother.

And that was what Judith did. The result was "The Taproot Diary," one of the most remarkable series of undergraduate poems I have ever read. No sooner was it completed than it was published as a whole — all fifteen poems — in *Escarpments*, a periodical published at SUNY Buffalo and edited by Carol Sineni:

THE TAPROOT DIARY:

THE LANDSHIPS
Diary Entry; May 1st, 1850.
LaPorte, Indiana

The landships traveled waving
their floating gray sails through

the endless desert sea. The wheels
rutted the arid soil cutting the tumbleweed
waves; they broke against the side.

"Onward they went towards
the promised land of Honey
Lake; where they were bound by
the tales of golden wealth. The
wild mountains lay before them."

Looking Back
Diary Entry; May 4th, 1850.
LaPorte, Indiana

The prairie schooners were anchored by hemp rope
in front of the general store. We loaded up
the crafts with flour, coffee, muskets, and blankets,
along with other supplies.
The wagons were weighed down heavily.
Teams of oxen were hitched to the rigs
pulling the schooners through the cloud of dust.
Father sat at the helm, steering us on the journey.

The Journey
Diary Entry; May 10th, 1850.
  Sedley, Indiana

Ahead of the fleet,
scouts searched out safe routes
of travel, to insure no indian
pirates lurked on the rough roads before us.

Our journey was slow.
Somedays only ten mile
was covered before the sun
sunk slowly beyond the westward horizon.
Under the stars we rested 'til dawn
opened our eyes.

The fire was smoldering
when we woke, bellowing high
white smoke. It was a sorry
sight, the fire dying where we spent a
restless night.

THE SWARDLANDS
Diary Entry; May 20th, 1850.
  Illinois

Spring grasses grew around
us, as we walked along
side of the wagons.

The sun sent its ruling rays
down, beating our backs, heads
and shoulders.

The road was overgrown
with grass and rocks. Not
a tree was in sight.

No shade was found
on the swardlands. Miles and miles
lay before us, trudging on shank's mare.
The mountains and valleys were
no where to be seen.

NIGHTCIRCLES
Diary Entry; May 25th, 1850
  Illinois

We made camp on
the setting of the sun.
The six wagons in our party
circled the nightfire.

The scouts came back
from a large buffalo kill.
The fresh meat was roasted over
the glowing embers of dried grass and wood.
The fuel for the fires is getting low.

The wind blew through
the grasses, making our bones
chill to the marrow. The coyotes
howled from off in the distance.
We huddled together for warmth.

THE STORM

Diary Entry; June 3rd, 1850.
  The Prairie

Morning broke with a
thundering bang. The air hung thick
in the sky.

The lightning scared the
horses, they reared up with
whinnying moans.

In the Northwest
red balls of fire rolled
along the prairie floor.

Thin stalks of rag grass
burnt like torches lighting
up the brown earth.

When the rains came,
we took shelter under the
canvas of the wagon,

crouched together for comfort
in the cramped space.

WASHDAY
Diary Entry; June 8th, 1850.
   The Prairie

The men found a small clear spring
welling up from the ground.
We gathered some buckets together
for some fresh cooking and drinking water.
Then, we commenced to wash the clothes.

The milliner washed her bonnets
with strong lye and laid them
on a big rock to dry.

We scrubbed the clothes
on the rocks with soap and
rinsed them in the spring.

I hung my clothes on the whiffletree,
to let them dry in the fresh, sweet
breeze of honeysuckle.

THE CROSSING
Diary Entry; June 18th 1850.
   The Prairie

The mountains seemed no nearer, as we crossed
wearily through the endless field of yellow
straw. Dust rose up underfoot, the wind
blew it in our faces.

The soles of my shoes wore thin from the long
walk across the plains. Small stones stabbed

the bottoms of my feet, making the walk
almost unbearable.

THE AGUE
Diary entry; June 25th, 1850
  The Prairie

The peepers squeaked their
eerie song from a swamp
filled with black water and
tall weeds, by our camp.

The mosquitoes swarmed our
campfire like bees swarming to
a honey tree. They must have
smelt the human skin.

The wheel wright got the
ague, from a bite on
his neck. He shook day and
night with the fever.

The journey took its
toll. The men dug a
shallow hole with axes and shovels.

We stood and prayed
for the soul of the wheel wright,
whose body was left in a
hollow unmarked damp grave.

THE SIGHTING
Diary entry; July 6th, 1850.
  The Prairie

Above the horizon peek the
blue and white snow capped tops
of the mountains.

The distance between us and the
land is still great, but we are getting
closer to the new found land of promises.

THE DESERT
Diary Entry; September 1st, 1850.
  The Black Rock Desert, Nevada

The heat is like an
open hearth burning the land.

There is very little good grass
growing on the crusty soil.
Burned out wagons line the trail.

Hundreds of ox skeletons
are scattered on the ground.

Not the rustle of a leaf or
the hum of an insect breaks the quiet.

It is only us
who break the still air.

THE DIGGERS
Diary Entry; September 3rd, 1850.
  Deep Hole Springs, Nevada

Shrieks were heard outside of the
wagons, in the still darkness.
Night had fallen when the
Diggers made a raid upon our camp.

They tried to drive the oxen
off the site and into a deep pit
for an easy catch.

When they found that they couldn't,
the Diggers crept behind
the sage, armed with bows and arrows.
They shot two of the animals
and a watchman.

The man was struck in the shoulder,
but somehow managed to fire his gun.
He killed one of the Diggers,
the rest ran off. It won't be the last of them.

THE ARRIVAL
Diary Entry; September 10th, 1850.
  Honey Lake Valley, California.

We've reached the promised
wilderness of Honey Lake.
A few miners have settled
here in log cabins.

The only bands of people
we see are travelers,
indians and miners.

There is plenty of water
and the land seems fresh
and bountiful.
Father started to build
us a cabin, and has set his
mind on becoming a rancher.
I do not know why they call this
"the land of the never sweats" (Sineni, 5-15).

One never knows what a student is going to look like, either, or when someone will decide to become a student. Charlie Davis, a legendary character in Oswego, New York, and in the worlds of folklore and jazz as well, turned from music to business to poetry and fiction writing and editing. He established his own publishing company, Mathom, in 1977.

For many years Davis had been a partner in a local business firm, and when he decided to return to college in the mid-1970s he was half-retired. Retirement for Charlie simply meant expanding his horizons — not that they had been previously very limited. One might say he now had more time to devote to his vocations. Two of these had always been music and verse composition. He began by taking courses in poetry writing with Roger Dickinson-Brown, then a member of the staff of the Program in Writing Arts at the College at Oswego.

Davis had grown up in Indiana. His father had been a close friend of a neighbor, James Whitcomb Riley, the "Hoosier Poet," and Charlie early came under Riley's benevolent influence. Later on, Charlie graduated from Notre Dame University and, upon his graduation, organized a group of musicians during the hey-day of the Big Bands — he wrote about it in his book, *That Band from Indiana* — and was very successful on the swing and hot jazz circuits. One of his compositions of the period was "Copenhagen," a jazz classic that has been performed by nearly all the famous swing and jazz artists since it was introduced. The composer in 1990 still drew royalties from it twice a year.

The first course Davis took was titled "The Nature of Poetry." It was a beginner's course, but stringent and technical. In it the student must write verse exercises in every prosody, schema, and genre imaginable, including parenthetic prosody. At one point in the course students were even required to invent a prosody of their own, as Russell Salamon had done when he was an undergraduate.

Davis did well for Dickinson-Brown, and he began to involve himself in the extensive literary scene on campus. He gave readings with other students, and his work was always popular because it was..."quaint" is the only word to describe it. The Riley influence was clear, at least to the faculty if not to the students, who had never heard of the Hoosier Poet.

When Davis asked to take the second course in the sequence of three undergraduate poetry courses in the Program he was asked whether he had ever completed a B. A. He replied that he had a Ph.B. in business administration from Notre Dame, and he was denied permission to take the course, but he was told that he could enroll in the graduate seminar titled "Conference Course in Writing Poetry," which he did. He was told that the project of the course involved writing a long poem, something he had never done, and he was (atypically for the class) given a proscription: he was not to write a single rhymed couplet. Instead, he was going to do something difficult. Difficult for him, that is.

"But what?" he asked, baffled.

"Well, have you ever heard of William Carlos Williams?"

"No, should I have?"

"Yes, since he's a famous contemporary of yours. Your first assignment is to read Williams' *Paterson*."

Davis did so. No sooner had he digested the book than he began to write ...*And So the Irish Built a Church*, a story about Oswego written, like *Paterson*, in prose and verse, with diary entries, newspaper clippings, songs, and what-have-you (it is impossible for the reader to identify what Davis invented and what he researched), tossed together in a seemingly random, but for all that, nevertheless, highly wrought melange of lore and character and incident. Davis got so carried away that he even composed a pseudo-nineteenth century musical piece and copied it out on aged paper suitably charred to look as though it had been saved from the conflagration that had consumed the original church.

The other members of the class were no less busy than Charlie Davis, and as the semester developed it became obvious that this was a remarkable group of students doing fine things. The Davis piece was not the first work to be published from that class, but he was without doubt writing the longest work — it turned out to be 120 pages in length — and the most popular. Everyone was interested in reading the next installment though Charlie, doing something totally new and experimental for him (except where he managed to sneak in a rhymed song against orders), could not believe his classmates were not dissembling when they applauded him. Here is a sample of Charlie's epic:

Lewis Turco

    Peter Lappin and the sixteen families grouped together to form a parish, hoping to bring a local or traveling priest to Oswego for regular or at least occasional services. The following names, found on the sand and wind-burnished tombstones in the oldest part of St. Paul's Cemetery, are probably the names of the sixteen:

Shephard	Navagh	McCann	Carlin
Lappin	Murray	Allard	Fineran
O'Connell	McCarthy	Burnes	Dailey
Kenefic	Reilly	Costello	Galvin
Mullen	Farrell		

They became noted for their
ability as fighters. And later on became
fighters in the ring, the prize ring; for money.

Names like John L. Sullivan,
Bob Fitzsimmons and Sharkey and Irish
Mick Kelly.

All got their full page
pictures in the Police Gazette.
The Lapides, the Ostrynskis,

The Cohns and Schmidts,
all changed their names to
O'Brien, Murphy and Irish Bob

Delaney and Killer O'Neal
so they could get
their pictures in the Police

Gazette and make
it big in the ring.

A Sheaf of Leaves: Literary Memoirs

Within sixty days of their application, the Bishop wrote the good news: Reverend Father Donahoe (sometimes spelled Donahue) who was covering the central tier of New York State (Auburn, Rome, Camden, the villages of Central Square and a few small hamlets)...would come to Oswego, say Mass and hear confessions every three months beginning at once. Father Donahoe said his first Mass late in 1830 and his second in early 1831. He traveled mostly on horseback...sometimes in daylight...sometimes at night.

> Patsy Fineran speakin' . . ."what
> a year it was! Seems just like
> yesterday. Made enough money
> to fill a corn-crib doin' nu-
> thin' but shootin' the pesky
> timber wolves. Put a musket
> ball in fifty of 'em that
> year. Put fifteen hundr'd
> American $ bills in my
> money belt. They've
> gone now to where
> it's a mite health-
> ier. Last year I
> only got two.
> This year
> I got
> 0"

Since its publication in book form, there have been people who know W. C. Williams who claim that ...*And So the Irish*... is more readable than its model. Since *Paterson* is a modern classic, this opinion is heretical. The main criticism of the Davis opus may be that it begins to a degree shakily. Riley is recognizable in the sentiment, and Williams in the form: the two do not mix well early on. But as the book progresses, Riley and Williams disappear and Davis rises above his sources to become one of the most engaging literary personalities of recent years, just as the man himself was larger than life.

The town of Oswego comes alive. People emerge and turn real before one's eyes. Davis managed to build a microcosm that is convincing and engaging. How many poets could claim that in the twentieth century? And how many teachers can hope to have a pupil like Charlie Davis more than once in a career? Yet it happens all the time.

A Remembrance of
Howard Nemerov

When I heard how sick he was, I wrote Howard this letter datelined Oswego, New York, 1 June 1991:

Dear Howard,
I'm 2/3 of the way through teaching a "pre-session," 3-week summer school course called "The Art of Poetry," which ought in fact to be called "Everything You Ever Wanted to Know about Poetry but Were Afraid to Ask." Most of the students are adults, people in a program that is designed to turn arts & sciences graduates into school teachers.

So I thought I would drop you a note to tell you that I have used more of your poems in the class than those of anyone else in the world — "Angel and Stone," "The Companions," "A Primer of the Daily Round," "The Goose Fish," "The May-Day Dancing," "The Dial Tone." It's a magnificent body of work you've produced, Howard, and I for one (and only one) am as grateful as I can be that you've produced, and are continuing to produce it.

I use your poems as models of bardic craft, but their true value lies in the help they give your readers; help in getting through the ordinary day, through depression and crisis — getting through life a little easier, with a little more insight into the human condition. I tell my students, and I show them how you do it, that no one I know of can take a common situation and add to it incrementally until, suddenly, we are spinning around the sun, as in "The May-Day dancing," or listening in to the power of eternity, as in "The Dial Tone," or facing the fact of our self-delusion without illusion, as in "the Goose Fish" — not even Wallace Stevens ever did that last any better.

I must sign off and get on with it, and let you get on with it as well. Although we've seen too little of one another over the years, I wanted to let you know that I count you as one of my dearest friends. I'll never forget the first time I heard you read, at the Poetry Center in Cleveland back in the early '60's. Up to that point I'd not paid your poems much attention, I'm afraid, but when I heard how they were supposed to sound I went home and re-read them, hearing them in your voice now, and I was stunned to discover, to understand, how magnificent they are and how solid and down to earth at the same time. I've been unable to live without them since then.

Love,
Lew

On the evening of the fourth of June 1991 I came home from school to find this phone message from Howard on my answering machine:

Lewis, this is Howard Nemerov. I just this morning got your wonderful letter, and I'm glad you had your phone number on it because I'm much too enfeebled to write a letter back. But thank you ever so much. Now...well, I'll talk to you some time. Regards. Love to Jean.

The next day I wrote and sent this reply:

Dear Howard,

I'm very sorry not to have been home last night when you phoned, but I got your message on my answering gadget. I was in the class I told you about. I'd love to talk with you, too, but I don't wish to impose upon you. Perhaps, if you'd like to chat for a couple of minutes, you might have a member of your family drop me a postcard with a time and date on it that would be convenient for you, and I could dial you up. If you don't feel up to it, though, please don't exert yourself. Just know that I'm thinking of you.

And now I'm going to tell you something that I've not told you in nearly thirty years. You came to Cleveland early in 1964, as I recall it, and you stayed with us. I don't know if you recall our conversation about *The New Yorker*, but I maintained that there was such a thing as a *New Yorker* poem, and you adamantly denied it. If so, you asked, what were its characteristics?

At the moment I couldn't answer, but when you had gone home I went to the library and got a bunch of past issues of the magazine and went through the poems in them. I made a list of the characteristics of a typical *New Yorker* poem:

Most of the poems were written in meters, but the rhythms were easy and the diction was conversational on an intelligent and educated level. There was rhyme, but the rhymes were often consonances, and there was a fair amount of light rhyming.

The settings of many of the poems were spots in Europe. There was often water. There were animals and birds, but all of them were small. the colors were muted, the tone pensive.

Once I had figured these things out I sat down and wrote a poem titled "Pompeii: The Fountain" (I had been to Pompeii while I was in the Navy in the early 'fifties; I couldn't remember if it really had a fountain in the square, but I needed the water) that had all the qualities I'd listed. I sent it to *The New Yorker*. Here is a copy of the final version of the poem, titled simply "The Fountain": I eventually disguised it in quantitative syllabics to hide its rhymes and meters, and I collected it in *The Weed Garden* (I think you have a copy). Following the poem is a photocopy of the letter about it I got from Howard Moss:

Lewis Turco

THE FOUNTAIN

        The ashen birds light
      out of the air. The sun fires
an ultimate fusillade into the fountain
      where the seagulls gather to wish
        the world goodnight: they are furnished with rainbows

        for a moment. An
      aubade shall issue from them
tomorrow, burnished sparks of matinsong banked now
      for the evening in shadows and
        dust. The square fills with strollers. In the near distance

        night flings a star skyward.
      An eruption of silence faults
for a moment this murmurous village of strangers.
      In the cafes, lights now — and in
        the fountain perpetual rain whose mist withers

        among footfall and
      laughter. But the girl who leans
against the curving basin, among the gulls, seems
      not to hear the curious voices
        of the square. No footfall disturbs her musing:

she holds the water's fire. She is beautiful.

A Sheaf of Leaves: Literary Memoirs

THE NEW YORKER
No 25 WEST 43rd STREET
NEW YORK, 36, N. Y.

OXFORD 5-1414

10 March 1964

Dear Mr. Turco,

In spite of admiring many things in *Pompeii*, I'm sorry to have to say that we finally decided against it. We've published so many poems on places in Europe, Italy in particular, that we're cautious about buying others. This may be more of a problem of ours than of yours or anyone else's, but I did want to tell you so that you would understand our reasons and not think we rejected the poem because we didn't like it. We just feel that only poems we really can't resist of this kind should appear in the magazine, since I think that we've covered the whole map of Europe over the last ten years.

[An irrelevant paragraph has been deleted here.]

Thanks for sending us these poems, and please keep trying us with others.

    Sincerely,
    /s/ Howard Moss

I thought Moss' answer was hysterically funny, and I felt vindicated, but I didn't want to offend you, so I never told you about it. Now, though, I think you'll find is as humorous as I did then.

There is, however, a sequel. One day while I was in Hillsdale, where I went from Fenn later in 1964, I wrote another poem that I thought *The New Yorker* might like, but I had nothing to include in the same envelope except "An Ordinary Evening in Cleveland," a long poem I'd sent around and around — twenty-two times! I couldn't imagine *the New Yorker* liking it for various reasons including its length, its melancholy mood, and its surreal imagery, but I decided to use it as an envelope stuffer anyway.

And that is how "An Ordinary Evening in Cleveland" became the first poem of mine that *The New Yorker* ever published. So you see, Howard, you were vindicated as well. There *was* such a thing as a "*New Yorker* poem," but the magazine also published lots of poems that were not at all typical of its typical poems.

With constant good wishes for you, my friend,

Lew Turco

And with that, our correspondence ended.

THE HILLSDALE EPISTLES

August 2, 1964
Prof. Arnold Tew
Department of English
Fenn College
Cleveland, Ohio

Dear Arnold,

    Well, how are things back there at Old Swampy College? We're starting to settle in here at Hillsdale, and it should be a real experience next month when school opens. It's pretty hot here right now, but not half as hot as in Cleveland, I bet. At least we've got grass and trees and a big front yard now. Man, are we glad to be out of that crummy third-floor apartment. Hillsdale College has given us a big seven-room house right on the campus — no more driving ten miles down the freeway for this kid! Nothing but squirrels here (we've got a black walnut tree right out in the front yard)!

The guy who lived here before us asked me how come I got special treatment on the house. When I said I didn't know I had, he asked me my name. I told him and he said, "Oh, the new celebrity!" Dig that, me a celebrity! He told me the College had been wanting a poet on campus for a long time...and I'm it! Quite a different attitude from Fenn, eh wot? But that's all water over the dam. Here we are in our Midwestern Valhalla, at a neat little liberal arts college, and I'll be having real students with backgrounds for a change. Give our best to everybody. Jean and Melora send their love to Sheila and the girls.

Best,
Lew

P. S. You know what the graduating class here painted on the front stairs of Central Hall (with its big old wickerwork Victorian tower)? "The world's never-closing door / Is open to the class of '64." That sounds a little funny to me. Oh, well.

September 18, 1964
Dear Arnold,

It sure was nice having you visit us last week, but I'm sorry I was away at the Faculty Pre-Opening Conference so much. I promised I'd give you a run-down of what went on. It was quite a conference. Well, first of all, the title of President Phillips' talk was, "Why Mediocre Men Succeed." I was interested in the topic, and I sure wasn't disappointed, either in its content or its delivery. I've got a theory that some speakers can be inspired by their topics, and this was a case in point. After he was through the Academic Dean, Dr. Kolivosky (who is rumored to be writing a "Big Book" — he's in sociology), got up to say a few words. "Thank you, President Don," he murmured in a rather unctuous manner, which is his way, "for sharing" (that's his favorite word) "your thoughts with us." Then, turning to us: "Yes, the thing we must all remember about Basic Principles is that they are so Widely Applicable." I don't remember what else he said because I started mulling that over. I wonder if he helped the graduating class write its verse for the stairs?

Later in the session we got another chance to hear Dr. Phillips. He had heard, it seems, that some professors had criticized his having a small ("second-hand") refrigerator, paid for by the College in his (WOW!) office. He explained that the reason he had it was because if "Johnny's parents" come to visit him to talk about Johnny, and if Johnny were with them, why, while the older folks were talking he could offer Johnny a bottle of pop. Because that's what it was filled with...soda pop! I got the impression he doesn't much cotton to faculty criticism. As he said, everything reaches his ears in the end.

"All it takes is a shift in allegiances among you," he pointed out, "and I hear everything." Friendships don't last forever; you lose a pal, and others gain a confidant. At this point I began to get a little shaky and I started to look over my neighbors pretty carefully. They were all busy looking over their own, though, so I quit just in time to see Dr. Kolivosky get up again and pin me to the wall with his eyes.

I didn't know what to expect, and I was feeling kind of worried, frankly, when he said, "Well, Professor Turco, how do you like Hillsdale?" You know I'm not much on social niceties, and when somebody asks me a question, I answer it. Besides, the Dean took me by surprise. So I gathered up my nonpluses and replied, "I don't know yet, but I like some of the people I've met."

That seemed to set him back a minute, but — in a somewhat threatening manner, I felt — he stared at me and said, "You'd better, Professor Turco. You'd better...because we like you!" Glad in my heart of hearts, I smiled at him. In fact, I nearly winked at him. I'm glad I didn't, though. I have this kind of eerie feeling...well, drop that. It's only a feeling.

This letter is getting long, so I won't tell you about the guest speakers, a husband and wife team of educators from Michigan or Michigan State, except to say that the lady in question told us she doesn't like to socialize with students because it lowers her dignity. I'm getting a sort of peculiar feeling about this place. If it develops I'll let you know.

Best,
Lew

November 3, 1964

Dear Arnold,

Well, here it is Election Day already, and a lot of water under the bridge. You know that queasy feeling I told you I was getting about this place? It's developing fast. You know, this is a liberal arts college, and — stop me if I'm wrong — such a school is supposed to have its eye on academics primarily — right? I'll assume you answered "yes" and go on: something is wrong! There's some kind of political point of view stressed around here, it looks like. Now, you know I never was much up on politics, but I did vote for Eisenhower twice and Kennedy once (though I almost skipped the Kennedy-Nixon one: Tweedle-dum and Tweedle-dee, far as I could tell), and it's not as though I don't care, so maybe you could put a name to what's going on just to clear things up for me.

The college administration has been putting out quite a lot of literature lately, but the most seminal piece boils down to this: "**MMW = MR + HE x T**." This is called, locally, the "Log Cabin Theory," and it translates out to "**M**an's **M**aterial **W**elfare *equals* **M**aterial **R**esources *plus* **H**uman **E**nergy *times* **T**ools." Some guy named Robinofsky, or something like that, invented this formula, and it is evidently very big around here, especially with a professor in economics named Campbell. What it looks like is that the whole school is devoted to putting this "idea" on the market and selling it to parents who then send their poor little rich kids here to have the formula branded in glowing letters on their memory lobes.

The whole thing reminds me, kind of, of that Cleveland corporation with the funny signs they used to hang on the gate of their plant. You remember, one went, **There Were No Fringe Benefits at Valley Forge.** Is that outfit still on Fenn College's board of trustees? No kidding, it's like old home week around here sometimes.

Oh, that reminds me — you recall the rhyme the kids painted on the stairs of Central? Larry Bouquet, a guy in my department, has thought up one for next year: "Undying Ideas Are Still Alive / For the Class of 1965." I'm trying to rig up a formula to fit some of these ideas. All I've managed to come up with so far is this: **BP + WA x UI = NFBaVF(oAE) √MM** or, in layman's language, **B**asic **P**rinciples, *plus* **W**ide **A**pplicability *times* **U**ndying **I**deas *over the square root of* **M**ediocre **M**en *equals* **N**o **F**ringe **B**enefits at **V**alley **F**orge (or **A**nywhere **E**lse). But that seems kind of cumbersome. Let me know if you think of any refinements. We go in big for simplification around here.

One other piece of information. You said you saw my poems in the Fall issue of *The North American Review* — did you see the two articles pro and con Goldwater in the same issue? One was all about how college profs ought to consider Barry seriously, and the other was nothing but Goldwater quotations that spoke for themselves to damn him in his own words. Well, today all us "employees of the College" came over to our mailboxes in Central, and there were reprints of the pro-Goldwater article waiting for us, initialed by President Don. It's illegal for an employer to do that, isn't it? Anyway, I kept turning it around and over, but I couldn't find the other half of the argument. I guess they didn't have room to print it on the same sheet. Maybe we'll get it later on — next election, perhaps.

Well, I'll see you. For a while there I thought I'd skip this one, but now there's a crowd of us going down to the polls to vote for Lyndon B. Johnson and Hubert H. Humphrey, so I've got to close. Here's one last formula for you: **AuH$_2$O-65 / NFBAVF = LBJ + H^3** or, in other words, **G**oldwater in **1965** over **N**o **F**ringe **B**enefits at **V**alley **F**orge *equals* **L**yndon and **H**ubie.

Best,
Lew

P. S. Did you know we have our own Presidential Candidate here on campus? This is no joke! Earl Munn, Assistant Academic Dean, is running (again) on the Prohibition Ticket!

December 20, 1964
Dear Arnold,
Thanks for your letter, but what's a Birch? We've got a lot of nut-bearing trees around here (and a whole bunch of squirrels), but I haven't seen any birches that I know of, especially none that look like johns. Besides, tree-dwelling rodents aren't sophisticated enough to belong to societies, are they?

Anyway, it's Christmas vacation at last, and not a minute too soon. I've finally figured out what they wanted a poet around here for — I just came from the President's (WOW!) office (no, he didn't offer me any pop). I was called in to check his Christmas card verse, to make sure it scanned, I guess. It didn't, but I'm getting too cagey to be caught in untenable positions, so I said he certainly had talent, yessirree.

I've been learning a lot this year, and it's been the students who've been doing most of the teaching. You remember I said they'd probably have backgrounds? They sure do. Only most of it seems to be in high school courses in extra-curricular activities like Arbor-Wrestling (the Arboretum is right around the corner from here — the matches are all mixed singles and Dead Soldiering. My daughter has been picking up a lot, too — she's getting big and going to the College Nursery School (don't ask which one), and that's where the trouble lies. This is a small town, and man, they live on rumors around here. The newest rumor is that I've got a foul mouth.

We live on a street that's almost nothing but fraternities and sororities. Every night there, before it got too cold, bunches of fellows would come marching up the street in the dead of night, counting cadence. Well, as a former Navy boot, I'm interested in that sort of thing (though not to the extent of losing much sleep over it). Here would come this gang, and by the time they got to our house they'd be all juiced up (bottles all over our lawn the next day) and screaming. If my wife and I are awake, naturally, so is Melora, and she's got ears. There's one outfit that ties the record Company "A" held at Bainbridge Recruiting Station for foul language. I'm a student of literature and a writer, but I want to tell you I'm amazed at the number of four-letter words that fraternity crew can pack in between the numbers. So are the freshman girls next door at Mauck Hall, by the way.

At any rate, Melora goes off to school the next day with a whole new vocabulary, and I'm given the credit for it. Oh, well, I'm planning to leave Hillsdale anyhow, but I'll save that story till next time. Best to everybody,

                Lew

P. S. Dr. Kolivosky's long-awaited contribution to scholarship has finally been published, to much local fanfare in the Happy Daley News. What it turned out to be is a handbook on interior decoration and furniture sales for the National Institute of Furniture Salesmen, believe it or not. I'm planning on reading it just as soon as we buy a new sofa.

December 30, 1964
Dear Arnold,

I don't know what you're so frantic about, but just to calm you down, okay — I'll tell you about why I'm leaving.

Back at UConn (bless her green lawns) Jean was a member of Kappa Kappa Gamma. As soon as the local chapter here heard about this they asked us to chaperon a dance, which we did. It was a first for me, and, naturally, right off the bat some gatecrasher began smuggling liquor in to the band, right by the door of the room we were all sitting in — three house-mothers and another set of chaperons. Well, I didn't want to bother the kid, particularly as the house-mothers were telling such fine stories — one was about a girl who came in drunk one night and beat up the third-floor proctor over at West Hall. But finally Jean made me get up and do something about this kid.

It took me three hoots and a bellow to make him stop. I warned him, he said (over his shoulder), "I gotcha," and I thought we had the whole thing cleared away. I was wrong. You know about three strikes and out? Well, I caught him two more times and then gave up.

I turned him in next day. Nothing happened, of course...not until the Bouquets chaperoned another dance a week or two later in Toledo. When they got on the chartered bus to come home one of the drunks said to Larry — I think I told you he's in English with me — "I see you brought your snatch along." Sarah Bouquet, by the way, teaches here too. She broke down and they were hooted off the bus. They got on another one with the Pledges, but that was no better. Nobody seemed to want to do anything about it, so Larry and I decided to write separate letters to the school paper — which is supposedly censorship-free — about student drinking and disrespect.

If all Pandemonium didn't break loose! The letters were intercepted by Dean Hendee — the students call him the Green Dean because of this double-breasted khaki suit he always wears, like a uniform. This man is "Dean of Students," but "President Don" has him on every "faculty" committee in sight, particularly the ticklish ones. (He spends his spare moments ticketing student cars in back of East Hall.) Larry and I were hailed in before Kolivosky, the Green Dean, and Prof. Applegate, one of the innumerable retirees from other places who swarm Hillsdale. Applegate is Faculty Advisor to the Board of Student Publications, and he nods a lot, and smiles.

The upshot was that they wanted us to withdraw our letters on the grounds 1) we don't "wash our dirty laundry in public," and 2) Bouquet had been seen with his wife and the other chaperons, on two occasions — once before, and once during the dance — having cocktails in the public lounge of this hotel where the shindig was going on. It seems the College didn't want Larry's reputation besmirched.

Larry kept telling them there was this little difference, see, between an adult having a cocktail in a public lounge and a bunch of rowdy drunken fraternity minors on a public conveyance engaged in interstate transportation. But the deans weren't having any of that.

Applegate sat and nodded every so often when Hendee glanced at him. The Green Dean kept saying there were College Laws against chaperons having a cocktail. If so, nobody ever told any faculty about it, we replied, and anyway, such strictures would be College Rules. The kids had broken the law, not to mention College rules. "They are College laws!" Hendee pointed out. "Rules!" I intimated; "Laws are enacted by duly constituted public legislative bodies." It didn't make any difference, "They are LAWS!!!" the Green Dean implied.

This line of interrogation was getting me nowhere, so I asked what possible reason they had for wanting my letter withdrawn, besides that about dirty laundry. But they went on to other things, so I asked Applegate, and he nodded amiably at me.

Every time I asked the question they went on to other things, until finally I said I believed in open debate of issues and the free exchange of ideas. They all looked at me, and I was pleased to be back in on the conversation. The next thing I saw was the ash tray on Kolivosky's desk jump two feet up in the air. The desk itself was reverberating like a drum under Greeny's ham fist, and his purple mouth was hanging wide open. There, in mid-atmosphere, hung his words in quotes: **"IT'S AGAINST THE PHILOSOPHY OF THE COLLEGE!"** And then his eyes bugged back in and he sat back.

When I could talk again I allowed as how I was terribly sorry to hear that, and could I please be excused. It turned out that I couldn't, and things went on a while longer, but I didn't listen much. I was thinking over how I'd phrase my resignation. As it turns out, a lot of us are thinking about it, and Old Man Rumor's gotten back to Kolivosky. He told me the other day — smiling, like, you know — that rather than see me go, the school would give me bad credentials. He's said that to several others, too — all in fun, of course. What a card he is — nothing but good times. Let me know if this letter gets past the Tinsel Curtain.

Best,
Lew

February 4, 1965
Dear Arnold,

A new year, and what a drag it's been around here. If John Ciardi hadn't shown up I don't know how we'd have spent the time. At a reception for him at one point he was holding forth on something that I thought was rather speculative, and when he had finished I said, "John, that's highly suppository." Hillsdale does things to one's brain, I think. He talked at Chapel in the morning about Ralph Waldo Emerson and read some of his own poetry in the afternoon. At the morning session he said, "To quote Emerson, 'It is the not-mes in my friend that delight me.' But Emerson didn't go far enough — I have discovered that there are no not-mes." Well, the *Hillsdale Daily News* sent over their finest to cover the story — an old lady with an ear trumpet, and it showed up in the paper like this: "To quote Emerson, 'It is the knock-knees in my friend that delight me.'" And it went on, "But

Emerson didn't go far enough — I have discovered that there are no knock-knees."

Of course I approved of that, so I wrote the paper to suggest some more revisions of famous quotations. I said, how about, "Dump the torpedoes! Full speed to bed!" Or even, "In your Hertz you know his ruts" which, since that's a takeoff on Goldwater's campaign slogan, "In your heart you know he's right," was taking my life lightly. They actually printed it, and the next day I got a call from the public library which wanted me to help them locate the quotation. I asked why, and they said they'd been having a run on Emerson since my letter appeared.

I also got an "Apprecia-Gram" the other day — from President Don — for something I did. It read,

Hillsdale College APPRECIA-GRAM

We appreciate you!

[*There was a message in this space, and then down below,*]

"Kindness is the oil that reduces the friction of life"
D. J. P.

That made my day, let me tell you. We've got a custom around here of giving standing ovations to our speakers who, outside of Ciardi and one or two others, are people like the Founder and Director of the Institute for Straight-Thinking (I kid you not! as Jack Paar used to say).

The English Department (all four of us including the chair, Edwin Dike, Dan Wheaton, Larry Bouquet and me) have decided they're not really ovations but "Apprecia-Stands," and what we do on our feet is "Apprecia-Clap," known in the aggregate as "Appreciapplause." This mostly occurs over in the College's new Leadership Development Center, in the room called the Discussatorium.

Did I tell you I'm getting up a Conference of Midwestern Poets here? Shades of the old Cleveland Poetry Center! Well, the Conference will be held at the Leadership Development Center in

a place called the Mirror Room: a big conference room with a balcony fronted by one-way glass mirrors so that observers won't disturb conference participants. The observers are supposed to be students — this is the gimmick the school sells parents, but Hillsdale's so far off the beaten track that they can't get many conferences in, despite the sign at the edge of town that says,
        HILLSDALE: GATEWAY TO MICHIGAN.
There are microphones in the ceiling so that you can hear as well as see behind the mirrors. More later.
        Best,
        Lew

P. S. Did you know that Rubinofsky (the Log-Cabin boy) has written a book titled, *How to be Popular though Conservative*? I hear they're planning to give him an honorary degree in June. Meanwhile, on Sunday, January 3rd, the Charleston, S. C. *News and Courier* carried an article on page 6-B titled, "Conservative View Stifled on Campus." It was written by a guy named Rose, in our Hillsdale College Department of Languages.

April 12, 1965
Dear Arnold,

    Well, the Conference was over yesterday. You probably heard about the tornadoes we had in the evening, but I swear to you I wasn't responsible. Matter of fact, Jean and I slept right through them while they were smashing up the outskirts of town. I got up the next day and went over to have breakfast at the snack bar. I sat with a couple of colleagues who were discussing the storm, and I looked up at them and said, "What tornado?"

    They looked at me as though I were from Mars. "It tore up the east side of town," one of them told me.

    Later on, Jean and Melora and I took a drive to see for ourselves — it was amazing! A new runoff system was being installed at one spot where big corrugated galvanized metal pipes had been lying the day before. Now, some of them were twisted around trees and telephone poles as though they were ribbons. One house we looked at had been picked up off its foundation, moved a couple of feet, and set back down.

Hillsdale was full of rumors and stories. The woman at the checkout of the market we use said that at the sound of the sirens she and her husband ran down into their cellar, but that he had gone back upstairs after something. He called to her to come up, which she did, and just then the tornado hit their house, collapsing the wall which fell into the cellar just where she had been standing. Another fellow, a farmer, had just sat down to eat his supper and he glanced out the kitchen window at his flock of chickens which were standing around their trough eating their own meal. He next looked out that window the next day, and was amazed to see the chickens still standing there, so he went out to check them out — they were all dead, standing in place! The tornado had driven their legs into the ground.

But the *worst* story was this: a steeplejack had been up on the belltower of the Baptist church when the tornado touched down. It grabbed him, drove a leather lace through his chest, tore off one leg and half of another, and threw him to the earth. He died with a thong in his heart and ex-spired with a thigh.

All went well with the Conference, except that Kolivosky wouldn't let one Beatnik register because he sent in some poems that had those words the fraternity boys use in their cadence-count. He wrote the rejection letter and wanted to know if I cared to sign it!

We've taken to holding our Faculty Meetings in the Mirror Room lately. Before the last one somebody put it out that a High Administrator observes these sessions (President Don never appears at the meetings). During the meeting I thought I saw a flare behind the glass, as though somebody had lighted a cigarette, so I told my neighbors, and we all sat around casting fishy glances upward and saying nothing about Mike Moore's trouble, about which everybody thought there'd be an explosion. After the meeting a bunch of people were standing around gossiping. One guy said, "Did you know somebody is up there listening to us?" He pointed, but everybody thought it was a joke and went on talking. Just then a door slammed hard up in the balcony behind the mirrors. Is Somebody Up There Watching Us?

            Lew

P. S. Campbell just published a high school economics text under a grant from the Grant Foundation (so help me). He wrote it with two school people from Houston, and on its front jacket it has the Log Cabin Theory and the Hillsdale crest. On the back is a blurb by Phillips; on the inside jacket is all about Happy Dale College and Campbell and Phillips. Its title is *Economics and Freedom,* and I guess the idea is that any high school that adopts it will have a lot of students who want to come to Happy Dale. They're going to give Rubinofsky a Doctor of Semantics degree! What is the meaning of all this?

May 2, 1965
Dear Arnold,

    Didn't I tell you about Moore? — he's been "let go." Nobody knows why, but it seems to have something to do with things he said in passing in his American Heritage class. I gather that some of these things were that George Washington wore wooden choppers, Ben Franklin liked to play around with the ladies, Woodrow Wilson had bunions, and Thomas Jefferson had a black mistress. All of these things, of course, are true. However, the Administration has also hinted that Moore was being given the sack for "personal" reasons as well.

    Now, this is an odd thing. Mike is a married man with a new daughter; he is a pillar of church and community, a Doctor in History from Western Reserve University and, to top it all off, a teetotaler. A lot of the faculty and some of the students got pretty mad at the insinuations, but some of us treated it as a joke. Some independent students demonstrated on the steps of Central (a first!) while fraternity boys counter-demonstrated with signs like, "Does your nose itch? Then picket." The independents are busy getting their transfer transcripts in order.

    Anyway, lately Mike picked up a rumor on campus, told his wife about it, and she went downstairs to ask the landlady, whose husband is a Trustee, if she'd heard that the "reason" was that Mike liked to get all dressed up in women's clothes. The landlady said yes, she'd heard it from a member of the Board of Women Commissioners, who had gotten it from the Chairman of the

Board of Trustees who evidently believed it. After a little nosing around, Mike managed to trace the source of the rumors to...ME!

And I admitted it. It seems that a bunch of us were sitting around a table over at the Center just after the administration came out with their insinuations. I remarked to the gathering that I knew what the reason was. Everybody was all ears.

"He's a transvestite," I said, and leered. "I heard that too," a student replied, "and the only reason he was caught was because the Green Dean made a pass at him." At the time, we all laughed.

Which reminds me of something else that happened earlier in the year: Ralph Reynolds, the pastor of the College Baptist Church, and Ed Dike, the Chairman of our English Department, were to stage a discussion titled "Sex and Common Sense" at Ed's home. they put up posters, but the school made them take the signs down because of that word. Some time later, another group wanted to discuss "Miscegenation and the Pill," but they were worried about the fate of their signs. They asked me what I thought and I said, "Put them up."

"How come?" they asked.

"Because nobody over at Central is going to know what *miscegenation* means." They had a fine big turnout, I understand, and nobody touched their signs.

See you. Don't wink at any strange ladies.

Best,
Lew

June 13, 1965
Dear Arnold,

Well, it's all done. Over a dozen faculty (nearly one-third of the staff) are leaving for new jobs, and they gave that Rubinofsky his honorary Doctor of Semantics degree at commencement the other day: **MM = D. S.**

Man, I am going to miss Hillsdale College. I've got me a job in a state college in New York — I've had a liberal dose of private Liberal Arts as she is practiced in the great Heart of America. When we come trailing through Cleveland we'll stop by to say hello. Meanwhile, love to all.

Best,
Lew

A Sheaf of Leaves: Literary Memoirs

April 6, 1966
Dear Arnold,

    It's been a long time since I've written you...almost a year. I hear that Fenn College now has a new name: Cleveland State University! Quite a step up, I'd say. Well, I've taken another step as well — all the way to New York State. I like my new job here at S.U.N.Y. College at Oswego, and everything's going fine. But you know, I have kind of a nostalgia for all that madness that took place last year at Hillsdale.

    I'll fill you in on what happened after my last letter: nothing much. I taught summer school to get enough money to move. Everything kind of died out. The A. A. U. P. investigation never came to anything — that grand old Professional Organization again did nothing, as they did at Fenn when I got booted out. Nothing ever came of the investigation by the accrediting agency, either. The widow of a former U. S. ambassador died and left the College 2.2 million dollars, just at the wrong (from our refugee point of view) moment.

    But nothing happens at Hillsdale without a sign from Heaven. On the last day of summer school or, rather, that night, we had the most incredible sheet-lightning storm. Jean, Melora and I cowered under a table in the cellar waiting for the world to come to an end. Then we tore out of town for good the next morning. Frieda Reynolds, wife of the pastor of the College Baptist Church (and you haven't heard that story — but it's too long and involved to go into here), wrote us to say the dust had no sooner settled behind us than they came in to tear down our house (they couldn't wait, she said) to build a new Nursery School.

    And now here it is a year later. The gang is scattered far from Fantasyland in Michigan...but Hillsdale's back in the news, as no doubt you know. this time it's on a national level: they've got FLYING SAUCERS floating around over the Arboretum! Did you hear Johnny Carson on the "Tonight Show" give the Hillsdale dogcatcher a "Stupidity of the Week Award"? Seems as how the next time the dogcatcher sees a UFO he's going to take a pot-shot at it with his 30.06 rifle. I guess he carries it around to knock off mad dogs (hope he doesn't go too near Central Hall).

My replacement (or somebody's) in the English Department has hit *The New York Times* no less! Seems she had her English classes sitting around in the trees waiting for the men from Mars so that they could take notes on these extra-terrestrial phenomena. If you haven't caught the story out there in Limbo, try to dig up a copy of the *Times* for March 23rd and turn to page twenty-two.

It's a crazy kind of nostalgia I feel right at the moment, but I guess it's time to close this letter and go back to hiding in my office. I'd like to get through the first year here, at least, without attracting any attention. Love to Sheila and the kids. Jean and Melora send their regards.
       All best,
       Lew

December 6, 1999
Dean Emeritus Arnold Tew
Cleveland State University

Dear Arnold,
 How long has it been since we've seen each other? Thirteen years? I visited you when I finally came back to Fenn College oops! Excuse me, I mean Cleveland State University, don't I? in 1986 for the silver anniversary of the Poetry Center I founded, and I guess that's the last close contact we've had except for the annual Christmas cards. But the Millennium is just around the corner, and I simply had to write you to ask if you've seen the latest episode in the grand tradition of Hillsdale College.

If so, you'll know that even though all the old cast of characters is gone, the newest crew has managed to outdo the old ones in bitter sleaze. It seems that Lissa, the forty-one-year-old daughter-in-law of George C. Roche III, the President of the College for the last 28 years, "shot herself to death in a gazebo in the school's Arboretum" (remember the flying saucers?). Afterward Roche's son, George the IVth, a forty-four year-old "lecturer in history and exercise physiology [!!] at the school, publicly accused his father of having had an affair" with Lissa, an affair that had lasted for nearly all of the more than two decades of the son's marriage! The story is in *Time* magazine, the issue of November 29, 1999, on page 6, so you can check it out for yourself if you haven't already seen it.

Afterward President Roche is said to have "denied the affair to the board, 'invoking God as my witness.' Then two weeks ago, he abruptly retired, walking away from a job that made him the fifth-highest-paid college president in the country, with salary and benefits that *Forbes* magazine estimated at $524,000 last year."

"'Together we have built a wonderful dream,' Roche said in his resignation letter. 'We have proved that integrity, values and courage can still triumph in a corrupt world,'" if you can believe it. The students are disillusioned (again): "'He's made this school and the whole conservative movement laughable,' said history senior Chris Ratliff, 20." Others, according to *Time*, "stopped looking up to Roche last year, when he and his wife of 44 years divorced in the midst of her battle with liver cancer." He married another woman five months later.

Former Secretary of Education in the Reagan administration William J. Bennett, who is Chair of the College's Presidential Search Committee (and, it turns out, a notorious gambler), has decided to celebrate this latest achievement in conservative education by turning in his resignation as well.

How did I learn of this? I was out in Scottsdale, Arizona, on November 29th and 30th, giving a reading and a master class at Paradise Valley Community College as the guest of one of my former students, Steven E. Swerdfeger, who teaches there. He graduated from S.U.N.Y. Oswego in 1970, and he remembered the original "Hillsdale Epistles" when he saw this new story. He clipped it out and gave it to me. Steven said he knew I'd want to bring the Epistles up to date, and he was right, but I wish America weren't this insane.

Did I ever send you a copy of my last published volume, *A Book of Fears*? It came out in 1998. I never felt that it was finished, and the week or two before I went out to Scottsdale I began writing more poems in the series, one of which was titled,

Lewis Turco

IDEOPHOBIA: The Fear of Ideas
for George W. Bush

What good were they? The only thing they did
for him was make his poor head hurt like hell,
batting about between his ears, back and forth,
bounding off the walls of his skull, making his eyes
go spinning in circles like some cartoon of Elmer

Fudd after he'd been hit with a hammer. If he had wanted
to study stars he'd have become an astronomer...
or was it *astrologer*? He didn't know. Who cares?
He'd hated high school where they tried to make
you actually remember some of that stuff,

like economics and current affairs. College was great!
Beer and pot, girls and games, parties and brawls
until you woke in the morning, your poor head hurting
like hell, bells bounding off the walls of your skull,
batting about between your ears, back and forth

until the day he had to go to class—
or get kicked out. But what the hell — no pain, no gain,
is what they say. As little as possible, though,
that's his motto. "Make love, not war," but do it smart,
don't stand for anything, just do it, get it done.

I read the poem as part of my program at Paradise Valley before Steven gave me the clipping. It's the paradigm of the type of student one used to find, and probably still does find at Hillsdale College. Isn't it fun to think that soon our country may (again) be run by one of these people?
    With best wishes for happy holidays and the next thousand years,
                                  Lew

GREAT POETS I ALMOST MET

Over more than four decades as a writer I have met many poets, but it is those that I *almost* met that make my memory itch. Jean and I were graduated from high school in 1952; she went to the University of Connecticut while I went into the Navy for those same four years, and when she graduated I entered UConn myself. My poetry teacher there was John Malcolm Brinnin, the man who had brought Dylan Thomas to this country and who subsequently wrote *Dylan Thomas in America* . Unfortunately, it was while I was in the service that Thomas had visited UConn. Although I had bought Thomas' *Collected Poems* at the Yale Co-op early on, while on leave or a weekend pass, I never managed to see him or hear him read. By the time I attended UConn myself he was dead.

His legend continued to live, though, and there were some of us who would have emulated him if we could. When I retired from teaching in 1996 R. S. Gwynn was the master-of-ceremonies at my retirement banquet at S.U.N.Y. Oswego, and he put together some remarks and comments made by people who had known me over the years. He got Donald Justice to contribute this ancecdote:

"When Lew was in graduate school," Justice tells us, "he was the champion of two parlor tricks for which alone we would never have forgotten him, even if he had written nothing: one was the trick of being able to recite anything backwards, and to do it instantly; the second and more impressive was the trick of improvising on the spot a Dylan Thomas poem, not ever one we could quite remember, though each new Turco-Thomas poem did sound at least faintly familiar and certainly authentic."

At Bread Loaf in 1961 the late Robert Huff and I used to have Dylan Thomas sound-alike contests — of course, we had listened to his recordings. Huff was good, but I had the advantage of reading original material, for the year before, in my *First Poems*, I had published my

Dirge a la Dylan

When I was a curled boy, short and long-
    shadowed beneath an apple moon,
I peeled my dreams out of cider skies
    and toasted them crisp each fiery noon.

When I was a birch young man I pruned
    my dreams until they grew green and tall.
I plunged brown seed upon mossy days,
    urged them to lunge and be done with the fall.

Then, when I was a hairy man,
    I grasped my past by both its ears
to feed it on cabbages and grass
    until it turned pink-eyed with the years.

> Ah! curled small lad; O birch young man,
>   hairy elder: apple hours
> are lying, prune-dry, upon cellar shelves,
>   choking black seed within vinegar cores.

Many years later I was still at it. At a party in Oswego, New York, at the home of the novelist John Herrman, I said to him that if Dylan Thomas hadn't lived, I could have written like him all day long. Herrman scoffed. I said, "Okay, I'll prove it. Give me paper and a pen." He did, and I wrote a poem in quantitative syllabics (as I had been doing since 1959) just as Thomas did, and when I was through I read it to the assembly. They were impressed, but I had to do something more with it, so the next day I disguised the syllabics by writing the poem out in prose lines. And then I submitted it to *Poetry*, which accepted it. Later still, I rewrote it and put it back into a form of verse:

AN ARRAS TAPESTRY

>   In clockstruck Arras stars
> come broaching the frames where grave
> folk lie waking. In the least
>
>   of rooms, stretched among sheets
> and chimes, body like the weft
> of an old design, there lies
>
>   the beginning of the
> gravest — a child threading dreams
> as shadows loom and shuttle
>
>   in the stone shires.
> In the hempen hours, grieving
> for light among his graylings,

> flesh taut upon the bed-
> frame, boneframe, stead shaking in
> shadow, he shall pass beneath
>
> the steeples' bobbins
> tracing dream and age upon
> a warp of hours — all folk
>
> woven in the tapestry
> of town and star: for silence
> shall comb this waking and his
>
> sleep, the gathered umber
> be raveled, strand and chime.

When the poem was published I gave an inscribed copy of the magazine to Herrman.

The next poet I almost met was E. E. Cummings whose poetry I had been reading and admiring for years. At UConn I was chair of the committee that brought poets to campus. One of my professors was the Cummings scholar Norman Friedman, and it was he who suggested that if we would like to have Cummings come to campus, I need look no further for an agent than Norman Friedman. Of course, we jumped at the chance, for Cummings was not only famous, he was elderly and quite feeble, and who knew how long he would be around? I worked through Friedman, and in due time the program was arranged. I was to introduce Friedman who was to introduce the poet whom he was shepherding.

Cummings read his work in a tiny, piping voice, nearly inaudible in the Student Union auditorium, even with amplification. Friedman had said that Cummings would need a break after a half hour, and he was not to have people pestering him, so when the time came the professor whisked his poet into the United Nations room nearby. I stood at the door looking through the glass panes at Cummings and Friedman, and then, when it was time to resume the program, Friedman whisked him back onto the stage.

One of the things we students liked to do when we had a poet visit was to ask for a poem to publish in our undergraduate magazine, of which I was the editor. Prof. Friedman came through for us, and we were able to publish in our periodical what was destined to be a famous Cummings poem, "l(a" — the sort of thing that I remember the poetaster Stanton A. Coblentz having railed against in some little magazine or other as a typical Cummings super-Modernist brain twister, but E. E. Cummings was in many ways a sentimental poet, and he hid this sentimentality with all sorts of typographical, grammatic, syntactic and rhetorical tricks and, sometimes, with a rather slangy and "wise guy" level of diction, though that is not the case here. Complicating his essential sentimentality was his sarcastic view of life: Cummings did not care for what he called "mostpeople" who, it seemed to him, were against culture and art and too wrapped up in the quotidian — Cummings' "mostpeople" were what H. L. Mencken called the "booboisie."

A poem I wrote at UConn under the Cummings influence was this one, which appeared in my *First Poems* in 1960:

A TALE OF RIVERS AND A BOY

Long once ago in our town was a boy
moon blue grass sparse as August's thirsty bones
who down to rivers ran to sense them flow
between all acorns grown as tall as high
to saline waters difficult to con
down dawn thin valleys down the arching land
through evenings bridging hamlets inland up
with hills along the pulsing bays

                                                    New moon
plus booked Septembers watched the boy turn his
new leaves now olding out to fall upon
the bent back of an autumn wild with wind
and soft with warm ideas lately fact
to find if underneath were not the core
that bore the trifling nut of everything
his lonely rivers were

                          Then when the moon
was snowy as the skeleton of worlds
entombed in catacombs of seasoned bones
the boy down slid to know the rivers' ice
to touch intrepid soles to surfaces
of fluid solid as a skin may crust
and wonder when would this bleak water heave
down patient banks

                        The moon switched green at last
among the drops of cloudy rivers down
upon their muddy parents falling out
of springing skies and also on the boy
attentive now to tributary suns
who stood on brinks and dams with eyes to note
the rivers molt and snake away again
toward the bays where moons conceive

                                       But now
there's no more in our anytown one boy
no moon blue boy for flesh has grown and gone
along the riverflow long down ago
to reassert the disbelief of minds
and find again that rivers cannot go
but round and round as moons go round and round
to chase the seasons through subsiding years

    After his reading, Friedman whisked Cummings away again — who knew where? — and I went home. A day or so later Friedman asked me, "How did you like Cummings?" I said I'd greatly enjoyed the reading, but I wished that I had been introduced to him. "Didn't I have you meet him?" I shook my head. "No." Perhaps he apologized. I don't remember.
    Later, while I was attending the Iowa Writers' Workshop we heard that there was to be a reading in Chicago by T. S. Eliot, sponsored by *Poetry*. Several cars full of Workshoppers drove up from

Iowa City, and Paul Engle got some of us invited after the reading to a reception and cocktail party on Lakeshore Drive at the home of Thomas Lannan, the largest patron of the magazine. I remember the cavernous modern apartment as being wall-to-wall carpets and floor-to-ceiling works of art. I knew that Eliot was present somewhere, so I wandered through the rooms one by one, looking for him. I stumbled over famous writers everywhere, and I thought that I hit every room in the complex. I remember seeing Oscar Williams sitting like a small troll on a piano bench with a poetess on each knee — I believe one of them was Claire McAlllister — but Eliot had been well-hidden, and I never laid eyes on the great man. The only thing of note that took place was that one of the caterer's waiters propositioned me in the men's room.

During my last year in the Navy — 1955-56 — while I was stationed at Arlington Naval Barracks and working at the Bureau of Naval Personnel, Ezra Pound was still interned at St. Elizabeth's Hospital in Philadelphia, but at the time it didn't occur to me to attempt to visit him, which would have been easy for me to do: I frequently drove to Connecticut on weekends and passed by Philadelphia regularly. But many years later, while I was teaching at S.U.N.Y. Oswego, one of my colleagues, the late Gerhard Zeller, a Pound scholar, said that he had corresponded with the poet for many years. He said he thought Pound would be glad to hear from me, and he gave me Pound's address in Rapallo, Italy, where by this time he was spending his exile.

I had been thinking about visiting Italy on my sabbatical, so I wrote to Pound asking if I might drop in one day. Since I was an undergraduate I have collected books in my field, and whenever possible I like to have them signed by their authors, so I included in the package a copy of his paperback *Selected Poems*, which I had had as a textbook in Friedman's Modern Poetry class and that I had bound. I asked him to sign it, and I included sase for its return.

One day the envelope came back. I saw that Pound had written out his name and address by hand in the upper left-hand corner. I opened it to find that the poet had inscribed his book for me in the same hand. He hadn't written me a note or a letter responding to my request for permission to visit him; instead, he had enclosed his calling card and had written out in hand on it his home address which,

I understood, was an old-fashioned European way of saying, in effect, "Certainly, drop by if you are in the neighborhood."

But I never was. Though in the nineties my wife and I did manage to get to England at last, for some reason every time we planned to travel abroad our ancient sewer line would collapse, or we would need a new roof, or one of our parents would die. I never got to meet Ezra Pound, but Ger Zeller had even worse luck: his apartment building burned down and destroyed not only all the correspondence he had conducted with his poet, but his unfinished doctoral dissertation on him as well.

Conrad Aiken died of a heart attack on Friday, August 17th, 1973. In his *New York Times* obituary notice of Sunday, the 19th following, Alden Whitman wrote, "As the years wore on Mr. Aiken came to have hardly a kind word for anybody or anything except comic strips, martinis, and John O'Hara's short stories. In an interview with this reporter in 1969, he wrote off contemporary American poetry as having come to 'a temporary pause' and dismissed Archibald MacLeish, Robert Lowell and Allen Ginsberg, among others, as over-estimated." I am sorry the *Times* obituary is the last impression the public had of the end of a great poet's life. On August 26th of the year of Aiken's death I wrote Mr. Whitman a letter — never acknowledged — in which I corrected his vision of the poet as a bitter old man who had lost his interest in poetry.

In the fall of 1970, nearly a year after the reporter interviewed Aiken, I found a first edition of the poet's *The Coming Forth by Day of Osiris Jones* (1931). Aiken is one of my favorite authors, and I had several other of his books, among them his 1961 *Selected Poems* which I had praised in a review I'd done for *American Weave*, the magazine of my friend Loring Williams when we had both been living in Cleveland in the early 1960s. In October of 1970 I wrote Conrad Aiken a letter to ask if he would be willing to inscribe a book or two for me if I sent them along with return postage. I hoped to get a favorable response by reminding him of my review.

On October 29th Aiken replied that he would be "glad to sign it. And thanks," he continued, "for reviewing me. Maybe now again?" For it appeared that Oxford University Press had on 27th August 1970 published his *Collected Poems 1916-1970* and committed the error of printing on the title page, "Second Edition." Aiken was considerably upset that they had done so without consulting him and without mentioning that the new volume contained "FIVE more books than the 1953 edition," he wrote, adding, "They are going to correct it but too late. It will get NO reviews. Ars lunga etc."

As soon as I got his card on November 2nd I sent Aiken two of his books, *Osiris Jones* and the *Selected Poems*, and I included a letter. I said that I was enclosing two of my own books "as a gift — one just out today, *The Inhabitant*." The other was *Awaken, Bells Falling* (1968).

I also wrote Daryl Hine, editor of *Poetry*, to ask if he'd like me to review the new *Collected Poems*, as Aiken had requested. Hine responded quickly in the affirmative, even before I had gotten the review copy. I wrote to Aiken to tell him that I would do the review, but I was not prepared for the note I received from him — he didn't even mention the review. The postcard was datelined "Brewster, Mass., Nov. 20 70":

> Dear Mr. Turco: <u>The Inhabitant</u> is the best new poem I've read in something like thirty years — profoundly satisfying to me, speaks my language, such a relief to have WHOLE meaning again, instead of this pitiable dot-and-dash splinter-poetry, or sawdust cornflakes which we usually get. And you're <u>all</u> good. You give me courage to <u>read</u> again, and even to believe again in myself. So you see how handsomely I'm in debt. Thank you! You should be, and will be, better <u>known</u>. The Coll Poems are being sent, but don't feel you must like me because I like YOU — gawd ferbid.

Before the mail had arrived at my family's apartment in Oswego, New York, on November third, I had written a note to tell Aiken that I had received the signed books; after the mail came and I had gotten over the first effects of Aiken's letter, I sat down and wrote him again on the same day to tell him how much I appreciated his remarks about my books. I said that *The Inhabitant* "will have a very small circulation, but I'd rather have your single opinion than a thousand readers." I told him his comments would have no effect on my review, as I had long been his admirer anyway, and had said so in the earlier review.

I added, "I'd like very much to meet you some day. My home town is Meriden, Connecticut, and we spend our summers in Maine.... Perhaps, on a trip someday from here to there, I might visit with you for a few minutes?"

The review copy of Aiken's book finally came, and I sat down to write the review for *Poetry*, which had set fairly stringent space limitations for the piece. When it was finished I sent it off to Hine, and by the end of January 1971 I had received a formal acceptance of it, together with a note of thanks from Hine, one sentence of which read, "Belated thanks for this review, which manages to say so much in such a short space."

The next communication I had from Aiken was datelined Savannah, Georgia, March 8, 1971, and it was also a surprise: "I'd like to nominate you for the Loines Award, of the National Institute of Arts and Letters," he wrote, "for an American or English poet whose work has not been too much recognized." He said he didn't have my books with him, though, and wondered if I wouldn't send the Institute copies and tell them he'd told me to do so. "Don't hope too much!" he wrote. "You must know as well as I do what happens on these damned committees. I served on one at the Institute which tried to give the Gold Medal for fiction to K A Porter instead of Faulkner! But I proceeded to nominate F and of course when it came to a full vote of the Institute he walked away with it, thank you. Disgraceful...[.]" He suggested further that I look up a critical piece on his new book that had appeared in the *Saturday Review* for January 30, 1971. He ended with, "We're here til May, then to the Cape end of that month. Communicate, and try to come by at Brewster. It would be nice to see you."

I knew that one couldn't apply for the Loines Award oneself, and I felt diffident about sending them my own books. I wanted to avoid any appearance that I was responsible for initiating this nomination; therefore, on March 10th I wrote Aiken, to say I appreciated his efforts in my behalf, but suggested that I send him the books to forward. I enclosed a copy of my review of his book, though I'd not yet received proofs from *Poetry*, I told him. I said I'd look up the *Saturday Review* piece, and I ended with, "I'm looking forward to the summer. I intend to take full advantage of your offer while we're on our way down to Maine."

On March 13th Aiken responded with "...thanks for books and the review." He agreed that he himself had simultaneously decided that his sending in the books to the Institute "might be more tactful! I'll send 'em on to Insti. Your review is very good, AND kind — I only regret that you can't have been a LITTLE more specific about early, middle and late, etc etc. But VERY useful. And I'm glad you slapped O U Pee on the wrist...and yes, a martini next summer!"

I replied on the 9th of April with thanks for his last card. I wrote that I would have liked to have more space in my review, "but the enclosed correspondence from *Poetry* will explain things, I said. "I'm working on a book of criticism," I continued, "and I'll get a chance to expand on your work, I'm sure.

"I don't know when the book will be finished, but I'll let you know when it is — and when and if it's published." I ended with, "Looking forward to summer, and our martini —" Unfortunately, my *Visions and Revisions of American Poetry*, with its comparison of Aiken and Wallace Stevens in a chapter titled "A Modernist Coin," wasn't published until 1986.

On May 20th of 1971 I wrote Aiken again to give him the news and to say, "We'll be leaving for Maine in a few weeks." I gave him my summer address and phone number. I told Aiken I'd be on sabbatical in the fall, and might stay on in Maine for a while. I enclosed a copy of the first review of *The Inhabitant* to be published.

Aiken was back in Brewster by June 1st, which is when he next wrote me. He quibbled a bit with the review of *The Inhabitant*: "But does he quite see that it's ONE POEM**?? I wonder! Don't know about seeing you this month — the trip up took a lot of whey out of me, I'm still weak and shaky — could you perhaps call me to see what's what a few days before you start—?" He gave me his phone number and suggested that perhaps the fall would be better for my visit, "as June looks now as if it might be a little crowded. Sorry — let's wait and see. I'd very much like to meet you."

I replied over a month later, on the 8th of July. I thanked him for his card and said that of course I'd come down whatever month he wished. I also thanked him for having Oxford send me the new edition of his impressionist autobiography *Ushant*, which I was reading and enjoying. I told him I'd have Jerry Patz, publisher of *The Inhabitant*, send him a copy of my new book, *Pocoangelini: A Fantography and Other Poems*, when it appeared in September. "I read proofs on your review in *Poetry* not long ago. It should be out this month or next.," I wrote. Aiken replied on July 30th that he looked forward to October and my visit.

I was apprehensive about Aiken's health, and I did not want to tax him during the month of August by writing him letters he might feel obliged to answer. During this period, though, the review in *Poetry* appeared and I sent him a copy. On August 13th Aiken dropped me a card from Brewster: "Thanks!" he said. "The review is damned good, and Allen Tate said so in a note this morning. He sent me a copy." Aiken said he would see me in October.

Not long after, I sent him a copy of *Pocoangelini*, just out: Jerry Patz had asked Aiken for permission to use his letter of praise for *The Inhabitant* as a blurb on the new book, and it appeared on the back cover of the paperback edition. Aiken replied with a card dated September 9th: "Many thanks for the little angels, which I haven't had time for yet. We're a hospital at the moment, and I have no mind or energy." He wasn't as intrigued with this book, though, and of course he was right, for all three of the series comprising the volume — "Pocoangelini, A Fantography," "Bordello," and "The Sketches" — had been written earlier, some of them much earlier, than *The Inhabitant*. However, the latter had originally been published as a chapbook in 1962, and it had received good reviews. The middle series, a short one, had never appeared as a set before, and it was subsequently to be picked apart again as individual poems were picked up and anthologized frequently. "But don't believe anything I say! For I don't either," he wrote; "I'm a little out of my mind." I took it that he meant that he was feverish.

David M. Ungerer of Reston Publishing Company had a bit earlier flown to Maine to ask that I turn my S.U.N.Y. correspondence course study-guide into a college textbook, and I had just signed a contract to write *Poetry: An Introduction through Writing*. I planned to go home to New York State, where my professional library was located, to work on it, so I wrote Aiken before I had received his card, on September 11th, "I'll be leaving here to return to Oswego about October 17th. Would it be possible for me to drop in on you in October before then?"

When I finally got his card, I dashed off a note on September 13th to hide under nonsense how upset I felt about his health problems. It was meanwhile becoming clear to Aiken that the National Institute of Arts and Letters wasn't nearly as enthusiastic about *The Inhabitant* as he was, for on September 22nd he wrote to say that he'd written a letter to the secretary of the Institute, Felicia Geffen, "for the committee, but don't know if it's now too late. [Malcolm] Cowley was here a week ago, but was offhandedly noncommittal about it all, so I haven't too much hope." He said further that "my wife is better, but as we're both shaky, I fear we must again postpone positive decision about seeing you next month — hope we'll be in the clear for lunch or a drink. So let's reappraise round Oct 9th or 10th."

Obviously, Aiken was still expending energy in behalf of my book, and I wanted to spare him and reassure him that I wasn't very much concerned about the Loines Award. Literary politics has never been of interest to me, any more than it was to Aiken who had always been something of a loner. On the 24th of September I wrote, "I'm tremendously pleased to hear your wife is better and that you're feeling better than you sounded in your last card." I told him not to worry about the award, for his praise was better than any award I could receive.

Of greatest concern to me was Aiken's health and the often-deferred visit I was to pay him. It was put off for a final time when, on October 3rd, he wrote from Brewster, "Dear Lewis: This is sad, and I'm sorry, but I fear it can't be helped." Besides Mrs. Aiken's ill health, the poet himself had "...gone and had another heart flurry." The doctor told him he simply had to slow down and specifically not see people, as excitement sent his blood pressure soaring. "So, forgive me," he wrote, "but we'll just have to put it off for another year." He and Mrs. Aiken had "sorrowfully decided to leave for the south, and more clement weather, earlier than we'd planned. Don't hold it against me. And forgive me too," he continued, "if I don't correspond, for this too has become a burden, my desk is a snow-drift of unanswered letters. Hell."

The next note I wrote, on October 7th, was brief for two reasons: I felt I had been bothering Aiken excessively, and I didn't want to add to his problems. The other reason was that I was deeply disappointed, although I didn't want to show it. "Dear Conrad," I said. "You have my love. We'll see each other next year. Meanwhile, my very best to you and Mrs. Aiken."

After quite a long lapse I wrote Aiken again the next year, on March 10, 1972. "Please don't feel you have to answer this letter," I said. "I just feel like writing you. I thought you might not mind hearing what I've been doing...." I gave him the news and wrote, "I look forward to the summer, of course, which isn't far off now." I added, "Perhaps we can see each other then. I hope so."

I received no response, and I judged Aiken was still quite ill. A couple of months later I sent him another letter, dated May 15th, telling him I'd been "scouring the bookstores for Aikeniana." I asked if he'd be willing to sign some bookplates for me, and I sent him a copy of a poem I'd written. On the first of June 1972 Aiken wrote me his last letter, from Savannah.

It was as I had surmised — he had been "ill since fall, prostate with complications, had to delay trip south, and now the doctor won't let me travel. Nor can I walk, or read with intelligence...." He enclosed the signed bookplates — "that sounds like fun," he said. "Don't know when, if ever, we'll get back to the Cape. Meanwhile our house has been brutally robbed of most of its objets d'arts, lifetime collection. Sickening."

Conrad Aiken lived for a bit over another year. That he was a harried, disillusioned man with overwhelming health problems is true, but that he ever lost his interest in literature and life is not. He left as a legacy to us a trove of poetry, fiction and autobiography that few writers have equaled in quality, and fewer have surpassed. He left, as well, the memory of great vitality to the end.

The last great poet I "almost met" was Hart Crane whom I could not possibly have met under any circumstances because he died two years before I was born, but I came close to meeting him through Loring Williams, Crane's uncle by marriage to Alice Crane Williams, Hart's aunt, and my association with Loring was early, though neither of us knew it until I got my first teaching job in Cleveland at Fenn College in 1960.

A Sheaf of Leaves: Literary Memoirs

When I was a child my father was a counselor for a year or two at Royal Ambassadors Boy's Camp at Ocean Park in Maine — I was a camper there myself. Ocean Park was, and it still is, an interdenominational summer enclave, with a weighting toward the Baptists, on the Maine coast near Saco, a mile below Old Orchard Beach. It is also the site of one of the oldest writers' conferences in the country, the State of Maine, co-founded by Adelbert Jakeman and Loring, a native of South Berwick, Maine, who was largely responsible for the publication of my first book in 1960, and wholly responsible for my second major effort two years later.

With George Abbe and Clarence "Red" Farrar, publisher of Golden Quill Press, Loring Williams served on the board of The Book Club for Poetry which chose my *First Poems* as a Club selection while I was still a graduate student in the Writers' Workshop of the University of Iowa, before I knew I would be teaching in Cleveland where he had been living for many years and serving as editor and publisher of American Weave Press. As soon as I got to Cleveland Loring and I became close friends, and I would go over to his house in Cleveland Heights once or twice nearly every week. When I founded the Cleveland Poetry Center at Fenn, he became the moderator of the Poetry Forums, and I would see him there as well. In 1962 he published *The Sketches of Lewis Turco and Livevil: A Mask* as an American Weave Award chapbook.

Whenever I visited Loring at home I would say hello and a few words to Alice Crane who was a musician and composer of short pieces and hymns. She had never had to work a day in her life, for her family was wealthy, owners of several buildings in Cleveland that brought in a constant flow of revenue. Her marriage to Loring was one of convenience, I believe, for Loring took care of Alice in every way — he cooked the meals, cleaned the house...he even had to turn on the television for her as she seemed not to know how to do it. I never heard a word of complaint about the situation from Loring; in fact, he seemed quite fond of Alice whose head was always in the clouds. She was the perfect paradigm of Victorian refinement. She died as she had lived — in her sleep — several years after I had left Cleveland. Loring subsequently moved back to South Berwick, Maine, where I visited him once before he, too, died. Then, in 1979 I wrote this poem, part of a manuscript titled *Letters to the Dead*, recalling my visits to him in his Cleveland home:

Lewis Turco

LETTER TO AN EDITOR

Our Hero conjures up his ancient friend,
The literary Weaver, editor
And correspondent, in his printery
Belowstairs in the house were East Cleveland
Becomes the Heights. He was the guarantor
Of evenings filled with printer's deviltry

And conversation — nights that otherwise
Would have been lost in smog and Erie mist.
Dear Loring, he implores, *I've missed you well
These several years. I know that you despise
Shows of emotion. Forgive me. You don't exist,
So I must follow though I go through Hell.*

*I dream about your office down below;
The flywheel of your press turning around,
The fonts of type, the tubes of murky ink.
Upstairs your fabled wife treads to and fro —
Hart Crane's aunt, billowing like a mound
Of lace and lavender, attempts to think*

*Of one more bar of music to compose.
Turn off the press — it rumbles to a halt.
We sit and talk among those paneled walls —
Cleveland recedes and starts to decompose.
The strokes of fate are muffled in your vault,
And we can barely hear her siren calls.*

*I count it as a personal offense,
Loring, when someone dies, someone I know,
Particularly you. What did you get
Out of this retreat? It makes no sense.
How can I calculate the tab I owe
And pay you back? You've buried me in debt.*

I must resort to dreams. I turn within
My winding sheets and wait for you to come
To stand beside my stead. You proffer me
A book you've set in leaden type, but on
Those pages there is emptiness. I thumb
The volume through. I read that you are gone.

One evening, during one of these visits, Alice Crane quite unexpectedly descended the stairs heavily, came into the den, sat down, and for unknown reasons began to talk about her nephew. Hart Crane, though he had been born in Garretsville in 1899, had lived with his mother's mother in Cleveland from the ages of ten through sixteen when his parents were divorced. At that point he left home and high school and moved to New York City to become a Great Poet. Unfortunately, his father had to continue to support him until they had a falling-out in 1921 and he was forced to make it on his own. But these are details to be found in any biography. Alice Crane's conversation was much more intimate and interesting.

These were the early 1960s when the technology of the tape recorder was primitive and expensive. I didn't own one, but even if I had, I wouldn't have known enough to bring it with me that evening. Alice was clearly baffled by Hart. She talked about his behavior as a juvenile and adolescent, how he was battered by his parents' constant battles; how he stood up to his father in trying to protect his mother from his verbal assaults; how, though he loved her, she sent him away to live in Cleveland. She talked about the candy factory Hart's father owned, about how his aunts and uncles had no clue how to approach him, how he was clearly unappreciative of the family's efforts in his behalf, how he wound up writing such incomprehensible poetry. And when she was finished, Alice arose, moved slowly up the stairs, and never repeated her descent into the nether regions while I was present.

Lewis Turco

A Friend in Need, a Friend Indeed

Edward Cifelli, in his 1997 *John Ciardi, A Biography*, did what a biographer is supposed to do. He captured the spirit and essence of his subject. Nearly the whole man is there: the braggart who constantly boasted of being the richest poet in America, the super-overachiever, the workaholic, the public orator and dictatorial director of the Bread Loaf Writers' Conference, the loving but seldom-present father who was what the social workers these days call an "enabler," one who conspires to enable another person or other people to continue in self-destructive behavior, as Ciardi certainly did with his children, perhaps in an attempt to make up for his non-presence, either physical or mental, while he rambled around America and the world making money or sat alone in his study pouring out columns, poems, articles, lectures, book after book.

If my thumbnail sketch leaves a negative taste on the tongue, it is a deliberate effect, intended to mirror what I think may be the effect of Cifelli's biography on the reader. I can hear that reader saying, "If this is what he was like, then Ciardi deserved to speed downhill, out of control, after his heyday in the 1960's. He was clearly out of touch with the times, a personality that mirrors all that was worst about the generation of World War II ex-GIs who came home to make a cozy, unthinking success of things."

But that's essentially a false impression of John Ciardi. What I miss in the biography is a sense of his sense of humor. It is utterly true that he did all the things Prof. Cifelli says he did, but Ciardi did them drolly, with an air of self-deprecation and satire. He knew he was acting the boor, but he hated boors, and he let you know it. Cifelli properly noted that Ciardi had many, many friends, but the reader may have a hard time understanding why they all loved him so much, so long and so deeply. I would have liked to see more anecdotes in this book, such as this, for instance:

At Bread Loaf in 1961 Robert Huff, Richard Frost and I shared one of the little cottages near Treman Hall. One night we were sitting around reciting limericks to one another and, of course, laughing and carrying on after each one. We were making enough noise to arouse the ire of some women who lived in another cottage close by, and they complained to John that we were making too much noise. John came by — it must have been after ten p.m. — to do his duty and tell us to quiet down. He asked us what we were doing, and after he had fulfilled his function as policeman he sat down with us and began to recite limericks himself from his prodigious memory, most if not all of them original, just as Cifelli has described Ciardi's doing on other occasions. All those present became, over the course of the next several hours, hysterical to the point that our sides ached. We were making much more noise with John present than we had been making before he arrived. I have no idea what the women did, or how they managed to get any sleep at all that night.

It is true, too, as Cifelli pointed out, that there was a hierarchy at Bread Loaf, but it was much more malleable than it appears to be in this book. That same year, as one of the Poetry Fellows, I was expected to put in time at Treman Hall with the faculty and the other Fellows. Scholars, such as A. R. Ammons, who were a step below, were not allowed in, nor were the Waiters or the conferees of various types, including Contributors and Auditors.

The evening that Robert Frost came by, he was seated in an armchair with a shawl over his knees on one side of the room. I was astonished at the super-sophistication of the staff and fellows: no one except John seemed to pay any attention at all to him. But that there was great awareness of Frost was clear if one looked at what was happening, for the conversation and drinking and walking about were as usual, but there was a clear line of demarcation over which no one stepped: a semicircle around Frost's chair. Everyone was careful to pretend indifference to Frost. It was a form of fright.

I stood at the edge of the circle staring at Frost who looked very lonely. John went to him and said something and then came toward me. He said something like, "Why don't you go and talk with Robert? He's being ignored." But I was too timid.

John left, I continued standing until I heard Frost mutter, "Won't someone talk to me?"

I gathered up my courage and went over to introduce myself. "What will we talk about?"

"You start," he replied, so I told him a story about a woodchuck that had chased my wife once in Connecticut. He responded by telling me something about his adventures the first time he had gone to England. Soon we were joined by two young women, sisters whose names I forget. We talked with Frost almost the whole evening; hardly anyone interrupted the whole time.

Hardly anyone. During the course of the conversation I told Robert that a namesake of his was at the Conference, the young poet Richard Frost who was attending on a Danforth grant, not one of the official Conference fellowships; thus, he was barred from Treman. I asked Ciardi if it would be all right if I brought Dick in to meet Robert, and Ciardi gave the okay. I went and got Dick and a copy of my *First Poems*, recently published, which I gave Robert as a gift (I was too shy to inscribe it to him) after I had introduced Dick. They exchanged pleasantries, decided that they weren't related, and Dick left after an interval.

At one point Ciardi came by again and said, "Robert, the Waiters want to sing a song for you."

Frost said, "All right," and Ciardi waved the young people in from the front door where they were clustered.

They came in, gathered around us in a semicircle and sang, to the tune of "Hernando's Hideaway," "Whose woods, these are, I think I know. / His house, is in, the village though. / He will, not see, me stopping here, / to watch, his woods fill up with snow, Olé!"

Those are some of the reasons *I* had for loving John Ciardi, who was an unstuffy, funny son-of-a-bitch who would do absolutely anything he could for you if he liked you and if you needed help. Cifelli in his book notes that after that same conference he gave the broke Miller Williams and his wife money to get back home. It was the least he could do since he had talked Miller into coming to Bread Loaf in the first place. That two hundred dollar investment was one of the best Ciardi ever made, and he made many — he wasn't called "Lucky John" for nothing — for after Ciardi's reputation had run down to a trickle, Miller kept it alive as publisher of the University of Arkansas Press, a position that was the direct result of the contacts and friendships Miller made at Bread Loaf that year, for at the time he was a high school biology teacher. Within the next year or so Miller made the transition to teaching college English, and Williams in 1997 retired as a Distinguished Professor. It is Arkansas that published Cifelli's biography, the edition of Ciardi's *The Collected Poems* that Cifelli also edited in 1997, and many other books including Vince Clemente's *John Ciardi: Measure of the Man* (1987).

Even on the public rostrum, which is mainly how he made his money, Ciardi could be very funny in the midst of a serious lecture. In Cleveland in the early '60's he was giving a talk at John Carroll University. He was doing his famous discussion of Robert Frost's "Stopping by Woods on a Snowy Evening," in which he pointed out that the form of the poem was an interlocking rubaiyat which should have ended by circling back, in the last quatrain, to the first stanza to pick up the main rhyme again. Instead, Ciardi said, Frost broke the form, and in breaking it made the poem a hundredfold more effective than it would otherwise have been had he maintained the requirements of the rubaiyat.

The house was packed. One of those present (besides my wife and myself) was a woman named "Yetta Blank" (that was really her name), one of those whom Cifelli in his biography characterized as an "arm-grabber." John recited the first two lines of the last stanza of Frost's poem, then the third line, "And miles to go before I sleep." He paused dramatically, looked at the audience and said rhetorically, "Now, how would you have ended that poem?"

Yetta Blank leapt to her feet and called out, "And now I lay me down to sleep?" In the hall, dead silence. Ciardi leaned across the podium, rested on his forearms, lanced her with his gaze and said, "You really think so, huh?" Bedlam. I don't know how many minutes it was before order was restored, but it is the funniest moment I can recall at a public program, and I have spent a lifetime attending them.

If it is objected that the inclusion of more such incidents (Cifelli does include some) would have unconscionably lengthened the book, then my reply is, cut out some of the many catalogues of Ciardi's itinerary. They are not exhaustive, but they give the impression that they are. One can only begin skipping and scanning when they arrive periodically throughout the book.

On October 8th 1997 my wife and I went to dinner at a local restaurant with one of our former colleagues at SUNY Oswego, a professor of music. When she asked what I was doing at the moment, I told her I was reading the biography of John Ciardi. "Who is he?" she asked. I could hardly believe she didn't know. When I told her about the poet's many books, his magnificent translations of Dante's great poems, his television program, his "Manner of Speaking" columns in, and his poetry editorship of, *The Saturday Review*, his radio program on PBS, his books of poetry, of etymology, of children's verse, his directorship of Bread Loaf, she just shook her head. Then I said, "Don't you recall that huge flap about Anne Morrow Lindergh's poetry?" That, finally, rang a bell, but evidently not a very loud one.

The one incident that most clearly showed how far from his palmy days as a public figure John Ciardi had fallen took place after his death, at a NEMLA meeting in Boston in 1987. There was to be a session on Ciardi during which Vince Clemente's book, *John Ciardi: Measure of the Man*, was to be published by Arkansas. At that time both Vince and I were employed by branches of the State University of New York, and we had both been invited to a conflicting SUNY Writers' Festival in Binghamton where we were to read and where Allen Ginsberg was to be the featured guest. Vince chose to go to Binghamton to read his poetry instead of attending the NEMLA convention to be present at the birth of his book. I sat with Judith Ciardi and her family while X. J. Kennedy read the main paper of the session. Aside from those people who were officially a part of the program or were associated with the University of Arkansas Press,

I was the only member of the audience other than the Ciardis. Judith turned to me and said, "I guess it's a good thing the family came."

POETRY, THE TAG-END OF THE ENTERTAINMENT INDUSTRY

Dana Gioia wrote a book, *Can Poetry Matter?* (Graywolf, 1992). Perhaps it can, but it doesn't, not any longer. It used to be, when there was no written literature, or very little, that poetry was at the center of culture. Then, it was poetry that carried the culture, passing lore and mythology on from one generation to the next. The elements of civilization were borne by the mnemonic devices of language — by meter, rhyme, repetition and the other sonic devices that have always been associated with "poetry" — the art of language — until the 20th century when it all went by the board. At best, poetry in the twenty-first century is the tag-end of the entertainment industry.

The death of poetry began in America with Walt Whitman in the 19th century and in Europe with the Symbolists who decided that they would write their "poetry" henceforth in *"vers libre,"* ignoring the traditional French system of syllabic prosody. Whitman himself was incapable of writing traditional verse. Anyone who doubts this may look at his early verses published in *The Brooklyn Eagle* and elsewhere. They are appallingly bad. His most famous metered poem is "O, Captain! My Captain!" So he did what the Symbolists did, he began writing prose poems. This is not necessarily a bad thing, but prose provides no boundaries for the poet to inhabit as verse does. To write prose poems one must have the ability to edit one's own work stringently. Whitman did not. He didn't even keep the editorial acumen he exercised as a newspaperman. As a result, he became prolix and spongy.

After Whitman along came the Modernists, many of whom espoused writing in many different prose forms which only Amy Lowell had the good sense to call "polyphonic prose" rather than "free verse" which is a contradiction in terms. According to our dictionaries verse is defined as "metered language" and prose is "unmetered language." Verse counts syllables; prose counts nothing; thus, "free verse" is an impossibility — one can't both count and not count simultaneously. But although the Modernists wrote in prose forms, some of them, like William Carlos Williams, tried to find "free verse" systems that would be the equivalent of the supposedly passé traditional metrical systems like iambic pentameter. As a result, various prosodies were cast under the rubric of "free verse" that were actually variable accentual prosody, syllabics, and so forth. This knowledge was lost upon succeeding generations, but not on every individual.

Like other members of his poetic "Post-Modernist" generation, Karl Shapiro was of two minds, literarily speaking — he grew up during the Modernist revolution reading and admiring the great experimental poets of his day, but in the high school and college classrooms he read the traditional British and American poets and was trained in their methods. Shapiro was a stranger neither to formal craft nor prosodic experiment. His *Essay on Rime* (Reynal, 1945), in fact, was a study and consideration of the traditional approaches to poetry, the entire volume itself being written in verse rather than in prose mode, a feat not to be equaled until John Hollander wrote his *Rhyme's Reason* nearly forty years later.

During the 1960s many of the formal poets like Shapiro were persuaded to the new view of the "Beats" and the Black Mountain poets that metrical versewriting was no longer relevant to the times, which were calling for harangue and confession, oriented to social activism and reform. Poetry was being politicized and "democratized." Karl Shapiro was one of the first of the formalists to adopt the new stance. He gave a lecture in the early 1960s at various universities, including the Fenn College (now Cleveland State University) Poetry Center, that resurrected the theories of the nineteenth-century British satirical novelist Thomas Love Peacock to the effect that mankind ought to have outgrown traditional poetry which was no more than the nursery rhymes of an infant society. Shapiro said that if poetry was that which was "lost in translation," then he wanted his work to sound as much like translations as possible, for he wanted no part of rhymes and meters and such linguistic tinkletoys any longer.

Shapiro joined the Beats, also, in making the connection between formal poetry and the "military-industrial complex" when he wrote in *College English*, the issue of October 1964, "An overnight collapse of the stanza might be as dangerous as the abolition of the Army. Poets still need close-order drill and the barracks mentality. It's too bad that they do. Novelists don't nor does any other kind of artist I know of. But poets are still the hostages of convention." Kenneth Rexroth had been saying exactly the same thing for years.

This was not the Shapiro to be found in *An Essay on Rime*. In his volume of prose poems *The Bourgeois Poet* (Random, 1964), Shapiro tried to out-Beat Allen Ginsberg. By the time *White-Haired Lover* appeared, however (Random, 1968), Shapiro had done another about-face and was writing sonnets again, at least part-time, just as Peacock — despite his haranguing on the subject of formal poetry — had sneaked sonnets into his novels.

By the 1970s poetry had lost all semblance of an art form. There were many members of at least two generations of "poets" who were completely innocent of the knowledge of their craft. But perhaps Shapiro had been correct about nursery rhymes, for children continued to love the sounds of the language if no one else did. In fact, children want no part of poems that aren't rhymed and metered.

How many of us haven't read at least one book about teaching poetry to children that makes such points as these: Poetry is that which is washed out of children by education. Education, including the learning of metrics, is responsible for killing poetry; therefore, we ought not to force children to learn the techniques of versification, because poetry is a spontaneous activity — whatever children write is the stuff of poetry?

If that is so, why do children demand nursery rhymes still? Why did my three-year-old son, Christopher, love to sway to the heavy beat of rock and roll and why, as an adult in 2003, is he a professional rock musician? Why did his original vocalist and songwriter, Ben Doyle, take courses from me in poetry writing and, in 1999, win the Academy of American Poets' Walt Whitman Award with his first book, *Radio, Radio*? Why do all pop songs still rhyme and meter? How is it that all the generations since the Beats of the 1950s want to write unmetered poems while their PR men make vast claims that the songwriters are the new, true poets of the age, and that formal poetry is dead as a doormat? If that makes sense, then I don't know what doesn't.

Something's truly wrong here, and I think I know what it is: We are the victims of propaganda — all of us except the children. The propaganda serves the purposes of people who have tin ears but want to write "poetry" anyhow. It's a very simple thing to tell when a rhymed, metered poem is a failure, much more difficult when there is no rhythmic structure against which to measure the ineptitudes of the would-be poets who can't make the English language do what they want it to do. It's all very democratic — if poetry is treated as the subjective welling-up of the unconscious, then the results can only be judged subjectively, and no one is a failure, because at least our mothers and our friends will like our literature (or say they do).

I should have said we are all the victims of propaganda except the children and the rock poets. One even wonders if it isn't the rappers and hip-hoppers who finance this media blitz, because if people begin writing good metrical verse again, it will immediately become obvious that the tinny effusions of the songsters are written at a very low level of competence. As long as no one challenges them, people are going to believe they are the last of the old-time bards, these bumpers and grinders.

The best thing that could happen in grade school English lessons would be teaching children the methods used in writing the kinds of poems they most enjoy. Of course it would be difficult to teach, and to learn. So is taking piano lessons. And not all children are going to turn into poets, nor would we want them to. But it wouldn't hurt the young folk to learn something about how to write in their native language and tradition.

"Native language" — there's something wrong with that phrase, too. Nobody has a "native language." One is not born knowing English or French or Russian or Tagalog. One learns it. There is absolutely nothing automatic or "natural" about learning to speak and write. It is not one's subconscious mind that figures out how to put words together. A child consciously learns his language by imitation, rote memory, trial and error, and parental correction. If a poet is one who, as Auden said, "refines the dialect of the tribe," then he or she has learned to do better what the tribe has learned to do well. *Learned.*

These things are so obvious I blush to say them, but the rock and roll PR and the psychological and sociological educationese are so loud that I must say this, I'm afraid: He or she who is the best poet is that person who has learned best how to say what must be said.

And you can't fool the children. They are bored by unimaginative writing; by slack writing; by unclear writing. I don't know how anyone is going to train our poets to be imaginative, but they can certainly be trained to be clear and rhythmic. Enough, however, about meters and forms and sounds, all of which fascinate children.

Perhaps a word ought to be said at this point about the flagrant dishonesty of poetry reviewing in America these days. Critics of novels feel few compunctions about airing their opinions. Theater and cinema critics have been known to deliver a blast when they hear a bomb drop, but reviewers of poetry for many years now have tiptoed around, trying not to offend anyone who might possibly sit on a panel that hands out prizes and fellowships. Without people telling the truth about bad writing nothing is going to change except that the writing is going to get worse. In his review of Charles Wright's *Appalachia* in *The New York Times Book Review* for Sunday, March 28th, 1999, Adam Kirsch wrote that, unlike Matthew Arnold who "refused the completeness of spiritual conviction, but embraced the completeness of poetic form," "Wright, like many serious poets today, refuses both kinds of completeness." "These poems do not want to be made things, beautiful in their wholeness." Why not say outright what he means? That, like the productions of the many prose-chopping "free verse" writers who wouldn't know iambic pentameter from a pair of suspenders, Wright's "poetry" is flaccid and boring.

Not long after this review appeared it was announced on PBS that Robert Pinsky had been reappointed for "an unprecedented third one-year term" as "Poet Laureate." Mr. Pinsky is the same type of poet as Wright. (Both are winners of the Pulitzer Prize!) His "free verse" is merely chopped prose. He has no ear whatever for the rhythms of the English language. His work is as dull as a board; worse, it is filled with stale "insights" and soppy sentimentality.

It is appalling that the Librarian of Congress, of all people, had so little insight into what constitutes language art that he appointed a hack writer — the 20th-century American equivalent of the 18th-century Englishman Colley Cibber — to the post of "Poet Laureate" once, let alone three times, to the detriment of the profession of letters. Is the public to assume that American poetry is so poverty-stricken that James H. Billington couldn't find someone worthwhile to honor? Perhaps so.

A week later PBS did a piece on both Wright and Pinsky pointing out that the former was quite reticent and often unwilling to read his work in public, but that Pinsky, to the contrary, took every opportunity to push poetry as THE democratic art, wishing to put material called poetry on buses and billboards, to expose everyone to the wonders of this art form. The only problem is, of course, that no one wants to read this stuff. It is uninteresting.

And then Billington did it again. A good definition of poetry is a simple one: *Something said well is something well said, but something said superbly is a poem.* Mary Jo Salter wrote, in her *Times* review of the new Poet Laureate Billy Collins's *Nine Horses* (Sunday, October 20, 2002), "Usually, the enthusiastic questioner can't call up Collins's exact phrasing. The poem remembered is the one about shoveling snow with Buddha, or the one about listening to jazz while musing on the three blind mice, or the one about undressing Emily Dickinson, or the one — we forget what it's called — about forgetting.

"If you often think of such poems but can't quote from them, that's partly because you don't go to Billy Collins for complex metrical effects or rhyme schemes, either of which might be usefully mnemonic. His pacing and sense of proportion are rhythmic and graceful, but their effect feels as tossed off and elusive as conversation. Nor can you often turn to Collins for much in the way of assonance, alliteration, wordplay, or even for a venturesome vocabulary. It's fair to say that you wouldn't want most poets to disregard so many tools of versification."

Ms. Salter finally came to the conclusion that, in his new book, Collins had, perhaps, written one real poem, "Litany." Then what are the rest of the items in *Nine Horses*? It's fair to say, probably not *something said superbly*, but more likely the productions of another of the run-of-the mill prose-poetasters the current Librarian of Congress has appointed to act as the spokesman for American poetry in our literary democracy.

As early as 1986 Diane Wakoski, at least, was willing to go on record in a straightforward if misguided manner when she published an essay titled "The New Conservatism in American Poetry," (*The American Book Review*, November-December 1986) in which she launched an *ad hominem* attack on "John Hollander as Satan" and on Robert Pinsky, "a nice man, even a good writer, but NOT one of the searchers for a new American voice." Despite the fact that Pinsky wrote what he considered to be "free verse," Wakoski maintained that he, and others like him, were representative of conservative literary legions who were making an assault upon "the free verse revolution, denouncing the poetry which is the fulfillment of the Whitman heritage, making defensive jokes about the ill-educated, slovenly writers of poetry who have been teaching college poetry classes for the past decade, allowing their students to write drivel and go out into the world, illiterate of poetry." Perhaps this description fits Hollander who, in his *Rhyme's Reason* (Yale, 1981), duplicated Shapiro's feat by writing a poetry handbook entirely in meter, but certainly not Pinsky who believes himself to be a Whitmanian.

The last time the Beat poets and critics had attacked what was then called "academic poetry" and equated it with "Fascism" and the "military-industrial complex" their ploy had worked. Rather than be perceived by their students as members of the American Nazi Party or the Ku Klux Klan, poets on college faculties everywhere during the activist 1960s abdicated their responsibility to provide their pupils with substance and became a caste of "nurturers" rather than teachers: the pedagogical philosophy of the late William

Stafford became the rule, and students tended to become imitators of their teachers, many of whom were themselves imitating him.

Stafford was from the beginning a proponent of what has been called the "organic" poem, the theory of which was first enunciated by the 19th-century critic Ralph Waldo Emerson in his essay titled "The Poet." The idea of organic poetry is that the poet is not responsible for writing the poem which "chooses its own form" and grows like a plant or a conch, "naturally," in effect making itself up as it builds. The poet's job, then, according to this theory of irresponsibility, as enunciated by Stafford in a Brockport "Writers' Forum" interview and in print (in that interview published as "Keeping the Lines Wet" in *Prairie Schooner*, Summer 1977), is merely to listen, to feel his or her way into the language, to leave him or herself open to "encounters with language" so that the poet may respond when he or she feels a "nudge" toward some "larger pattern" — by which Stafford evidently meant something mythopoeic or archetypal. It then becomes the poet's job to record that pattern, though perhaps imperfectly.

The holder of a Ph. D. from Iowa, Professor Stafford also held the pedagogical opinion that teaching creative writing is impossible; all an instructor can do is encourage a student to encounter language and search for organic and mythopoeic patterns in his or her own way. In an essay, "The Minuet: Sidling Around Student Poems," written for Alberta Turner's *Poets Teaching* (Longman, 1980), Stafford said, "My first impulse, when confronted with a student's writing, is to become steadfastly evasive until some signal from the student indicates a direction where the student is ready to go. I want to become the follower in this dance, partly because of some principles about what can be truly helpful in such an interchange, and partly because I have learned that the area between us is full of booby traps: the writer may have many kinds of predispositions, hang-ups, quirks, needs, bonuses. How the student comes toward me across that area is a crucially important beginning for whatever dancing there is going to be." And he continued, "The first move is the student's move, not mine." The young person who wants to learn something about writing from an elder is out of luck and on his or her own.

By the time she wrote her jeremiad Wakoski was unable to perceive that her generation of anti-intellectuals was the "conservative" generation and that the consideration of craft and structure was new, even revolutionary, to younger poets. But it is too late. Poetry is no longer at the center of culture and now we have dozens of media to carry our civilization, everything from print to electronic methods like the internet. Poetry, if it is to survive, must entertain, like basketball or the movies, or MTV or prose fiction.

The problem is that the poets don't know how to entertain the reader any longer. They have forgotten how to sing. All they want to do is talk about themselves in the most "sincere," flattest voice they can develop. In this they have succeeded. At the same time, the "profession" of poetry has become totally democratic. All the writing programs in the undergraduate and graduate schools have "taught" the young people, even those with no talent for writing or ear for the language, that whatever they turn out is going to be poetry. As a result, nobody buys or reads poetry because it has no entertainment value, but, paradoxically, everybody writes and publishes it; there are thousands of subsidies and book publication prizes because people need credentials to get jobs teaching so that they can keep the engine of ignorance chugging.

When our civilization crashes and we are swept back into barbarism, perhaps poetry will resume its place at the center of culture. One needs no special equipment for it, not a computer or word-processor, nor a pencil and piece of paper, not even a cave wall. All one needs is intelligence, mnemonic devices, and a voice. Until then, if poetry is to survive as an art, poets are going to have to rediscover how to entertain the reader, how to "sing" without music, using only the language itself. It can be done. In 1990 Bill Baer founded *The Formalist, A Journal of Metrical Poetry*. When he had seen it, the playwright Arthur Miller wrote him, "I am sure I will not be the only one who will be grateful for it. Frankly, it was a shock to realize, as I looked through the first issue, that I had very nearly given up the idea of taking pleasure from poetry." As has nearly everyone else, if they knew in the first place that language art can be entertaining and enjoyable.

Works Cited in "Upstairs"

Vince Clemente, "The Writer as Hyphenated-American," *The Boston Book Review*, 1996.

Fred Gardaphé, "In Search of Italian / American Writers," *Italian America*, ii:1, March 1997, p. 6.

Robert Hayden, "The Poetry of Robert Hayden," Writers' Forum video archive, SUNY Brockport.

Jerre Mangione and Ben Morreale, *La Storia, Five Centuries of the Italian American Experience*, New York: Harper, 1992, pp. 430-434.

Christopher Ricks, "Preface" to T. S. Eliot, *Inventions of the March Hare, Poems 1909-1917*, New York, Harcourt, 1997, p. xiii.

Felix Stefanile, *Italian Americana*, I:2, Spring 1975.

WORKS CITED IN "MUSING ABOUT STUDENTS"

Charlie Davis, ...*and so the Irish Built a Church*, Freeport: Bond-Wheelwright, 1975.

Russell Salamon, *Parent[hetical Pop]pies*, Cleveland: Renegade Press, 1964.

Carol Sineni, ed., *Escarpments*, 4:1, Autumn 1983.

Alberta Turner, ed., *Poets Teaching: The Creative Process*, ed. Alberta Turner, New York: Longman, 1980, pp. 49-51.

Lewis Turco

ABOUT THE AUTHOR

Lewis Turco, Professor Emeritus of English Writing Arts, is perhaps the most widely respected poet-scholar in the United States. He took his B. A. from the University of Connecticut in 1959 and his M. A. from the University of Iowa in 1962. In 2000 he received an honorary degree, Doctor of Humane Letters, from Ashland University in Ohio.

Founding director of both the Cleveland State University Poetry Center (1962) and the Program in Writing Arts at the State University of New York at Oswego (1968) before his retirement in 1996, he was chosen to write the major essay on "Poetry" — as well as a dozen other entries — for *The Encyclopedia of American Literature*, and was himself included in it as a biographee. His poems, essays, stories and plays have appeared in most of the major literary periodicals over the past half-century, and in over one hundred books and anthologies.

Lewis Turco's classic *The Book of Forms: A Handbook of Poetics* has been called "the poet's Bible" since its original publication in 1968, through three editions and many printings. A companion volume, *The Book of Literary Terms, The Genres of Fiction, Drama, Nonfiction, Literary Criticism and Scholarship*, received a *Choice* award as an "Outstanding Academic Book" for the year 2000. A third book in the series, *The Book of Dialogue* will appear in 2004. His first book of criticism, *Visions and Revisions of American Poetry*, won the Melville Cane Award of the Poetry Society of America in 1986, and his *A Book of Fears: Poems*, with Italian translations by Joseph Alessia, won the first annual Bordighera Bilingual Poetry Prize in 1998. Poems in his book of poetry, *The Green Maces of Autumn: Voices in an Old Maine House* (2002) won both the *Silverfish Review* Chapbook Award for 1989, and the Cooper House Chapbook Competition for 1990. In 1999 Prof. Turco received the John Ciardi Award for lifetime achievement in poetry sponsored by the periodical *Italian Americana* and the National Italian American Foundation.

A Sheaf of Leaves: Literary Memoirs

www.ingramcontent.com/pod-product-compliance
Lightning Source LLC
Chambersburg PA
CBHW022109150426
43195CB00008B/334